THE REFERENCE SHELF

Vol. 14 No. 8

INTERNATIONAL FEDERATION OF DEMOCRACIES

(PROPOSED)

COMPILED BY
JULIA E. JOHNSEN

NEW YORK
THE H. W. WILSON COMPANY
1941

Published April 1941
Second Printing December 1941
Third Printing October 1943

Printed in the United States of America

INTRODUCTION

Among the various suggestions for a new world order when present wars shall cease, among steps urgently stressed even before peace is won, proposed as a gateway out of the seeming impasse in which civilization finds itself today, is the idea of international federation. Envisioned from time to time by dreamers and statesmen of past centuries, accentuated by the troubled and torn world spirit of today, the thought has taken wide possession of men's minds that some form of international cooperatin is politically realizable, that a brotherhood of men is possible, a unity of nations, a oneness of life in which all men can live at peace and turn their inventiveness, constructiveness, creativeness toward higher possibilities of living, toward more pervading human welfare, toward the flowering of civilization, instead of contributing to the recurring vast leakages of human powers and values in destructiveness and strife.

In its most recent and most widely popularized form today international federation is engaging the attention of many thoughtful people and of many expanding organizations as essentially, at least in its initial stages, a federation of the democracies. This idea one of its more prominent advocates, Clarence K. Streit, an American journalist who was for a decade a correspondent of *The New York Times* at the League of Nations, has worked out in his book *Union Now,* 1939, and his more recent *Union Now With Britain.* Streit's plan has been widely acclaimed and discussed. His solution would be based on an international organization analogous to our national government, but forming a union of nations instead of states. Originally his proposal included sixteen initial democracies. Of these only Britain, her Dominions, and the United States now stand as possible bulwarks against the invasion of a totalitarian world. The idea of a union of the democracies has been an underlying concept in many public discussions, has been alluded to in many public debates, as in those of our lease-lend bill and all-out aid to Britain, and has colored various formulations of war aims and peace proposals alike by nations at war and in our own gropings for some sound pattern of a new world order that will ultimately contribute to security and world peace.

It is not, however, the Streit plan or any other concrete plan that is the basic idea behind the conception of a federation of the democracies, but the abstract ideal of international spiritual cooperation, of some form of unity of nations, some scaling down of national sovereignties to the point at least of giving emphasis and weight to a supreme international law under which nations as well as men can live under a common peace and order, that may be taken as the embodiment of the idea known under such various designations as Union Now, a Federal Union, a Union of the North Atlantic States, an English-Speaking Union, and a Federation of Democracies. In such an ideal is intended to be presented a common front of liberty-loving nations against outlaw concepts of national force and violence, against the submergence of democratic ideologies, against the sacrifice of what men value most. What form, in detail, such a federation may take is to many of less importance than the realization of its practical functioning as worked out in the ultimate, in any case, if the time comes when it is to be realized, by practical and, let us hope, far-visioned statesmen.

To some the thought of international federation under the leadership of democratic nations is the supremely urgent step today, that the western nations may the more immediately salvage what is left of their democratic concepts and practices; to others there looms the threat of its antithesis, a seemingly inevitable Germanic world. Some adherents of federation would pattern international union on a continental basis, as suggested by our Pan American or Western Hemispheric unity, and they envision a federation of Europe, once popularized by the French statesman Aristide Briand, and now again examined in the light of the conditions of that war-torn continent. Still others look upon lesser regional units as being called for, Central European, Baltic, Balkan, Danubian, Russian and the like, as being more practical and realizable, such units to retain, at the same time, the potentialities of again uniting under a larger continental or world federation. And finally there are those who would dispense with any intermediate steps and support a forthright world federation under a plan open to all nations. World federationists point out, among other things, the possibilities still inherent in a reconstituted League of Nations and the value of retaining the international activities already developed under that world organization. They call attention, also, to some major world needs for international government, more particularly an effective World Court, and an international police that can enforce, if need be, a world order.

This number of the REFERENCE SHELF is an attempt to bring together some of the more timely and outstanding concepts of international federation. The historical background is given and some representative forms of federation or proposed federation are touched on. Special stress is given to a proposed union of the democracies, including prominently the Streit plan, together with some outstanding affirmative and negative discussion. A summary of arguments on this aspect is given, and a classified bibliography is presented for those who may wish additional selective reading and materials for debate. Limitations of the compilation have precluded any attempt to more than touch upon side aspects, such as regional federations. The same considerations have made it desirable to center attention for the most part, on the more timely and up-to-date materials.

April 7, 1941

JULIA E. JOHNSEN

CONTENTS

BIBLIOGRAPHY

GENERAL DISCUSSION

THE NEED FOR WORLD ORGANIZATION[1]

The necessity for world organization grows out of the fact that modern technological developments have transformed the world into a compact neighborhood. In the interest of peace and security, it is imperative that the world-neighborhood be organized to prevent anarchy and to preserve law and order.

It is no longer possible for any nation to find security in isolation. Economic self-sufficiency is a dream impossible of fulfillment, in an economically interdependent world. No one nation is really secure unless and until all are secure.

In his testimony before the Ways and Means Committee of the House of Representatives on January 11, 1940, Cordell Hull, Secretary of State, said:

> The experience of the two decades which elapsed between the end of the World War and the outbreak of a new war in Europe has brought out in sharp relief the validity of two basic propositions. The first is that our nation, and every nation, can enjoy sustained prosperity only in a world which is at peace. The second is that a peaceful world is possible only when there exists for it a solid economic foundation, an indispensable part of which is active and mutually beneficial trade among the nations.

Cultural and political, as well as economic, relations among nations in the modern world require some form of international organization, on a world scale, if the values of civilization are to be preserved and extended.

Recognizing that world organization is a necessary requirement for world peace and security, our purpose in this discussion is to show the historic movements, precedents, and proposals looking toward world organization. Then to evaluate present achievements of existing institutions in regional or world organ-

[1] By E. Guy Talbott, California. Regional Director, National Council for Prevention of War. *World Affairs Interpreter.* 11:287-95. Autumn, 1940.

ization, with some estimate of what changes or additions are indicated in such agencies as the League of Nations. Finally, to suggest certain contributions the United States might make in the field of world organization.

I. Historic Movements Toward World Organization

The great German philosopher, Hegel, in closing his monumental *Philosophy of History* said: "The history of the world is nothing but the development of the Idea of Freedom." This "Idea" expresses itself in ever-expanding social institutions and governmental organizations, the ultimate goal being world unity.

There are seven well-defined movements or trends toward world organization, beginning with the family, sometimes in the form of a patriarchate and sometimes a matriarchate. The development of the social organism has been upward through the clan, the tribe, the nation, the empire, federated states, and culminating in the League of Nations. These historic movements or trends toward world organization have largely been an unconscious, undirected expansion. Only in comparatively recent times has mankind begun consciously to direct the development of social and governmental institutions.

America's great sociologist, Lester F. Ward, basing his teaching on the analogies of scientific control in the field of botany and biology, taught that mankind can rapidly attain the goal of human unity through the conscious direction of social progress toward that goal.

China is perhaps the best example of a living nation, whose development can be traced to earliest antiquity, representing the historic movements toward world unity. All of the steps toward unity can be traced in the written history of China, including loyalty to the ideals of the League of Nations.

The last Plenary Session of the Central Executive Committee of the Kuomintang held November 20, 1939, adopted a manifesto which declared:

Having fought for more than two years, China is today more than ever alive to the fact that all countries must share security and well-being in common if any one of them is to enjoy these things. . . . We are strongly of the belief that when the two wars now in progress come to an end there will arise an effective and genuine system of organized security such as may give the nations the opportunity of living side by side in peace and enlightenment.

II. Historic Precedents for World Organization

The attempts by a single ruler to control the world, as represented by Alexander and Caesar, are hardly in the field of precedents for world organization. There are, however, many actual instances in which groups of city-states or nations have cooperated for common ends, and those organizations, however tenuous or short-lived, do form precedents for world organization.

The Achaean League (368-146 B.C.) was composed of twelve Greek city-states, and was an effective cooperative league functioning as a supergovernment.

Co-existent with the Achaean League was the Amphictyonic Council, representing the same twelve city states, but functioning primarily in the religious realm.

Following the Treaty of Utrecht (Dec. 22, 1713), a federation was created composed of those powers in Europe opposed to French expansion.

The American Federal Union (1776-1787) paved the way for similar governments and unions of states in the Western Hemisphere and in other parts of the world.

The Quadruple Alliance (1814) following the Napoleonic Wars was composed of Russia, Prussia, Austria, and Great Britain. Its function was largely political.

The so-called Holy Alliance (1815), composed of Russia, Prussia, and Austria, was primarily religious. It held somewhat the same relation to the Quadruple Alliance that the Greek Amphictyonic Council held to the Achaean League.

The Swiss Federation, composed of 22 cantons and representing three languages, was created in 1848. The Italian Federation, uniting the several independent Latin states, was formed in 1861, and the German Federation was completed in 1871, following the Franco-Prussian War.

The first and second Hague conferences in 1899 and 1907 represented the first major effort in modern times to bring together the civilized nations of the world for the specific purpose of creating cooperative institutions for the preservation of peace.

Following the World War, the League of Nations came into existence as the first world-wide expression of the solidarity of mankind. Its membership of 57 nations included all the major powers except the United States.

The British Commonwealth of Nations came into being at the Imperial Conference in 1926, and in effect assumed the prerogatives of the British Empire. The British Commonwealth of Nations received final sanction in the Statute of Westminster, adopted in 1931.

These various precedents in the field of international leagues, councils, unions, alliances, and federations prove that world organization is both possible and desirable.

III. Historic Proposals for World Organization

The idea of world organization to promote peace and human well-being is not new. It has been the dream of prophets, sages, poets, and statesmen throughout all history.

The "Grand Design" of Henry IV of France was prepared by the great French king in 1603, although it was not published for almost sixty years. It was a proposal for a general council of 15 European nations. Twelve of those nations were definitely committed to the plan, which included a common army and navy, before Henry's untimely death prevented the consummation of the plan.

The proposal of Crucé in 1623 was for a continuous Congress of Ambassadors representing all nations. The purpose was the settlement of disputes by the judgment of this Congress. Manifestly it was confined to Europe, as were most of the proposals of the seventeenth century.

Hugo Grotius, usually spoken of as the father of international law, in 1625 proposed the settlement of disputes through specially called congresses of the "Christian" powers of Europe. His proposal included a system of sanctions to compel recalcitrant nations to abide by the decisions of the Congress.

In 1693 William Penn proposed a "Grand Parliament of Europe." He was influenced largely by the "Grand Design" of Henry IV.

The proposal of St. Pierre (1714) was for a permanent union of European nations, the union to have power over the sovereigns. The union was to be composed of the nations created as a result of the Treaty of Utrecht (1713).

The Rousseau Plan proposed in 1761 was for a permanent diet of 19 European powers, forming a confederation. The confederation had power to outlaw any state and proceed against it with joint armed forces if the state refused to abide by a decision of the diet.

In 1784 Emanuel Kant published his *Essay on Perpetual Peace* in which he proposed a permanent international congress of nations with representative form of government. No state member was to interfere by force in the internal affairs of any other state.

In 1815 Simon Bolívar proposed a permanent league of American states, composed of those independent states in the Western Hemisphere. While his proposal did not bear immediate fruit, it paved the way for the existing Pan American Union and the current conferences of American states.

In 1838 Jeremy Bentham proposed his "Plan for universal and perpetual peace." His major proposal was a world court to settle disputes between nations.

In 1840 the American, William Ladd, in his essay on a Congress of Nations proposed both a court of justice among the nations and a congress of nations.

In 1910 Theodore Roosevelt, when he received the Nobel Peace Prize at Christiana, Norway, proposed a league of nations. He said:

> It would be a master stroke if those great powers honestly bent on peace would form a league of peace, not only to keep peace among themselves, but to prevent, by force if necessary, its being broken by others. . . . As things are now, such power to command peace throughout the world could best be assured by some combination between those great nations which sincerely desire peace and have no thought themselves of committing aggressions.

In 1911 the Belgian senator, La Fontaine, proposed a United States of the World, and in 1915 his plan was expanded into a document called "Magnissima Charta," a charter for world organization.

In 1915 the American organization called the League to Enforce Peace was organized by William Howard Taft, together with a large number of statesmen, educators, and business leaders. The educational campaign of this organization paved the way for the adoption of the Covenant of the League of Nations, under the leadership of Woodrow Wilson at the close of the World War.

In 1939 Clarence Streit, in his book *Union Now,* proposed a federal union of 15 North Atlantic democracies (including the self-governing dominions of the British Commonwealth of Nations). His proposal is a development of the American principle of federal union. At first restricted to the democratic countries, membership is to be open to all nations that later may qualify and desire to affiliate.

IV. Present Achievements in World Organization

In its restricted field, the Pan American Union and the Conference of American States represent outstanding achievements in international cooperation for common ends. It includes the 21 independent nations in the Western Hemisphere, except Canada. The plan of the Pan American Union might well serve as a pattern for regional organization in other areas. It involves no curtailment of national sovereignty.

The Permanent Court of Arbitration, which resulted from the first and second Hague conferences, and the Permanent Court of International Justice created by statute in 1919, are outstanding achievements in the field of arbitration and judicial settlement of disputes among nations. If the arbitration and juridical machinery of these courts were fully utilized, war would be unnecessary as a means of settling disputes among nations.

The International Labor Organization, called into being at the close of the World War, has achieved notable results in the field of international industrial and economic relations. The preamble to its charter states its purpose, namely, the securing of social justice as the necessary basis for universal peace. While it is directly related to the League of Nations, nonmembers such as the United States are also members. The importance of this organization cannot be over-emphasized in this technological age. If there were an international economic organization based on the pattern of the International Labor Organization, much more could be done to ease the economic tensions that lead to war.

POST-WAR INTERNATIONAL ORGANIZATION [2]

The marked success of federal governments of the Americas linked together in a Pan American Union based upon mutual respect and the principle of equality, has added impetus to the plan given wide publicity by Count Coudenhove-Kalergi for a United States of Europe; this plan in its later version would allow membership to the states of the old world, excluding

[2] From address of J. Eugene Harley, University of Southern California. *American Society of International Law. Proceedings,* 1940. p. 108-15.

Russia but including the United Kingdom. The Count's plan lay dormant for many years, and in the bright days of post-war international cooperation during the 1920's, when some 58 states were in the League of Nations and its activities were front-page news, in the days of the Kellogg-Briand Pact (1928), M. Briand revived the idea of a Union of European States. The Briand plan was launched in September, 1928, under the aegis of the League, with Sir Austen Chamberlain and Dr. Gustav Stresemann closely collaborating. Before the plan could get under way, the depression of 1929 came, and Stresemann died in the same year. The death of Briand himself was another blow to the plan.

The Briand plan stressed ultimate economic cooperation, but it contemplated political cooperation and security as a forerunner of economic rehabilitation. But the deep wounds left by the World War were not yet healed; and racial and national differences were too great to allow the plan to be realized. When the patient becomes ill, however, he begins to think of the doctor and the remedy. With wars raging, the peoples of Europe are again thinking of a way out of their sorry distress and their man-made troubles.

The various statesmen proclaim that they are fighting for a new order. The Germans say that they are fighting for *lebensraum* and for their share of trade and commerce. The Allies state that they are fighting for freedom and against Hitlerism and for real law and order in the world. Prime Minister Robert Gordon Menzies of Australia put it on a very high plane when he said:

> We are not fighting merely for the map of Europe of twelve months ago, or any of Europe. We have an open mind on all questions of merit. We hope the victorious Allies will proceed to re-erect the map of Europe with the idea of restoring, not the old boundaries, but true justice and independence, true lines of demarcation between self-respecting nations wishing to contrive salvation according to their own ideas.
>
> Finally, we should think how to prevent another war. We should not be skeptical of collective security, international agreements or the

League of Nations. What we did with the League was to ask an untrained man to do a record high jump. There will be no permanent peace through alliances and counteralliances. There must be some international outlawry of war to which every world power will subscribe.

The British Labor Party has come out with a strong program for "A New World Order." Mr. C. R. Attlee, the leader of this party, has spoken vigorously in Parliament for a new world order. The labor program for post-war peace and reconstruction as prepared by Mr. Attlee includes the following points:

1. There should be no dictated peace.
2. The recognition of the great principle that all nations large and small have a right to live and to develop their own type of civilization.
3. Aggression must be abandoned.
4. The use of armed force as an instrument of policy must be stopped.
5. War must be outlawed and law enthroned.
6. The rights of national, racial, and religious minorities must be recognized and respected, and, if necessary, upheld by effective international authority.
7. Establishment of an international authority operating in the political and economic sphere and endowed with power adequate to effectuate its authority.
8. A Federation of Europe. "Europe must federate or perish."
9. Abandonment of imperialism by extending and strengthening the mandate system.
10. Sanctions, including an international police force and economic pressure.
11. Drastic reduction of armaments.
12. Private manufacture and trade in armaments to be abolished.
13. Bold economic planning on a world scale.
14. Scope of activities of International Labor Office to be extended so that it would deal with "international minimum standards of wages, hours and industrial conditions, in order that, by increased production, by a more just distribution and by the wealth released from expenditure upon arms, the standard of living of the workers shall everywhere be raised. For peace depends on social justice within states, no less than on political justice between states.

President Nicholas Murray Butler would have a world federation for peace. In his *Annual Report* Dr. Butler appealed to the people of the United States to assume world leadership when the war ends and to bring forward a constructive policy of international cooperation as the alternative to chaos and disaster. He recalled and recommended again the program of the Chatham House Conference of 1935 as offering a "wholly practical plan of international cooperation, international organization and international stabilization." This program included: (1) measures by which the United States and Great Britain would enable debtor nations to pay with goods and services; (2) the formation of unions for low tariff or free trade; (3) stabilization of exchange on a gold basis; (4) strengthening of the League of Nations and the World Court; and (5) the cooperation of all nations to raise the standard of living.

Sir Norman Angell believes that although the British and French are now fighting for the principle of organized society and orderly civilization, they bogged down in their opportunities to uphold the banner of collective security by not taking a firm and timely stand for others—in China, Abyssinia, Spain, and Czechoslovakia—before their own national interests were directly threatened. He desires a strong international organization placing emphasis upon political structure first and accompanied by agreements on fundamentals of economic life.

The prolific British writer, H. G. Wells, warns that "if we don't end the war the war will end us." He believes that the world faces three alternatives in the shape of (1) world revolution, (2) political gangsterism, or (3) decadence and defeatism; and the only hope in the presence of a single world system that is breaking down is to set up a single economic control for the world. He fears, however, that a federation like that proposed by Mr. Streit will be illusory unless it is accompanied by socialism or collectivization (but not the type found in Russia). He insists on a bill of rights for man, to secure man's individual freedom.

Dr. William E. Rappard, a brilliant Swiss leader in the field of international affairs, sees international federalism as infinitely promising. He sees in it "the only happy outcome to the tragic chaos into which the anarchy of national sovereignties has plunged our contemporary civilization." He refers to the early experiences of the American colonies and the Swiss cantons with their systems of "popular" representation and "state" representation, and declares that "by a combination of these two systems in a bicameral régime" they found a "solution to which they have remained faithful since."

Dr. Rappard believes that a world court or other purely judicial organization is not enough. An adequate organization for peace must embrace also effective means to cope with political and economic problems and to promote prosperity for all. Peace must be secured with prosperity. He refers to President Butler's plan as envisaging a vast federation in which the United States will take a lead, with the liberal states of Europe at first included, but which later would become universal; he refers also to the plan of Lord Davies and his colleagues in the New Commonwealth group which contemplates a somewhat similar federation but with less intransigence towards the dictatorial states (*"avec peut-être une intransigeance moins absolue à l'égard des États dictatoriaux"*).

Professor Frederick L. Schuman (of Williams College) would have a "grand alliance" or confederation embracing the United States, the British Commonwealth, and France, together with as many of the Latin American States and European democracies as might care to join. But this type of organization of "good and virtuous democratic Powers," leaving out of the pale the "wicked totalitarians," was repugnant to Luigi Villari (a former member of the Italian delegation in the League of Nations Secretariat). Mr. Villari maintained that the only possible organization now would be one based on an agreement of the great civilized Powers who can make and carry out decisions for maintaining peace.

The Pan American Union as a regional plan of international cooperation has had the advantage of a common political system (constitutional republican); and historical and traditional factors, as well as geography, have militated in its favor. But in other parts of the world, regional unions based on geographical considerations alone would not coincide with nature ties now linking certain nations together. Moreover, regional units, unless in turn linked into a world federal arrangement of some kind, might create a new system of balance of power, a sort of exalted balance of power, with regions as the parties, rather than single states. Such possible drawbacks as these stand in the way of regionalism and point to the desirability of a single world-wide approach to the problem of peace and order. This world point of view is suggested further when attention is focused upon statements like that of Secretary of State Hull to the effect that a war in any part of the world engages the interests of the people of the United States, and President Roosevelt's recent declaration on Pan American Day, April 14, 1940, that whoever touches the interests of any one of the members of the Pan American Union touches the interests of all. The recent film entitled "Teddy, The Rough Rider" emphasizes President Theodore Roosevelt's insistence, at the time he received the Nobel Peace Prize, upon his view that he felt a war in Asia or elsewhere in the world engaged the interests of the people of the United States. The whole theory of collective security is logically predicated upon the world-wide point of view, rather than a regional one; since international law itself is world-wide in its scope, the peace and order which this branch of law serves should also be approached from a single global standpoint. Regionalism can never be the final answer to the problem of peace unless regionalism is in turn globalized or federalized to cover all of the world.

Careful students of problems of international organization are pretty well agreed that the fact that the League of Nations was tied up with the Versailles Treaty has in actual practice proved a great handicap to the League. In this connection the Government of Iraq observed that the incorporation of the Covenant in the peace treaties "tends to associate it with the advantages gained by the victorious nations." With this in mind, the Protocol for the Separation of the Covenant from the World War Peace Treaties was opened for signature on September 30, 1938, and now awaits ratifications sufficient to make it effective. Judge Hudson quotes from a memorandum of March 31, 1936, in which the German Government declared its willingness to reenter the League, but expressed the expectation that "within a reasonable time and by means of friendly negotiations, the question . . . of the separation of the Covenant of the League of Nations from its basis in the Treaty of Versailles setting will be cleared up."

A well-known authority like William E. Rappard has pointed out that the League of Nations was really "three Leagues" of Nations in one, *viz.*: (1) a League to settle international disputes; (2) a League to promote international cooperation; and (3) a League to enforce the provisions of the Versailles Treaty. This third League was the weak link in the chain of genuine international cooperation that is to be gotten rid of by means of the Protocol referred to above.

For some time it has been felt by many students of international organization that one of the great difficulties of the League of Nations—constituting, perhaps, one of the reasons for its non-universality—was the fact that in the Covenant and in the scheme of the League's organization, there was not a sufficient distinction made between political and non-political activities. For the purpose of improving the usefulness of the League, the Council, at its session on May 23, 1939, arranged for the setting up of a committee to study the development and expansion of the League's machinery for dealing with technical problems. On May 27, 1939, the Council approved the suggestion of Secretary-General Avenol and invited Mr. S. M. Bruce (Australia) to serve as chairman of the reorganization committee of seven members.

The Committee met at Paris from August 7 to 12, 1939. In its report it adopted the phraseology of "economic and social questions" to cover the scope of its activities, rather than the expression "technical problems." It praised the achievements of the League in this field, but pointed to the need for a distinction between political and non-political activities and the need for a wider, a more nearly universal cooperation in the non-political realm. The report contains a splendid summary of the social, economic, and humanitarian work of the League and affirms the need for a fresh stimulus to these efforts; it concludes that "the League's resources enable it in the most economical possible way":

(a) To collect and sift evidence drawn from all over the world;
(b) To obtain the services of the best experts in the world working without reward for the good of the cause;
(c) To arrange meetings between experts working in the same fields, enabling them to discuss their preoccupations, their successes, their failures;
(d) To provide the essential links between the experts and those responsible for policy;
(e) To provide constant and automatic opportunities for statesmen to meet and discuss their policy;
(f) To provide thereby means for better understanding of the aims and policies of different nations;
(g) To provide machinery for the conclusion of international conventions.

In this connection the Committee quotes from a letter of the Department of State of the United States to the Secretary-General of the League to the effect that

> The League of Nations has been responsible for the development of mutual exchange and discussion of ideas and methods to a greater extent and in more fields of humanitarian and scientific endeavor than any other organization in history.

The Bruce Committee recommended a Draft Constitution for the Central Committee for Economic and Social Questions. Specifically it would set up a Central Committee "entrusted with the direction and supervision of the work of the [League] committees dealing with economic and social questions." The Central Committee is to be composed of representatives of 24 states chosen for one year by the Assembly on the proposal of its

Bureau. The Central Committee is authorized to co-opt not more than eight experts appointed in a personal capacity. The Draft Constitution leaves the doors wide open for nonmembers of the League to collaborate in its social and economic activities. Steps are now being taken to carry into effect the recommendations of the Bruce Committee.

It seems clear that the future shape of international organization must be determined by a fresh consideration of the place of sanctions. We must reach a satisfactory decision as to whether sanctions are to be or not to be. If they are to be, then, in order to avoid the idea of *ex post facto* punishment, the program for sanctions must be more carefully worked out in advance so that the offending nations will certainly know what to expect and when to expect punishment. If the power of public opinion in checking aggression is not enough, the aggressor must face a more formidable deterrent in the shape of economic or military power. The New Commonwealth Society in England is taking a leading rôle in advocating a real international police force, and the French Government has consistently backed this idea. In this connection the use of a real international police force in the Saar Plebiscite is cited as a precedent. The strong indorsement of the idea of a police force for peace by President Theodore Roosevelt on the occasion of receiving the Nobel Peace Prize led to a resolution of Congress in June, 1910, looking forward to the reduction of armaments and setting up "the combined navies of the world [as] an international police force for the preservation of universal peace." The League to Enforce Peace, sponsored by former President Taft and Dr. A. Lawrence Lowell, favored the use of joint force to check peace-disturbers. President Wilson boldly stated in his speech to Congress (January 22, 1917) that if peace was to endure "it must be a peace made secure by the organized major force of mankind." The sanctions provided in Article 16 of the Covenant are still there. Shall they remain?

Future international organization for peace must be flexible enough to accommodate itself to "peaceful change"; if it is to be successful in substituting courts and conferences for bombs, bullets, and bayonets, it must take care of the legitimate economic needs of all nations; it must recognize once for all that it is too much to expect people anywhere to be sweet-spirited and peace-minded on empty stomachs and without jobs.

We may contemplate the future of international cooperation with genuine hope and expectation. That we shall move in the direction of *more* international cooperation rather than *less* of it is indicated, amongst other things, by two unanswerable considerations. (1) The greatest writers and authorities in past decades and centuries are theoretically agreed that the prospects for world peace will be immeasurably enhanced by some form of a world court or world tribunal to settle legal disputes and some form of world league to aid in the settlement of political and economic disputes. (2) Since it is now true that the vast majority—President Franklin D. Roosevelt puts it at 90 per cent—of the peoples of the world want peace, it seems clear that they will see the light and demand a progressive strengthening of the cooperation of civilized nations to promote their peace, their economic welfare, and their spiritual satisfaction in the building of a world worthy of men and women created in the image of Almighty God and entitled to a better deal than that offered to them by a handful of misguided, self-seeking leaders, whose false promises will fade away before the melting rays of God's truth as they illumine the principles of international law and equal justice and reveal the hollowness of the promises of these war-crazed pseudo-leaders. One of the greatest of these immutable truths was expressed by a great Frenchman, M. Léon Bourgeois:

When the President of the established Court of International Justice first pronounces the judgment which will express the will of all the free nations, his voice will be heard to the ends of the earth. . . . I see before us a star rising above the mountains; it grows clearer every day, and by this star people will find their way to their ultimate goal. "Ubi lux, ubi jus, ibi pax [where there is light, where there is justice, there is peace]."

DESIGNS FOR A WORLD ORDER [3]

It has been discovered that national groups subject to no law and no authority, and organizations controlled by no moral or spiritual principles, create the same anarchy and confusion that prevail in a primitive community of independent individuals under the same circumstances. So the questions are, what sort of organization or machinery is advisable or feasible, and how to persuade people to adopt it after it has been devised.

The exploration of this subject is being conducted methodically by every civilized country in the world. The Germans are perhaps more aware than anyone else of one evil of disunity due to intensely nationalistic groups. This is the growth of trade barriers, embargoes, currency manipulations, and all manner of restrictions amounting to economic war between territories. Their answer is relatively simple. They intend to get rid of the suffocating results of this stockade economy by conquering and, if necessary, enslaving a big enough territory to support an economic unit in a modern world.

This answer and this method appear to the rest of civilization to remedy one vice of the situation by increasing others. Violence in international affairs, and the tendency of national entities to disregard or abridge what are conceived to be the inherent and inalienable liberties and purposes of the individual man, are considered elsewhere to be even greater vices than economic isolation. So in democratic countries, neutral as well as belligerent, insight and discussion seek an answer which will rid the world of economic wrangles between groups, and at the same time eliminate force and war and increase and guarantee the personal liberties and opportunities of every individual.

[3] By Ralph W. Page, Journalist, Evening Bulletin, Philadelphia. *Annals of the American Academy.* 210:50-6. July, 1940.

In the United States and England the analysis of the difficulty and the possibilities of remedies are being explored with more thoroughness and determination than popular interest would indicate. The intellectual and moral elements of both countries are mobilizing to study every phase of this question. The foundation for general popular debate is being laid by innumerable groups engaged in research, study, consultation, and planning.

Among those in this country who are working toward some concrete suggestions or preparing themselves to appraise such suggestions are: nationwide groups conducted by the Committee to Study the Organization of Peace; the National Economic and Social Planning Association; the National Policy Committee; the American Association of University Women; the Provisional Committee of the World Council of Churches; the New School for Social Research; the National Peace Conference; the Foreign Policy Association; the Council of Foreign Relations; Inter-Democracy Federal Unionists; and the League of Nations Association. Joined with these, or in collaboration, are literally hundreds of other organizations, most of the authorities, interested scholars, and many men of affairs.

Preliminary surveys and tentative memoranda on the myriad subjects involved are the principal fruits of this work to date. But a few rash or courageous pioneers have presented fully developed plans for this new freedom, this new conception of the community of the world; and these at least pose the problems in concrete form and challenge the people to re-examine their complacent beliefs and accepted traditions, superstitions, and inertias.

The foundation of all thought upon the design of a new order is the great work of Lionel Curtis called *Civitas Dei,* or World Order. He says that the primary question in any human plan of action is, What is the purpose? In devising an organization for guiding the lives of vast populations, the question is no less than, What is the purpose of life itself? The nature and form of international organization must be determined by what men believe to be the nature of creation and their function in that creation. He reviews the entire history of thought and political forms of governing to demonstrate that there is only one purpose in life, and hence only one principle upon which men can build any successful institution.

Curtis' thesis is that to engender in men a desire to serve each other is the end and object of human existence. As he draws it, the drama of the world is the story of the gradual discovery that men grow to perfection in so far as they base their relations on the infinite duty of each to all. Men rise in stature, power, and understanding in proportion to their awareness of their unity and identity with other men. A completely impotent and miserable individual is one who conceives of himself as an isolated and complete unit, diverse in interest and hostile to every other living creature. Men achieve freedom and peace as their loyalties and their sympathies become progressively identified first with the family, then with the tribe, the state, the nation, the hemisphere, and finally expand to include the whole world.

Of all influences releasing men from the fears of savage ignorance and the selfish urges of pure animalism, the nature of the social organism in which they live is the most powerful. Curtis maintains that the only form which can accomplish the purpose of men's being is the Sermon on the Mount translated into political terms. Religion and politics, he demonstrates, are merely two aspects of life, a sphere viewed from two different angles.

It follows from this analysis that any political organization, whatever its size, should be designed entirely to provide the utmost freedom and opportunity for the individual to develop his sense of community and common interest with all mankind. It must then be based upon the direct participation and responsibility of the individual himself. It should be a commonwealth in that sense; and the perpetual striving and the ultimate purpose cannot be anything but a commonwealth of the world. One purpose, one interest, one loyalty, the brotherhood of man, is the only goal that enlists the life forces of the youth of the world. It is the sole realistic business of statesmen, politicians, and planners.

But Curtis believes that there exists today a great gulf in the minds of men. And this gulf precludes them from discarding the conception of the nation and the limited ideas of self and hostilities to others associated with the nation. People are obsessed with the notion that they can obtain selfish benefits from this grouping. Curtis concludes that any steps towards a world commonwealth will have to be gradual and groping. Consequently he thinks the maximum possibility is that two or more commonwealths, more advanced than the rest, might by some immense spiritual effort consciously merge their sovereignty into one international commonwealth.

Curtis' practical suggestion is that the experiment be tried by Australia or New Zealand or both, in combination with the United Kingdom. This new union, he thinks, will serve to demonstrate the principle if a minimum of sovereignty is relinquished to the common government. His formula for the first attempt is: (1) a legislature elected by and responsible to the people, (2) having final authority over peace and war and foreign affairs, and (3) having power to levy taxes directly on the people to exercise these powers. In addition, he would have an executive to carry out the legislative mandate. The distribution of voting power and burden of taxation and constitutional details he leaves to the negotiation. But the essence of the idea is that this new international commonwealth should extend a standing invitation to join, to all others who have the same purpose and beliefs.

In England, a semiofficial company of experts in economics, history, law, religion, and philosophy are producing a continuing series of tentative plans. They have no conclusion, but they have formulated certain principles. To begin with, they take a momentous step. They forswear any dominance of Great Britain in any properly reconstructed world. They discard any future combination of governments or peoples based upon common speech, economic interest, or geographical proximity. They would not make the form of government or the race the criterion of membership. The test they have arrived at is that any new federation or union should be composed of people who believe in the same human values. These, of course, are moral values. They can be maintained only by the compelling force of personal conviction. So in essence, their plans are based upon religious sanctions, and not upon mathematical or material considerations.

These experts conceive that the purposes of any plan are four: (1) upholding freedom of thought, expression of opinion, and movement; (2) upholding the rule of law, both nationally and internationally; (3) the use of the state, not as an instrument of domination or merely for the protection of private interests, but as an instrument of public welfare and cultural development; and (4) the organization of production and distribution for raising the standard of living and life of the people of the world. As a practical matter, they tend to the opinion that any union or federation for these purposes must be a growth rather than an immediate performance. As a basis, they expect and work for the amalgamation of the English and French peoples.

This has already reached the point of delegating authority to a Supreme Council, establishment of common shipping control, pooling financial resources and establishing a joint buying commission, a single military command, and a common center for training pilots. The idea is that this beginning will ripen into a fusion of these peoples for federal purposes, and at the end of the war all the people of Europe that circumstances permit should be called into an international reconstruction conference to decide on what form of government by the people on a partnership federal basis can be built on this foundation.

This plan and all English plans propose to carry on a remodeled League of Nations. The League is to serve its original purpose but without any attempt to require or enforce sanctions or military commitments. It will continue to be the center of universal contact and discussion—to mobilize technical information and recommend actions in fields of finance, transit, hygiene, economics, and intellectual and social pursuits. The International Labor Office will be continued and developed as an example of direct co-operation of peoples, to be ultimately followed in the conduct of other international affairs.

Meanwhile, the Institute of International Affairs, Chatham House, London, has produced two fairly specific proposals for a federation of peoples. One is by Sir John Fischer Williams and the other by Sir William Beveridge.

Williams calls for a written constitution after the American model. Membership would be open to those with a community of social and political outlook. The core, he says, might be states of western and central Europe and the British commonwealths. A New Germany would be highly welcome. Adhesion of the United States would be especially desirable—but, he adds, especially difficult. But a first essential is that there be enough membership to guarantee security. As much jurisdiction as possible over affairs federal in nature should be delegated. But he says that probably the practical limit is to create machinery necessary for action in foreign affairs. To include dominion over currency, commerce, and migration would be a great help. But he believes present opinion would prevent any country from surrendering any more sovereignty than control of foreign policy, armed forces, and a fund of money for defense.

Diluting an ideal constitution to meet present obstacles, Williams would provide either an assembly of delegates or a council to govern this federation. In either case, these would represent the constituent states in some proportion to population, modified in convention by negotiation. Each state would select its representatives as it pleased, the hope being that it would please to have them elected by popular vote. This council would be presided over by an elected chairman, and would itself appoint three executive ministers to conduct the foreign affairs, the military affairs, and the exchequer.

The size and character of the armed forces and the amount of money each constituent state would be called upon to provide would be incorporated in the original charter. Provision would be made for not too frequent revisions, with arbitration machinery provided in case of deadlock.

A Supreme Federal Court with final authority to settle disputes between states or a state and the federation completes the picture.

Sir William Beveridge proceeds further with the precedent of the American Constitution. His delegated powers include not only foreign affairs, control of the military, and funds to finance these, but also equal access to all colonies or dependencies. His constitution would create two houses, one an assembly elected by popular vote in proportion to population, and the other with equal representation for every state, selected as that state chose. He would have an executive, responsible to the legislature, and a supreme court. In addition, he would incorporate an equivalent of the American Bill of Rights in the organic law.

Beveridge despairs of including the United States, but he considers it essential to include Germany. The other members suggested are the same as everyone's list of democracies.

These plans might be discussed more specifically if two Americans had not adopted this idea of emulating the American Union and the Federal Constitution. They have gone about it in detail, article by article and section by section; consequently this approach to the problem is much more thoroughly covered in their schemes. Grenville Clark has offered for discussion a draft of a constitution for the Federation of Free Peoples. This is annotated and analyzed sentence by sentence. Clarence K. Streit has done the same thing, supporting his version by the remarkable volume called *Union Now*.

Both these planners have the advantage over the Englishmen. As Americans, they are not restricted by the exigencies of the war; and they have a people to address which is familiar with the necessity for the form and the operation of a successful federation. As a remedy for dissentions, hostilities, and trade barriers, and as a formula for common defense and the protection of personal liberties, nobody denies the potency of the United States Union. The transition from a confederation of quarreling and impotent sovereignties to a single powerful entity accomplished by the American states in 1787 obviously is the outstanding practical pattern to be followed in evolving any future union. . . .

[Streit's] proposal meets the approval of every theoretical presentation of this subject. Logically it presents a concrete scheme to accomplish at one stroke the objects advocated and dreamed of by all the authorities. But it is at once apparent that Streit has had either the courage or the foolhardiness to disregard the fears which have led others to tread softly and limit their immediate steps to what are believed to be acceptable politically by a pagan population.

Clark is an eminent lawyer. Although an idealist himself, he believes that the motive which will induce American citizens as well as others to embrace a federation is not the brotherhood of man or moral principles or anything else except their idea of what is to their enlightened self-interest. Whether they are enlightened enough to perceive their own patent self-interest seems to be the question.

Clark does not believe that our citizens would see the advantage to be gained by a wide custom union or an extended control of currency and citizenship and migration. He does think it possible to sell the idea of a federation to keep the peace and to safeguard free institutions. The cost and the dangers of war are terrifying everyone; and the threat to personal liberty is being driven home by every European dispatch. So Clark would use the American Constitution as a model to surrender only so much of national sovereignty to a central government as would be necessary to accomplish these two purposes.

The difference between these plans is the difference between a genuine union and a federation. The difference is accentuated by the machinery provided.

Streit's deviation from the American model is not material. He substitutes a board of five for the presidency, and allows this board to delegate executive action to a premier of its selection, who in turn appoints his own cabinet. The board has to dismiss the premier and appoint another, English fashion, if he loses confidence of either house. And upon occasion the board can dissolve congress or either house and call for a new election. However, these are details put forth for discussion and not vital to the idea, which is a genuine union of peoples with a constitution, a legislature, an executive, and a judiciary adopted from the American plan.

Clark, on the other hand, has set up not a government but an assembly and a court to execute a contract. In this contract the members guarantee all citizens the equivalent of the Bill of Rights and agree that they will settle all disputes without resort to violence. They also agree to refer all disputes to arbitration or else submit them for final adjudication to one supreme court. Further, they enter into a covenant to protect one another against aggression by the application of economic sanctions or military force as ordered by the congress.

To implement this contract, a congress is elected by popular vote and roughly numbered to represent population. This congress is authorized to levy assessments against each member to provide funds to carry on. It can also order the economic sanctions and the military maneuvers agreed upon. To enforce this prerogative further, it is authorized to maintain a military and naval establishment of its own, by calling on members for contributions of men as well as of money, and to name the commanders-in-chief of any forces. It can also recommend economic and social measures, and appoint the members of the court. The court's duty is to settle disputes between the members.

At this stage of the proceeding it looks as if the planners were torn between two desires. One is to invent some machinery that will really prevent wars, both military and economic, make power responsible to the people, and safeguard the personal liberties of these people. The other is to make no change that does not meet present opinion and prejudices. One might guess that both cannot be done at once. But it is to be hoped and expected that universal exposition and discussion will prepare the people of the world for some such miracle as happened in Philadelphia in 1787. What appears to be needed in addition to a plan is a Benjamin Franklin.

TOWARD A FEDERAL WORLD [4]

It is not generally realized that the government of these United States, which came formally into existence a century and a half ago, is now the oldest of all the governments existing in the world. It is the only one which has not been changed in essential principles or revolutionized during the past century and a half. This fact is, of itself, a tribute to the wisdom and the foresight of those whom we so gladly call the Founding Fathers. On the continent of Europe every government which has not been wholly made over since the World War, came into being in its present form only after the Napoleonic Wars, or, as in the case of France, after the Franco-Prussian War of 1870-1871. The government of Great Britain, responding to the pressure of the steadily growing liberal movement during the 18th and 19th centuries, was substantially changed both as to its center of gravity and as to its governmental procedure following the Reform Bill of 1832, the Parliamentary Representation Act of 1867 and the Parliament Act of 1911. The last-named act gave the relations between the House of Commons and the House of Lords their present form. Still later, in 1931, the Statute of

[4] Address delivered at the Parrish Art Museum, Southampton, Long Island, September 3, 1939, by Nicholas Murray Butler, President Columbia University. Carnegie Endowment for International Peace. New York. p. 1-9.

Westminster, an act of the greatest importance in the history of constitutional government and public law, brought into existence the British Commonwealth of Nations as now constituted. This act applied the federal principle to legislatively independent members of a great empire scattered all around the world. The governments of the Central American and South American peoples are all younger than the government of the United States. The governments on the continents of Africa and of Asia have been and still are in a constant state of flux, and it remains to be seen what their more permanent form is to be.

When the Federal Constitution had been agreed upon by the Philadelphia Convention on September 17, 1787, and submitted to each of the thirteen independent and sovereign states for their consideration and hoped-for ratification, Benjamin Franklin, most far-seeing of men, wrote these words to Monsieur Grand, a friend in France, under date of October 22, 1787, sending him at the same time a copy of the proposed new Federal Constitution for the American states:

> If it succeeds, I do not see why you might not in Europe carry the project of good Henry the Fourth into execution, by forming a federal union and one grand republic of all its different states and kingdoms, by means of a like convention, for we had many interests to reconcile.

It would seem plain, therefore, that those men who planned with so much wisdom and so much foresight the Constitution of the United States felt that they were dealing with forces and ideals which might well be not only American but world-wide. They were the very opposite of isolationists.

Something of the same sort characterized the chief spokesmen of the French Revolution. They, too, believed that they were building not for France alone but for all Europe. The quick outburst of reaction which marked the twenty years of the rule of Napoleon Bonaparte pushed any such hope and ambition far into the background.

As a result of these happenings of one hundred and fifty years ago and their influence, the civilized world seemed far on the way toward becoming a world in which the principles of democracy ruled and would express themselves either in the form of a democratic monarchy, as in Great Britain, Belgium, the Netherlands and the Scandinavian countries, or in that of a democratic republic, as in the United States, France and Switzerland. In almost every other country of the world, even in Germany and in Russia, there were clear signs that the principles of liberalism were, in one form or another, finding steadily increasing expression and influence.

When the Great War came a quarter-century ago, it was quickly interpreted by the President of the United States as fundamentally a contest between democratic and anti-democratic principles of government. His famous phrase, a war to make the world safe for democracy, was heard in every land and was almost universally accepted as both the explanation and the justification of that stupendous struggle. The contradictory and unhappy result is now so obvious as to need no comment. The passions and ambitions which were set loose by that great war have been operating and still operate to do the principles of democracy greater damage than has ever heretofore been inflicted on them from any source. . . .

What is the lesson to be learned from all this? Surely it is now the clear demonstration of more than a thousand years of nation-building that the doctrine of national sovereignty is both unsound and dangerous. That doctrine can only lead, as it has led, to the notion that each and every established government is a law unto itself and not subject to any limitations or control in its dealings with other governments. Put bluntly, this means that when two of these so-called sovereign governments cannot agree upon any matter which affects them both, then recourse shall be had to force, which is war. Constituted as they are, human beings in control of the administration of governments that claim to be sovereign will be constantly at war, regardless of the loss of life or of property which must always accompany war, whether successful or unsuccessful.

From a situation such as this there are but two paths of escape. The one is universal world domination by a single government. On a larger or a smaller scale, this end has been sought time and time again for fully three thousand years. Oriental peoples sought it; Alexander the Great sought it; Julius Caesar and his successors at the head of the Roman Empire sought it. Charlemagne would have been glad to seek it, as would Napoleon Bonaparte a thousand years later. The German Reichsfuehrer of today has it plainly in mind. Surely after all these illuminating experiences it ought to be obvious to everyone that the world cannot be unified under a single social, economic and political control. This could not be done when the world was relatively a very simple place, but now that invention and modern science have made it so complicated, as well as so interdependent in its every part, world domination by a single power has become more impossible than ever. The search for world domination or even for domination over a considerable part of the earth's surface means and must mean constant and almost continuous war. Different backgrounds of national history, of language, of social and political experience, to say nothing of climate and of the conditions of life, have made any such form of world unification as the ancient empire builders sought, a purely imaginary aim. It has and can have no relation to reality.

If, then, sovereignty be denied to governments of any kind, what is it that in last resort should rule and guide the action of men and shape the public policies of the governments which the several nations may from time to time set up? Obviously it is the moral law.

This moral law is not difficult to understand. Everyone, however great, knows when he is telling the truth, when he is acting in unselfish regard for the welfare of his fellow-men and when he is subjugating the gain-seeking or the power-seeking motive to higher and more constructive principles. The practical-minded man will see this. The theoretical person who loves to deal only with words and with the impressions of the moment, may take some time, perhaps a long time, to learn it. Unless it be learned, however, there is no escape from that barbarism which is return to the jungle.

The alternative to the hopeless attempt at universal world domination by a single government is that world-wide application of the federal principle which has already played so influential a part in modern political history and which alone has the power to make it possible for modern man to solve in permanent fashion, through the cooperation of nations, his unbelievably difficult and complicated problems, both economic, social and political.

The federal principle and its application upon an increasingly large scale have been before the minds of men for hundreds of years. One seer after another and one far-sighted statesman after another have proclaimed and interpreted the federal principle as essential to the peaceful, orderly maintenance and development of civilization. Few declarations of this principle are more significant or more definite than this prophecy written in autograph by Victor Hugo on the wall of the room in the Place des Vosges, Paris, where he died:

> I represent a party which does not yet exist: the party of revolution, civilization. This party will make the twentieth century. There will issue from it first the United States of Europe, then the United States of the World.

This federal principle must not be confused with group or regional alliances between governments for their own aggrandizement, no matter what may happen to the rest of the world. The federal principle, as supremely manifested in the Federal Constitution of the United States and in the Statute of Westminster which created the British Commonwealth of Nations, makes it not only possible but natural for a Vermont, a South Dakota, an Idaho and a Utah, or for a Newfoundland, a Union of South Africa and a New Zealand to enter a political partnership upon equal terms with a New York, an Illinois and a

Texas in the one case, or with a Canada and an Australia in the other. Under a properly organized federal system, the population or the wealth of a political partner gives no advantage in all that is essential to citizenship and to political liberty. The influence of the more populous and the richer peoples will always be dominant or nearly so, but that dominance will be exercised under the limitations of the articles of federation. This will involve no injustice and no discrimination against the less populous and the less wealthy members of the federation.

The practical question is, How can this tremendous and crucial problem be lifted from the region of discussion to that of early and definite action? It is plain that the world cannot wait.

One of the lessons which experience teaches is that in large matters of this kind too much must not be attempted at once. The overwhelming majority of men have to be taught, and it takes a long time to teach them. The Federal Government of the United States stands before the whole world as instructor in what the federal principle may accomplish over an enormous area with a huge and varied population. Nevertheless, if the attempt were made to organize the entire world in a satisfactory federation at once, it would probably fail, either wholly or in large part. The differences of background, of inheritance, of experience and of language might be found too great to permit an effective world-wide federal union at one stroke. The path of progress, obviously, is to promote the early organization of a world federation which would include, if not all European and Asiatic peoples, then those which are sufficiently self-controlled and like-minded to make a beginning possible. In due time and after the value of the federal principle had received new illustration, it would become practicable to go a step farther and begin to bring more of the national governments into a still larger union. There is no reason why those states which are called totalitarian should not be included in such a federal union, provided they will cease striving to extend their areas and their control by force, and will accept, honestly and completely, the principles upon which such a federal union is built. We need have no concern with the form of government which any independent people adopts for itself, if only it keeps its word and respects its international and federal obligations.

There is nothing new about this proposal to extend the federal principle. If mankind had shown itself capable of learning by experience, great progress would have been made centuries ago in developing a world system of federal unions which might easily have become a single world-wide union long before this 20th century. The story of these attempts and of the measure of success which they severally achieved will be found in very succinct form in the little volume entitled *Federations: A Study in Comparative Politics,* written by D. G. Karve, Professor of History and Economics at Fergusson College, Poona, India, and published seven years ago. It will surprise many readers of the present day to learn how clearly this idea of federation was in the minds of men almost from the very beginning of political organization. The Dutch Union between the provinces of the Lowlands, which lasted for more than two centuries, and the Swiss Federation, which is the oldest of all the existing federal states, are particularly rich in opportunity for study. In fact, the Swiss Federation and the United States of America may be regarded as the two most productive research laboratories in which the student and the builder of new federations may best carry on his work.

The history of Switzerland offers abundant material for guidance in dealing with this problem today. That country has many small towns and cities of only moderate size. Its physical formation, with high mountains, deep valleys, and many streams, provides almost compelling invitation to the development of many small communities, living largely in isolation and in independent social and political life. Some two-thirds of the population speak German and most of the remaining one-third speak French, although there is a very considerable number of those whose language is Italian. The population is divided almost equally between Protestants and Catholics, with a greater number of Protestants. These people, so placed and with such diverse backgrounds, have been successful, it would appear, in working out a plan for national unity which is wholly consonant with civil liberty and with local self-government. If the people of Switzerland have been able to achieve this great end, why should not others be able to follow their example and go and do likewise? Switzerland, of course, has passed through its difficult periods. These were in part due to religious strife, and in part to the rivalry between urban and rural cantons. But, taken as a whole and looking back over more than five hundred years, it is clear that Switzerland has a most important lesson to teach this modern world.

Had the Republic of Czechoslovakia, at the time of its organization in 1919, been based upon the cantonal system, its history during the past twenty years might have been very different and far happier. A Czechoslovakia composed of, say, five Czech cantons, two Slovak cantons, two German cantons, one Polish canton and one Hungarian canton, following the example of Switzerland, might well have been able to weather the storms which have marked the attempt to give to this splendid people the independent economic and political organization which they desire and should have.

In relation to this vitally important matter we have reached a point where the responsibility of the people of the United States is outstanding and imperative. As economic and political theories have developed and found expression in various governments, whether in Europe or in Asia, it has become impossible, at least for some time to come, for any other government than that of the United States to give the leadership for which the world is waiting. Had our American political acts during the past generation been true to our professions, and had the elected representatives of the two great political parties, when in office at Washington, kept the pledges which those parties had made to the American people in one political campaign after another, this world would today have been far on the way toward successful organization to promote prosperity and to preserve peace.

AMERICAN BACKGROUND TO BRIAND'S VISION OF A UNITED EUROPE [5]

We of the western world have had some experience in matters of federation and, as the American experiment is the only one which has hitherto survived its maker, it will perhaps not be considered impertinent to venture to suggest that America should not be overlooked in contemplating a *rapprochement,* however loose, of the nations of Europe. Of course, it would be preposterous to propose the acceptance of an American plan, however thoroughly it might have justified itself in this part of the world, because a country is not, and can not be, a free agent; it is conditioned by its traditions, from which it is difficult, if not impossible, to separate itself. Its past is in its present and the future must take note of each.

The Americans have had many and great difficulties to overcome; their past so infinitesimal, their traditions so recent as to be of their own making, that with good will they were able to form what they ventured to call "a more perfect union," which we of today would be inclined to speak of in the superlative. I would only venture to say that the American experiment has proved that states regarding themselves as free, independent and sovereign may live together, and in union, and under some form of a superintending head or government.

This is a fact which dare not be overlooked, for what one group of states has done, another may do, even though it be in a lesser and in a different degree. The past and the exigencies of the present must determine the form. What these exigen-

[5] By James Brown Scott, Honorary Editor-in-Chief, *American Journal of International Law. American Journal of International Law.* 24:738-42. October, 1930.

cies are, I may not consider. It is sufficient if I add that the form of government which the more perfect union was to replace had proved inadequate. It was a diplomatic association, rather than a union of states; and under these circumstances, it seemed to be impossible for the statesmen of that day to better the economic breakdown from which the states were suffering. The Declaration of Independence was of July 4, 1776, and it was exactly eleven years later that the delegates of the American states met in conference in Philadelphia to consider what could be done. It is eleven years since the World War, and the statesmen of Europe find themselves face to face with economic conditions which to them seem insupportable, if they do not indeed spell a breakdown, as was the case with us. It is, if I may venture to say so, well for the countries of Europe that their leading statesmen should likewise confer.

The American states had suffered from paper currency. They had not wholly recovered from the effects of a long and protracted war—almost double that of Europe in length, and under circumstances not less disastrous. Each state determined what commodities should enter and what should leave its frontiers, and the tariff to be imposed in either case. The result was that commerce was at a standstill, and that the sources of economic life were drying up. A merchant found commodities on hand a debit rather than an asset.

A few delegates had met at Annapolis the year before, ten years after the Declaration of Independence, to consider what could be done for commerce between the states; but the problems loomed so large that they felt that nothing could be done without a conference of the states; and accordingly a conference was held the ensuing year in Philadelphia, in which twelve of the states were represented by their official spokesmen. Last year—ten years after the World War—the statesmen of Europe began to discuss in Geneva, the possibilities of ameliorating the economic situation through a *rapprochement* of their various countries.

The cause of the American gathering of the states was, as I have said, and which I feel that I should repeat, commercial or economic; indeed the chairman, as we would say today, of the Massachusetts delegation, remarked on the floor of the Federal Convention that Massachusetts was able to defend itself and therefore did not need the protection of the other states; and that its whole reason for federation was the commercial situation.

What can be done, or what the men of light and leading in Europe should do, is for them and the peoples whom they represent to determine. It will not perhaps be considered immodest on our part to say that our Revolutionary Fathers thought themselves to be in the same condition and that they found a way out through union, which has proved satisfactory to their descendants.

There are four things which they did, and which, taken together, made a success of the experiment, for it was an experiment. Madison himself, whom a grateful posterity calls "the Father of the Constitution," saying that it was the first time that the representatives of states had met to deliberate on the form of government to be established in an accordance with their views and their needs. He went on to say, as I recall it, that the labors of their hands would be received with astonishment and admiration, were they able peaceably and freely and satisfactorily—I am quoting literally—"to establish one general government, when there is such a diversity of opinions and interests," when not cemented or stimulated by any common danger.

The first of the four things, whose conjunction has produced both astonishment and admiration, is that the peoples of the states reserved to themselves the powers of sovereignty, which they did not grant to a general government of their choice and creation. To such an extent is this true that, if the Constitution of the United States should be repealed over night, the forty-eight states of the American Union would appear before an astonished world as so many free, independent and sovereign states, with all the trappings and agencies of government.

The second of the four things is a plan of reaching the peoples of the state to the extent of the powers granted to the federal government, without the intervention or compulsion of a state. The state did not need to act, as the law of the federal government was to bind all inhabitants of each of the states, and the federal obligations were to be interpreted and applied through the federal courts to be created for this purpose. There is thus a local law of the state for purposes beginning and ending within the state; there is a federal law for purposes beginning, it may be, and ending within the state and yet affecting foreign nations; and the nature and extent and application of these laws are determined by courts of the federal government. There is here no force, no pressure, no compulsion upon the state; the individual obeys the federal government just as he had learned to obey the state government; there was to be a double allegiance—general to the state and special to the extent of the granted powers to the states in their united capacities.

The third of the four things is that the framers of the Union refused to have the capital located in any one of the states for fear that it would be dominated by the state in which it was situated. This seems simple today, but to them it was new and therefore difficult. It was a union of states, for the proclamation of independence found the colonies and the states without a foot of American soil which was not either held or claimed by one of the colonies and later by the states.

The Continental Congress, a body of diplomatic representatives, met in various capitals and towns, as the military situation permitted or required, and, as the government of the United States was not to be possessed of territory in its own right but to hold unsettled territory in trust for new states as the territory should be settled, it taxed the statesmanship of their leaders to locate the government somewhere in property possessed by the government and over which it should continue to exercise undivided authority. They hit upon a plan of authorizing the Congress of the Union to accept a strip of territory, not exceeding ten miles square, from one or more states which should be willing to grant it for that purpose. This is the District of Columbia, in which the government of the United States rules, as does the Pope in the still smaller state of the Vatican, in order to reach something more than one hundred millions in the one case and hundreds of millions in the other.

The last of the four things is that the states intended to and actually did organize the states of the Union for peaceful purposes. They contented themselves with militia. They renounced war between and among themselves, unless they were actually invaded and provided they did not have time to appeal to the government of their creation for protection in the hostilities which should arise between them. They had renounced the resort to war, and each state had renounced the right to make treaties with another. If neither war nor diplomacy were to settle disputes, what was to be done? They proposed, and they established, a court of the states which we know today as the Supreme Court of the United States, in which a state can sue and be sued by a state as ordinary individuals are sued in a court of justice. That this may be done on a larger and even more comprehensive scale is evidenced by the existence and successful operation of the Permanent Court of International Justice at The Hague.

So much for what may seem merely a domestic situation. Yet it is not without influence upon the outer world.

Canada was then an integral part of Great Britain, even if it be not so at the present time. Upon a matter of such delicacy I should not express an opinion. The fact is, however, that at a time when Canada formed part and parcel of what we call the British Empire the two countries agreed to live in peace with each other, so that, for the past one hundred years or more there has not been, and there is not now, a soldier or a fort for the more than three thousand miles of common boundary between the Dominion of Canada and these United States of America. There is not a soldier, nor is there a fortress, marking the boundaries between the Republic of Mexico to the south of these United States, and there is not a fleet on any of the inland waters of Canada and of the United States, through which, I am informed, commerce larger than that of the Mediterranean annually passes.

Law is better than force and justice better than law. We of the West, of European inheritance, have taken advantage of the newer traditions, and we hope that Europe will find it possible in some way to bend to its will the newer traditions of its own newer world, so that the actions of states, as well as of their peoples, shall be of law and of justice. It can be done because it has been done; those who did it felt that they were carrying into effect a European ideal, and that they were showing the possibility of its being done in Europe upon what was to them a larger and much more impressive scale.

THE PARADOX OF SOVEREIGNTY [6]

Whatever may be the immediate cause of any particular war, it seems clear that war as an institution could only persist in a world of sovereign states, each claiming the right to decide its own affairs as it sees fit, claiming in addition the right to decide where its "vital interests" begin and end, and refusing to recognize any authority as superior to its own. It follows that to a certain extent the institution of sovereignty is a cause of all wars, and that the most straightforward and only permanent way to abolish war is to abolish sovereignty.

This is easily seen if we compare Europe with the United States of America. The state of Connecticut does not think it

[6] By W. B. Curry, Director of Education, Dartington Hall, Totnes, England. Author of "The Case for Federal Union." *New Republic.* 102:176-7. February 5, 1940.

necessary to "defend" itself against the state of New York. Its children are not brought up to imagine themselves nobly sacrificing their lives for the honor or "vital interests" of Connecticut, or in defense of "gallant little" Rhode Island. European states on the contrary are in a condition of chronic "defense." . . .

It would seem that those who desire a lasting peace should also desire the surrender of the independent control of foreign policy, and the rapid creation of federal institutions for the whole world, together with the indispensable partial replacement of patriotic by cosmopolitan sentiment.

It is here that we come to the paradox in the present situation. If you ask a patriot why he objects to a World State, he will usually reply that he wishes his country to retain its independence of action, and, in effect, that he does not like the idea of its affairs being meddled with by a "pack of foreigners" sitting in Geneva. He will add that no sovereign state can be expected to surrender any of its independence unless compelled to do so by force.

Let us look a little further into this freedom that is so important that rather than surrender it nations are now risking final destruction in a world war. We are not to have World Government, it seems, because we must retain the right to manage our own affairs. In the years before the outbreak of the present war, the world was spending thousands of millions on armaments. Were these armaments part of a plan for the better management of our affairs? Did we enjoy them? Were they part of the pattern of life as we ideally wished to see it? In short, did anyone *want* these armaments? Apparently not, since when you asked the patriot whether he wanted them, he replied, "No, of course we don't want them, but we *have to have them because other nations have them.*" They are the result, apparently, not of choice but of compulsion.

Now there are some things we really do want. Think of the inroads on poverty, ignorance and disease that could have been made with those thousands of millions we were spending on armaments, and are now spending on "defense." Every slum in the world could be cleared for a fraction of this total. Think of what one percent of it would mean to medical research. Why, then, in the free exercise of our sovereign right to do what we like, don't we spend the money on education or houses or social services? The answer is that, being free and sovereign, *foreigners won't let us.* They compel us to spend money on armaments instead. So what our sovereignty amounts to is this: we waste our substance in order to preserve the right to be compelled to waste our substance.

Consider the question of trade. We all believe, or say we believe, that trade barriers ought to be reduced or abolished. We hold that a world of universal free trade, embodying, as it would, the maximum use of the principle of division of labor, would be better off than a world whose trade is choked with quotas, currency restrictions and high tariff barriers. England, for instance, would like to sell her goods as freely in Europe and the rest of the world as Connecticut sells her goods in the rest of the United States. But Connecticut does not wish, or at least has lost the right, to keep out "cheap foreign cars" from Detroit. Connecticut, having lost her freedom to impose tariffs, has retained her freedom to export her goods.

Or take the question of travel. Freedom of movement is surely a sufficiently elementary freedom, and yet in Europe it had practically died out even before the war, and what remained was accompanied by every kind of vexatious restriction. And all in the name of this precious freedom of sovereign states. How different, and how much freer, when states are no longer sovereign. You can travel from New York to San Francisco without once having your baggage opened and pawed about by a customs official, without any tiresome examination of passports, and without either having to change your money half a dozen times or being searched as you pass from Utah to Nevada in order to be sure that you are not taking too much money with you. In short, in the United States, human beings (for whose welfare states ostensibly exist) have retained the freedom to travel because the separate states have lost the freedom to annoy travelers.

The freedom conferred by sovereignty seems, therefore, to be a very queer thing. It compels us to do without things we want in order to spend vast sums on armaments that we don't want. It causes us to throttle each other's trade and to impede each other's travel. From time to time it causes us all to be conscripted and thus lose our freedom altogether. Finally it gives rise to periodic outbreaks of mass mutual homicide during which millions lose not merely their freedom but their lives. Is it possible to conceive of anything much more bound than this freedom of sovereign states?

Suppose instead that we lost this freedom. Suppose that, like the United States, *all* states had lost the right to maintain armed forces, the right to do what they like in matters affecting other countries, the right to impose tariffs or interfere with free travel. What a hideous state of slavery would result! We should no longer be liable to be conscripted in order to kill and be killed in conflicts arising out of imperial rivalries. The whole world would be our shop and the whole world our market. We should wander as freely over the world as Americans now wander over America. If we wished to tax ourselves in order to improve our roads, our schools or our houses, we should be free to do so, much more free indeed than if we had already spent more than we could afford, and borrowed the rest, in order to "defend" ourselves. As regards social life generally, why should we be less free than we are now? Individually we should be richer, happier, healthier and freer. Collectively we should have lost only the martial elements in national pride. What should we have lost that is worth preserving?

The interdependence of the modern world means that a world order sooner or later is inevitable. Either it will be imposed after the present period of slaughter and chaos, or it will come about later because we at last perceive it to be desirable. Which shall it be?

FEDERAL PRINCIPLES AND COMMON CONCEPT OF JUSTICE [7]

The foundations of peace must be the establishment and maintenance of an order so permeated by justice that the majority of men will not be moved to violence.

Since primitive times man has sought to find the means of getting along peacefully with his fellow-man. For this purpose he has formed such associations—families, tribes, villages, states and nations, and even leagues of nations—as seemed appropriate. In any such association, whether small or large, the primary purpose is to protect whatever the individuals consider their rights and interests. In order to do this successfully the individuals must agree as to what their rights are and what mutual obligations they will assume to protect them. This they can do only if they think fundamentally along the same lines—if "justice" means more or less the same thing to them—if violence among each other is outlawed.

Once this basis of common agreement has been reached, it becomes relatively easy to formulate laws for the protection of rights and interests and to maintain these laws by the common-consent use of force—in other words, police. If the laws are rooted in clear and firm majority opinion, their enforcement against the occasional transgressor is relatively simple. The trouble begins when laws are not supported by clear and firm popular opinion. This may happen from a great variety of causes, which the following random examples will serve to illustrate:

1. When laws are originally not arrived at by a democratic process but are promulgated by arbitrary authority; as, for instance, Hitler's laws today.

2. When laws are passed in a mood of popular sentiment which turns out to be temporary; as for, instance, our prohibition law, which gave rise to gangsterism.

[7] From article "Axis Defeat First But Not Ultimate Road to Peace," by James P. Warburg, Economist, New York. *New York Times.* Sec. 4. p. 8, 9. February 2, 1941.

3. When circumstances under which the law was passed have changed while the law remains the same; as, for instance, a speed limit of twenty miles an hour, which no one obeys and the police do not enforce.

One could give countless other examples. These merely illustrate the normal difficulties with which advancing civilization has had to cope. Every now and then there has been a failure, a resort to violence, and a setback. But, on the whole, western man had until recent times advanced fairly steadily toward the development of an order in which the resort to violence became constantly less necessary.

In recent years, however, the industrialization of the world, the elimination of time and distance, and the constantly increasing interdependence of the various parts of the world upon each other have vastly complicated the problem. Internal injustices within nations as well as external injustices between nations have become so aggravated that we have seen the gradual spread of disorder, and the breakdown of peace and justice engulfing almost the entire civilized world.

If we can in some small measure comprehend the basic nature of this disaster, we shall have taken the first step toward reconstruction.

Let us define one principle which—with all due respect to many contributing causes—seems to underlie the whole problem. This principle applies not only to the political structure within and between nations, but to the social and economic structure within nations as well.

The principle is this: An order permeated with justice demands that all those who are affected by the exercise of any power—political, social or economic—must have a voice in deciding to whom that power is delegated and how it is exercised. Whenever this principle is violated, injustice is created and the seeds of violence are sown.

We have sought to recognize this principle within our own country.

In our political structure we have evolved a formula which seeks, not always successfully, to combine the advantages of home rule in local matters with national unity under the federal principle. We have tried to recognize that the law-making and law-enforcing power should be coextensive with the area in which that power exercises its effect. City government is supposed to regulate matters whose effect takes place within city limits; state power pertains to matters which affect only the people within a state; and the power of the federal government is intended to be confined to matters which affect peoples in many states.

The power belongs to the people, who delegate it in accordance with the principle that power and responsibility to those affected by its use go hand in hand.

This is the political principle with which the Axis is at war and which it seeks to destroy throughout the world.

Where our political system breaks down occasionally it is due not so much to any fault of the structure as to the failure of the people to exercise the voice which the system gives them for their own protection.

But whereas we have come fairly close to achieving what most of us would consider "justice" in our political system, the same cannot be said of our social and economic structure. It is true that we have made great strides in recent years. We are groping our way forward. But the New Deal's much-discussed reforms are only first tentative steps in applying to economic power the same principles which we have long recognized as to political power. There are still great areas in our economic structure where power is wielded—sometimes arbitrarily—over people who have no effective voice in the delegation or exercise of that power. . . .

The path of further progress does not lead, as many fear, toward the dead hand of state socialism being laid upon the vital nerve centers of private enterprise. The path of further progress leads through enlightened self-interest toward a new, more socially conscious capitalism.

The solution is not to be found merely in further social legislation. Neither intelligence nor morality can be legislated. The soil in which new laws may take firm root must first be plowed and fertilized through the enlightenment of public opinion. The danger is that we shall lapse into an attitude of what has been called "preserving our social gains"—not recognizing that we have captured only a few outposts of the vast territory to be conquered.

The same basic principle of justice applies to the international order.

Just as within the nation we shall have to curtail the sovereignty of economic man and distribute economic power, as we have distributed political power—so we shall have to change and limit an outworn concept of national sovereignty. The government of a nation must have the power to do within its nation whatever the people of that nation desire it to do; it must not have the power to do things which affect the people of other nations without their too having a voice in the matter.

The application of this principle to international affairs has many implications, both economic and political.

It means that artificial barriers to the free flow of goods and services, or to the movements of people, must be recognized as matters which concern not one but all nations; that no nation shall have the right to erect such barriers—which include altering the relative value of currencies—without consultation with other nations.

It means the disarmament of individual nations, except for necessary domestic police forces, and the creation of an international police force strong enough to discourage any nation or group of nations from attempting to use force in the settlement of a dispute.

It means the creation of some sort of super-national machinery for the specific and limited purpose of exercising jointly and by mutual consultation the powers which, when exercised, affect the inhabitants of more than one nation.

It means not a league of sovereign nations, but the gradual extension of the federal principle by sovereign peoples actuated by a common aim of peace and a common concept of justice.

This is a stupendous undertaking. It cannot be accomplished overnight. It cannot be accomplished at all except in so far as there exists among the peoples concerned a more or less similar idea of what constitutes "justice." A super-national organism of this sort can no more exist "half slave and half free" than could our own Union.

This does not mean that, if the forces of democracy are victorious, they must seek to enforce democracy upon such peoples as may not be ripe or ready for it. Democracy can no more be enforced than peace, unless it corresponds to what a people's sense of justice demands.

It does mean that, when this war is over, the peoples who believe in democracy, who believe that the state is their servant and not their master, will have a chance, by banding together, to create an environment in which democracy can exist in peace.

Finally, let us face squarely what stands in the way of such a development.

The danger which threatens the continued existence of the order which we wish to preserve is the inherent weakness of nineteenth-century capitalism—namely, its tendency to become rigid, to deny change and to freeze to the status quo. This weakness can be overcome.

Neither the profit motive itself nor the inequality of wealth and power which it engenders is the cause of the trouble.

The trouble starts when those who have acquired power exercise it without sufficient sense of responsibility, without sufficient understanding of its ramified effects, and, above all, to protect their own position by erecting unnatural obstacles to change. When they do this they outrage the "sense of justice" of the masses and, by obstructing change, frustrate their efforts to remedy the injustice.

This is what destroys hope and leads to revolution—not the inequality of wealth and power, but their exploitation to prevent change and progress, which constitutes the denial of equal opportunity.

When those in power use their strength merely to entrench and fortify their privileged position, the common man rebels. He then becomes the prey of demagogues who promise him utopia, if only he will wear a shirt of black or brown or red.

It was not the common man who originally caused the trouble. It was the political man, the industrial man, the great landowner, the banker—all too many of whom placed concern for the maintenance of their own privileged position ahead of all other considerations. These men, and their social and economic parasites, were the original betrayers. Out of their selfishness were born the extreme mass movements of the left. Out of their fear, aroused by these movements, were born the reactionary dictatorships of the right.

We shall build a new and better world if the common man regains his faith, his hope of the future, and with it his courage to meet the present. He will regain them if those in positions of power and privilege share his faith and his hope—if they match his courage, if they realize before it is too late that progress can be guided but never thwarted—that the only way to retain power and privilege is to use them for the common good.

Our hope of peace is inextricably interwoven with the establishment of an order which will make recurring major conflicts unnecessary. There can be no peace for us alone in a world torn by war, nor in a world precariously balanced upon a knife-edge of constantly threatened conflict. We cannot withdraw from reality into a fancied dream-world of imaginary security. If we want peace we must do our share toward creating a world order in which there can be peace.

THE NATURE OF FEDERATION [8]

Federation organizes consent on the international scale while empire organizes coercion on that scale. Though coercion of the part by the whole is the essence of government, in the system of federalism that coercion can only be in accord with law, to which those bound have directly or indirectly consented. World federation, balancing the autonomy of the nation-state with the authority of the family of nations, was the system implied by the founders of modern international law after the breakup of the medieval empire. Organization to make international law effective was, however, hampered by exaggerated developments of the idea of sovereignty. A sovereign state, at the present time, claims the power to judge its own controversies, to enforce its own conception of its rights, to increase its armaments without limit, to treat its own nationals as it sees fit, and to regulate its economic life without regard to the effect of such regulations upon its neighbors.

These attributes of sovereignty must be limited.

(a) Nations must renounce the claim to be the final judge in their controversies with other nations and must submit to the jurisdiction of international tribunals. The basis of peace is justice; and justice is not the asserted claim of any one party, but must be determined by the judgment of the community.

(b) Nations must renounce the use of force for their own purposes in relations with other nations, except in self-defense. The justification for self-defense must always be subject to review by an international court or other competent body.

(c) The right of nations to maintain aggressive armaments must be sacrificed in consideration for an assurance of the security of all through regional and world-wide forces subject to international law and adequate to prevent illegal resorts to international violence.

[8] From Preliminary Report of the Commission to Study the Organization of Peace. p. 11-13. The Commission. New York. November, 1940.

(d) Nations must accept certain human and cultural rights in their constitutions and in international covenants. The destruction of civil liberties anywhere creates danger of war. The peace is not secure if any large and efficient population is permanently subject to a control which can create a fanatical national sentiment impervious to external opinion.

(e) Nations must recognize that their right to regulate economic activities is not unlimited. The world has become an economic unit; all nations must have access to its raw materials and its manufactured articles. The effort to divide the resources of the world into sixty economic compartments is one of the causes of war. The economic problem arising from this effort has increased in gravity with the scientific and industrial progress of the modern world.

Such renunciations of sovereignty for the common good will necessitate new institutions, world-wide and regional, to perform the services which can no longer be left to each state acting separately. The diplomatic system, international conferences, international tribunals with voluntary jurisdiction, international administrative unions, are steps toward a federal organization of the world, but they are not enough. International organizations must be created or developed from past experience. The following are essential:

(a) An international court with jurisdiction adequate to deal with all international disputes on the basis of law.

(b) International legislative bodies to remedy abuses in existing law and to make new law whenever technical progress requires the adjustment of international practice.

(c) Adequate police forces, world-wide or regional, and world-wide economic sanctions, to prevent aggression and to support international covenants.

(d) International machinery with authority to regulate international communication and transportation and to deal with such problems as international commerce, finance, health, nutrition, and labor standards—with regard to all of which the successful working of the constitution of the International Labor Organization offers valuable lessons.

(e) Appropriate authorities to administer backward areas ceded to the world federation. Such administration should give precedence to the interest of the inhabitants of the area, looking to their eventual self-government; assure all nations equal economic opportunity within the area; and should facilitate colonization and economic development of areas suitable for that purpose without injury to the native inhabitants. International corporations might well be encouraged to enlist world-wide support for the constructive task of developing such areas under supervision of such authorities.

Aristide Briand once wrote "There is not one peace for America, one peace for Europe and another for Asia, but one peace for the entire world." The nations of the New World cannot sever the links which bind them to those of the Old. The lesson which should have been learned in 1914 is being taught with greater suffering in 1940, that a threat to the peace, prosperity and the liberties of any part of the world causes profound economic dislocation and political fear in every other part of the world. While the Commission to Study the Organization of Peace recognizes this universality as fundamental, it also recognizes that there may be regional variations in any practical plan for world society. It is hard to see how Europe can emerge from its present catastrophe without sacrificing a greater degree of the sovereignty of its states than would be possible or desirable in other continents. International conditions have forced the nations of the Western Hemisphere to intensify the Pan American organization. The British Commonwealth is an essential and living organism and is a powerful factor for international organization, uniting the continents. The Soviet Union, the Far East, and the Near East, each constitute regions with distinctive characteristics; others may develop. While some rules of law must apply to all nations alike, in many matters variations must be provided within the distinctive regions.

POST-WAR WORLD [9]

World life will be entirely different after the present conflict from what it has ever been before. Whichever side wins in Europe or in Asia, we will have a new world around us. One epoch in human progress will have ended and another begun.

I am not thinking only of the conflicting ideologies and philosophies prevailing at the moment. What I have in mind is world life as a whole: its method, system, and organization. I shall try, after over twenty years abroad, to answer, without partisanship or pleading, some of the questions distressing millions of people today as to why the present world tragedy came about, how another can be avoided, and where this planet of ours is going.

Our starting point must be, I think, a recognition that the world's highways are becoming constantly more and more jammed. Distances are shrinking, startlingly; industry is reaching always farther afield; the world's population has jumped well over the two billion mark. Frontiers have passed not only for the United States but for the world.

Units of government are spreading out correspondingly. Germany stands astride Europe; Japan is reaching down from Manchuria through China towards the Dutch Indies; our own western hemisphere is moving outwards to global defense. We talk today not only of national, but of continental policies: of hemisphere defense, a new Europe, "a new order in Asia."

Whatever the outcome of the great conflicts now rending both Europe and Asia, we are apt to see agglomerations of power on a scale far transcending national lines. Large parts of both continents will be a shambles, looking outwards in distress for the most elementary necessities of life; martial law may be necessary merely to meet the primary needs of peoples; relief and reconstruction will have to be organized on an unprecedented scale.

[9] Radio address over Columbia Broadcasting System, by Arthur Sweetser, member of the League of Nations Secretariat since 1918. *Talks.* 5:41-5. October, 1940.

This will mean that international cooperation, far from being unnecessary, will be necessary to a degree such as we have never known. Despite the present holocaust, mankind stands on the threshold of a world era. The present conflicts are not only wars between nations; they are in a very real sense revolts against world society. The days of private or local wars are gone; a war today in any part of the world is a danger to all.

Twenty years ago, after World War Number One, the peoples of the world breathed a great hope. A generous armistice was signed; a great agency of peace was born out of the agony of desire to end war for all time. Many useful things were accomplished in the intervening years, yet the world is today in the grip of an even more bitter struggle.

The reason is tragically simple. The truest statement yet made about peace was that made to the American people by the President of the United States.

"Peace," he said, "must be affirmatively reached for. It cannot just be wished for. It cannot just be waited for."

That, in a nutshell, explains the tragedy of the past twenty years. The nations sought to secure world peace, the most precious of all things, for nothing. They made no sacrifice, gave up no sovereignty, abated none of their claims, accepted no outside judgment. What a travesty it is that, while peoples vote colossal taxes, conscription, or any other necessity for national defense, they fail to see that the very best defense against war is to prevent war! Very few make the mental effort to think out a positive, aggressive program of peace; they only too readily accept worn-out demagoguery from their leaders. One wonders, indeed, if deep in their hearts, they really wish peace as much as they profess; if they did, it would seem that they would demand an energetic, thoughtful policy, instead of vague emotionalism or weak defeatism.

Let him who doubts ask what has been the prime motive-force in the past twenty years. Has it not been that of every man for himself? Immediately after the last war, after just a flicker of idealism, the disruptive forces of selfishness and provincialism set in. First, the victor nations, exhausted, bitter, divided, proved unable to make a wise peace. Next, the United States, till then holding a beacon-light before the world, lost faith in its own proposals and withdrew into isolation without even giving them a chance or ever offering an alternative. Third, the Allies, driven back still further, were always late in their efforts at conciliation. Finally, other powers, driven alternately by feelings of injustice, economic pressure, and personal ambition, decided to hack out their futures by force.

The period 1920-40 was a tragic period of fear and distrust, not unnatural, perhaps, after a world cataclysm, but wholly out of line with the new world being born within it. Man's physical facilities had augmented enormously; his mental faculties lagged far behind. His voice began to span the world in a second's time; his airplanes crossed ocean and desert with fantastic speed, but his spirit huddled in fear and uncertainty. Still quivering from the repercussions of the war, frightened anew by the dislocations brought on by history's greatest economic development, he ended by standing paralyzed between the most extreme and contradictory challenges to all accepted dogmas of life, religion and government.

The League of Nations born out of the last war was sound in principle and in form. It had one desperate weakness beyond its own control: that it was never given the spirit and support which alone would have made it work. Certain nations were not admitted at the start; another nation disavowed its own creation; the others entered only half-heartedly. The spirit guiding its member states was not that of the community interest, but solely that of the individual government.

Back home, it was even worse. A statesman who showed himself supremely nationalistic and egotistic was cheered; one who proposed a generous gesture as in fact a long-range investment for his own people risked his political life. It was the hardest, not the wisest bargain that won acclaim; the selfish national victory even at the risk of a permanent enmity. Few of us can dissociate ourselves from a share in this responsibility; only too often we have failed to appreciate that an unwise victory today may prove to be a disaster tomorrow.

Money is not always a barometer of human motive; often, however, it gives a key to its intensity. Consider one small fact: the nations of the world put into their only general agencies of peace, League of Nations, International Labor Organization, and Permanent Court of International Justice, the paltry sum, all of them together, of but $7,000,000 annually. This year's arms appropriation for the United States alone, ten billions of dollars, would have paid all those contributions for nearly one thousand five hundred years. Or, put the other way around, the total expenditures for all these agencies during a year would meet this year's American arms bill for just about six hours. You cannot dam Niagara with a straw; you cannot get world peace for a penny.

Despite all this, however, and despite the present conflict, the fact remains that never in human history has there been such a concerted effort for cooperation between nations as in the past twenty years. The experience of the League of Nations, despite its major failure, has demonstrated that nations can work together, build together, plan together for the mutual good of all.

Each year for twenty years, some three score nations, with a thousand delegates and experts, have met in annual assembly at Geneva to discuss every phase of common international interest. Over one hundred times the more important of them have come together in the Council. Every day, year in and year out, some seven hundred international officials have worked together in a highly efficient international civil service. And from these central agencies have radiated out several scores of special agencies, whether autonomous organizations such as the Labor Office, the Court, and the various Institutes, or special committees on everything from the prevention of double taxation to the preservation of whales. And from them have sprung special plenary gatherings such as the World Economic and Disarmament Conferences and literally scores of others more modest.

These agencies have widened old channels of international cooperation and opened up new ones. Certain embryonic prewar activities for the prevention of the drug or white slave traffic were given an undreamed-of impetus.

Others wholly new to the international field such as nutrition and housing, were forged out of the confrontation of many minds and interests from all parts of the world, not least of all from this country.

Much of this is in silence today. The corridors of the League building at Geneva are sadly empty. The international officials gathered from all countries are largely scattered, some of them to that university town of Princeton, New Jersey, whence Woodrow Wilson became President of the United States. The light of organized international cooperation is dimmed.

But the spirit of all this can never die. A small embryo has been given life; it may be smothered for a moment, but it cannot be stifled permanently. The evils of the alternative method are now being written in blood.

Man has ahead of him the greatest intellectual and emotional effort in his long history. He must learn that beyond the nation is the world; that, whether he likes it or not, he is dependent on his fellow-man in other continents. He must either learn to work with them and prosper, or work against them and fight. He can, and he should, cherish the national, social and cultural traditions which spring deep out of his past, but he must appreciate that to the glory of national citizenship he can add that of world citizenship.

Here, indeed, is the last and the toughest lesson which mankind will have to learn. It cuts against age-old tradition, comparative inexperience in other methods, and a certain profound tendency either to ascribe all ills to some extraneous enemy or to run head first into a wall.

Man has not, despite all religion, laws, and police, ceased murder in the individual; it will take time, and perhaps, horrible lessons for him to cease it in the mass. Fortunately, out of the experiences of the past twenty years, he has many great assets on which to draw. Terrible as the present slaughter is, it may still have its value if it serves as the proving-ground whence issues forth a determination amongst men, both themselves to see the world in its larger form and to demand that their leaders do likewise. Man gets up the hill oft-time by a stumble and a lurch which still throw him forward. May we, this second time for many of us, learn that lesson and demand, each of us, a wise, generous and constructive international policy.

DIVISIONS OF PEOPLES, 1940 [10]

"Free"—ruled by parliamentary decisions
"Dictator"—ruled by executive decisions
"Captive"—democracies under foreign domination
U.S.S.R.—form, republic; substance, dictator
"Others"—miscellaneous classifications

"The Free"	*"The Captive"*	*"Axis"*
Australia	Belgium	Germany
Canada	Denmark	Hungary
Ireland	Finland	Italy
New Zealand	France	Japan
Union S. Africa	Holland	Roumania
United Kingdom	Norway	
United States	Sweden	
	Switzerland	

[10] From pamphlet "Basic Facts on Union of Free Peoples." Congress of American Professions. Cincinnati, Ohio. p. 5.

SOME MEASURES OF WORLD POWER

Measure	*"Free"*	*"Captive"*	*"Axis"*	*"USSR"*	*Other*
	Percentage				
Coal	51.1	6.3	15.2	10.8	16.6
Nickel	89.2	....	....	1.8	9.0
Rubber	53.7	39.3	....	....	7.0
Auto Products	77.1	5.7	11.1	5.3	.8
Gold Reserve	74.6	.9	2.2	14.9	7.4
Iron Ore	51.4	21.9	5.4	15.5	5.8
Tin	51.5	16.3	2.3	....	29.9
Petroleum	61.0	5.0	.4	10.0	23.6
Raw Cotton	58.7	....	.2	13.3	27.8
Steel	38.5	8.7	28.8	16.6	7.4
Wheat	34.0	10.6	16.4	11.6	27.4
Potash	9.4	18.7	63.6	7.5	.8
Aluminum	37.4	17.5	36.2	8.4	.5
Area	18.9	1.3	1.5	14.1	64.2
Population	10.9	4.1	12.8	8.6	63.6

"Free" and "Captive" Combined (Democracies): Larger population than Axis; nineteen times the land area; half of practically all essential raw materials; more than half of war materials; more than half world's trade; nearly all its gold; control of all the oceans; far superior in military power.

"Free" Peoples Alone (English-speaking): More powerful economically than Axis and "Captive" combined; military power rapidly overtaking them; United States and Britain control 27 of the world's 32 key naval locations.

EXCERPTS

The past twenty-five years and more have witnessed considerable agitation for leagues to enforce peace, world states, and other international enterprises to eliminate war and spread prosperity. And all these schemes, of which Mr. Streit's is the most recent, have attacked something called "nationalism" as the root of all evil.—*Quincy Howe, Author. Forum and Century. Jl. '39. p.* 31.

The task of trying to unite the peoples of the world has been blindly left by the democracies to the dictators. And the dictators are attempting to achieve this task, not by reason, but by brute force and the degradation of man; they are not working in the interests of human freedom and dignity, but are seeking everywhere to overthrow them.—*Hans Kohn, Prof. of History, Smith College. Vital Speeches of the Day. S.* 1, '40. *p.* 703.

During the great World War, the Allies, representing a major portion of the territory and population of the world, united in one central organization with one commander, or central authority, to overthrow the Central Powers. Just so the world can create one central organization, with one central executive authority, to win the great victory of peace.—*C. W. Young, Palo Alto, Calif. World Unity. Je.* '33. *p.* 147.

Intense nationalism, extreme insularity in outlook, and embittered political partisanship are the chief obstacles to the advancement of understanding, goodwill, and international peace. The inherent predilection of many for friendship and for peace instead of strife is apt to be submerged by egotistical eagerness to predominate rather than to cooperate.—*T. D. Young, President, Rotary International in Great Britain and Ireland. Rotarian. O.* '40. *p.* 7.

The task of creating a new world order is an onerous one, requiring every iota of knowledge, skill, devotion, determination and patience which mankind can bring to it. But it is a task which must be performed, for to fail in it will be to expose civilization to overthrow at the hands of ruthless force, while to succeed will be to free the tremendous stores of energy which have hitherto been consumed in mutual destruction for use in building up a higher type of human society than has ever yet been known.—*Frederick F. Blachly and Miriam E. Oatman, University of Oklahoma. Political Science Quarterly. Mr.* '19. *p.* 103.

The real international problem which confronts Europe and civilization today is not a choice between utopia and reality but between the psychology of conflicting interests and the organization of power politics on the one hand, and the psychology of common interests and the organization of international cooperation on the other. The transition to a durable peace and a more equitable social order must be in the sequence order, law and good government, as Sir Alfred Zimmern remarks, not law and then order. "No paper plan," insisted Lord Halifax, in a broadcast last autumn, "will endure that does not freely spring from the will of the people who alone can give it life."—*"Preparing for a New World Order." Nature. Ag.* 17, '40. *p.* 210.

Great Britain has come to believe that Hitler and Mussolini must be defeated before any proposals for the abolition of war can get a hearing. It is recalled that Mussolini has said: "Fascism does not believe either in the possibility or in the utility of perpetual peace. A doctrine that is based on the premise of peace is foreign to Fascism." Hitler's conquest of Austria, Czechoslovakia, Poland, Denmark, Norway, Holland, Belgium, Luxembourg and France appears to have closed the door as far as he is concerned to any program of peace now without victory. So, again, the war in Europe must end either with a victory for Britain or for Germany. That appears to be the tangible fact.—*Editorial. World Affairs. Mr.* '41. *p.* 6.

Since the outbreak of this war, a secret "peace department" of the Foreign Office, its personnel of experts known only to the higher-ups in Whitehall, has been busy studying data for the next settlement. It is concerned not with any "appeasement" now—it has been purposely kept under cover to prevent that misconception—but with helping to make the peace a lasting one when it comes.

This is the official body which is trying to put substance into the so-far vague aims expressed publicly by statement. Meanwhile—and nothing like so quietly—plenty of unofficial and near-official molders of opinion have been at work. Aside from such extremists as Pacifists, Communists, and Fascists, these fall roughly into two schools: the one advocating European federation; and another confining its aims to the "Delenda est Carthago" principle—that Germany must be destroyed.—*Newsweek. F.* 12, '40. *p.* 22.

International law has been too much inclined to take the unrealistic view that states alone are subjects of international relations. The democratic position should be followed that states *as such* cannot commit crimes and that, if crimes are committed in their names, they are to be attributed to the governments, which thereby violate not only international law but also the state's constitution, and therefore forfeit their right to govern. This was the principle on which Napoleon was eliminated from France and the Kaiser from Germany, and it is the principle which has been avowed in the present hostilities of France and Great Britain against the Nazis. It is the failure to recognize this principle which accounted in part for the failure of the sanctions of 1935, which should have been directed against Mussolini and not against Italy.—*Quincy Wright. Author. Asia. Jl.* '40. *p.* 392.

The history of humanity shows us a two-fold movement among the clans, tribes, nations and races which have occupied this planet. The first of these is the expansion of governments by the inclusion under one control of an increased number of social units. The causes for this expansion have been several, such as the ambition of rulers, and the necessity for combination in defence against a powerful enemy. The other movement shows a contraction or decentralization of government within such expanded area, whereby a variety of local business is entirely entrusted to a local sub-government. It is then often found that that local sub-government is more powerful in the preservation of peace and prosecution of prosperity than was the government of the region before the larger government had absorbed it within its greater power.—*Prof. Ernest Wood, Author of "A Text Book of Indian Citizenship." Advance! Australia. Ja.* 1, '29. *p.* 31.

The task which confronts our generation, not of cancelling (we hope) but of going beyond its national loyalties, is not something wholly new. Before we ever attained loyalty to a nation we had many frontiers to pass. Barriers between tribes, between hamlets, between cities, have been surmounted not so ill; we have kept something of the richness of the pattern while overcoming the prison walls. Now and then the walls tend to rise up again, yet on the whole we manage—the larger loyalties as well as the smaller are established. And I do not believe this can be answered by saying: Those transcendencies were of a different order, since we were passing only from a smaller to a larger closed community. I am sure that the dominant experience must again and again have been that of unclosing.—*"Bergson and World Loyalty," by Helen Wodehouse, D.Phil., Mistress of Girton College, Cambridge. Hibbert Journal. Jl.* '40. *p.* 462.

If we mean, after this war, to trudge along in the old ruts, always competitors, sometimes enemies, then we shall have power as it was in the ownership of many rival, independent states. Each will use it for his own ends. It will play its part in years of peace as well as in war. For let no one suppose that power is dormant and inactive during an armed peace. It gives resonance to a diplomatist's voice. No one listened to Mr. Eden or Lord Halifax as they might listen to a master of dialectic, or a golden-tongued orator. If their words had weight, it was because battleships and bombing planes were ranged behind them, and the wealth that could buy more ships and planes. When Herr von Ribbentrop and Lord Halifax exchanged notes, the result was hardly affected by the literary grace of their periods or the cogency of their logic. Two considerations counted: what armaments lay behind their logic, and had they the will to use these tools? That is always the hidden play behind diplomacy.—*H. N. Brailsford, British Journalist and Author. "The Federal Idea." Federal Union. London. p. 9.*

The necessity for world government results from the fact that the world has come of age. This is no figure of speech. It has a precise meaning. It expresses two facts: that the world has become a physical organic unit; and that it has acquired a consciousness of itself, or in other words, that it has become a thinking organic unit. Both these facts are evident to any person who observes contemporary events with a moderate amount of geographical and historical knowledge. The realities of geography are not grounded on mere mathematical distance and form. They depend on the quality and quantity of the obstacles raised by nature to human communications, and therefore they are bound to change with the progress of man's technique in the art of communicating. There was a time when Virgil described the British Isles as separate from the whole world. If we examine this expression, in appearance *merely* naïve, we find that it implies an important historical fact; that in Virgil's days there were in the world several lines of historical evolution running parallel to each other and with virtually no inter-communication or inter-influence—China, India, Persia, the Roman Empire, the Northern tribes of Barbarian Europe, America still behind the veil of mystery. Measured in terms of the time necessary to travel across it, the whole world is today the size Italy was in Virgil's days or for that matter in the days of Napoleon; while if our "yard-stick" is the time it takes to communicate—as by wireless telegraphy or telephony—between widely separated countries, the world is nowadays the size of a Greek city under Pericles or of an Italian republic under the Medici. These are the realities of geography.

The present international anarchy is not simply war, open or disguised. It is not simply the practice of power politics, failure to observe treaties and international law. All these things are but effects and symptoms of an anarchy more fundamental, an anarchy in which even the most pacific state has its share. For this anarchy is the mere existence of sovereign states. We are accustomed to hear the excessive nationalism of the age admitted and deplored. Nationalism is, however, already excessive when it claims for the nation independent sovereignty. What would be said of a claim by each family to be a sovereign community acknowledging no superior? Yet most men take it for granted that the national society must be sovereign and can admit no superior jurisdiction. It may be, and indeed widely is held that states have a moral duty to settle their quarrels by arbitration. Yet many even of those who believe this also think that, if an issue affects the vital interests of a nation, that nation is not bound to accept an arbitral decision contrary to what it regards as its vital interest. And in any case, a state must not be compelled to obey the umpire's ruling. For that would be inconsistent with its sovereignty. If there were a state whose citizens were not compelled to obey the judgment of a court of law, if and when they regarded the judgment as contrary to their vital interests, it is obvious to everyone that such a state would be in a condition of anarchy. Yet when states make precisely the same claim, it is regarded as right and proper, only what any self-respecting state should claim, and all loyal and patriotic citizens, it is held, not only may but ought to support such a claim, if need be with their lifeblood. Why? Why? Yet again why?—*E. I. Watkin, English Catholic Social Philosopher. Commonweal. Ja.* 5, '40. *p.* 237.

Suppose for a moment that the forty English counties were separate, independent countries—like the countries of Europe.

Think of forty different kinds of money, and tariff walls at every boundary! You could hardly do a day's hike without a passport and several kinds of money. Yorkshire, to encourage home industries, might set up little potteries; it would have to protect them from Staffordshire competition by heavy tariffs. Stafford, prevented from selling pots in York, would have no York money to buy York wool. It would have to start scrabbling for wool of its own, or some silly substitute. The net result: unemployed spinners and bad pots in Yorkshire, unemployed potters and bad wool in Staffordshire, increased poverty all around. Trade, of course, would be paralyzed. The unemployed, forbidden to take a paid job outside their own country, would have a still harder time of it. The burden of taxation would be unbearable. Every County Council, afraid of its neighbors, would be piling up tanks, guns, aeroplanes, ammunition. Every coastal county would have its navy and every inland county would claim its corridor to the sea. Precious little money could be spared for hospitals, or schools, or the dole. Every County Council would set up as sole judge of what concerned its vital interests; so that every petty squabble might mean war. Needing to be "strong" in self-defence, half the counties would be fascist. England, in short, would be a scene of poverty, fear and endless bloodshed, with nothing gained but the splendid "isolation" of the counties. Independence of the county would mean bondage of the individual.

That nightmare vision of the English counties is, thank heavens, only a nightmare; bad as things are, they aren't as desperate as that. But it is a pretty accurate picture of the nations of twentieth-century Europe.—*Raymond O'Malley. "Peace and Prosperity for the Asking." Federal Union Midland Branch. Birmingham, Eng. p.* 4-5.

To feel rightly about the world, to love what is good and to hate what is evil, to seek the highest when one sees it, is for most people no less important than accurate knowledge or trained skill. When a fact, or a group of facts, is linked with strong passion or emotion, it becomes the object of a "sentiment."

Patriotism is such a sentiment. World loyalty is akin to patriotism, but with all mankind for its object. It may be closely linked to a sentiment for God, the invisible King. "Religion," wrote Professor Whitehead, "is world loyalty." Indeed, the fatherhood of God and the brotherhood of man are facts that belong together, like electricity and magnetism. So religion comes into politics. Nor is this a modern doctrine. Pericles held that, if his dream of "a united Greece with Athens as its eye" were ever to come true, it must have behind it a religious motive. Something of the sort has already happened in the British Commonwealth of Nations where, as General Smuts has pointed out, there is not only a common kingship but also the invisible bond of ideals.

Unless this kind of bond unites the world, or most of it, and makes men *feel* for it as they now feel for their own nations, there will be no permanent union and no lasting world order. It is not enough for men to *understand* that the whole is greater than the part, that the world is greater than the nation, and that no nation can continue to live in isolation from the rest of mankind. It is necessary that the two constituent sentiments of patriotism and world loyalty should reenforce each other, as a Scotsman's British patriotism is strengthened by his love for Scotland, or as the American patriotism of the first citizens of the United States was evolved from their feelings for their own Massachusetts or Virginia or New York.—*Maxwell Garnett. In "World Unity." Oxford University Press. Lond.* '39. p. 29-30.

In the future days which we seek to make secure, we look forward to a world founded upon four essential human freedoms.

The first is freedom of speech and expression—everywhere in the world.

The second is freedom of every person to worship God in his own way—everywhere in the world.

The third is freedom from want, which translated into world terms, means economic understandings which will secure to every nation a healthy peacetime life for its inhabitants—everywhere in the world.

The fourth is freedom from fear, which, translated into world terms, means a world-wide reduction of armaments to such a point and in such a thorough fashion that no nation will be in a position to commit an act of physical aggression against any neighbor—anywhere in the world.

That is no vision of a distant millenium. It is a definite basis for a kind of world attainable in our own time and generation. That kind of world is the very antithesis of the so-called "new order" of tyranny which the dictators seek to create with the crash of a bomb.

To that new order we oppose the greater conception—the moral order. A good society is able to face schemes of world domination and foreign revolutions alike without fear.

Since the beginning of our American history we have been engaged in change, in a perpetual, peacetime revolution, a revolution which goes on steadily, quietly, adjusting itself to changing conditions without the concentration camp or the quicklime in the ditch. The world order which we seek is the cooperation of free countries, working together in a friendly, civilized society.—*President Franklin D. Roosevelt. Message to Congress, January* 6, 1941.

Many organizations and individuals are interested and cooperating in a real movement for a new world order and others are sending in their names daily. One of the best things along this line is now being developed by Prof. W. F. Gerhardt, of Wayne University, Detroit, where, interested in our problems from the social dynamics standpoint, they have a model world democracy project set up and in the making. They are taking also H. G. Wells' World Charter as an additional suggestion from which to proceed.

In such an all-embracing pact the rights and limitations of each and every people and nation should be clearly fixed, the principles underlying the relations of governments toward one another definitely laid down, and all international agreements and obligations ascertained and determined. This commonwealth must, so far as I can visualize it, consist of a world legislature, whose members will, as the trustees of the whole of mankind, ultimately control the resources of the component nations and will enact such laws as shall be required to satisfy the need and adjust the relationships of all races and peoples.

A world executive must aid in preserving the peace of the world and in seeing that its international laws are obeyed and its organic unity is safeguarded. A world tribunal must adjudicate and deliver its compulsory and final verdict in all disputes arising between the various nations. That would be better than settling disputes by war, would it not? At least that is the way we settle disputes in this country between states and between people, so I assume it is a qualified method.

A world script, a world literature, a uniform and universal system of currency, of weights and measures, will simplify education, trade, and business problems and will produce a better, friendlier understanding among the nations and races of mankind. In such a world society, science and religion, the two greatest forces in human life, could be reconciled and would work together instead of out of harmony as they seem to be now as we practice the art of war.—*John G. Alexander, U.S. Representative from Minnesota. Congressional Record. D.* 12, '40. *p.*21468.

Only Washington's personal intervention on the eve of the Constitutional Convention made certain the building of a government capable of serving such freedom throughout the vast area that was to be the United States. Only the stand Lincoln took was capable of continuing its unparalleled service to individual freedom. Different as were these two men in other respects, they stood on the same plane in their appreciation of their country's fundamental political need—federation. The appeal of these men, which emanates from the things they stood for, has long transcended national boundaries.

Britain's Lord Bryce, Austria's Count Coudenhove-Kalergi, France's Aristide Briand and Victor Hugo, Czechoslovakia's Masaryk and Beneš are among those who have offered expressed or implied tribute to the federal concept as worked out in America. The tribute continues as British and French leaders—and even German spokesmen in dubious echo—talk of the possibility of some sort of world federation after the war.

Europe since 1919 has been trying confederation, or the league system, as Americans tried it between 1777 and 1787. The League of Nations was a great step beyond the system of alliances and balance-of-power that previously served as a restraint on international anarchy. But the League had weaknesses which became apparent in crisis, and which become even more evident as the league system is contrasted with the federal idea. While each state reserved the right to be the final judge of its own actions, no association of states could have sufficient authority or power to preserve peace and guarantee justice among its members. Even such loyalty as the league idea demanded of member states proved too much for some of them, and indeed the United States refused even to undertake a League responsibility.

To have aimed at world federation before the world had tried confederation might well have been futile. Americans were ready to undertake federation only after ten years of sad experience with the confederate or league system. If the complacency of the relatively peaceful and prosperous post-Napoleonic century had not been shattered in 1914, perhaps not even a league system would have been welcomed in 1919.—*Editorial. Christian Science Monitor. F.* 10, '40. *p.*18.

"A composite state is one composed of two or more states. The character of the international person thus constituted depends upon the nature of the act by which the union was created and the extent to which the sovereignty of the component parts is impaired or taken away." The first type, the real union, exists "where states are not only ruled by the same prince, but are also united for international purposes by an express agreement. . . . Such a union is susceptible of great variation, and its character can be determined in each individual case only by the particular terms of the agreement." Examples are Norway and Sweden (1815-1907) and Austria-Hungary (1723-1919). Austria and Hungary had separate laws and administrative organization for many purposes but single ministers for foreign affairs, war, and finance. The second type, the confederation, is an association of states in a permanent manner "for the exercise in common of their rights of sovereignty for the general advantage." A common organization is provided by an agreement called a compact. The component states "retain their internal, and, to a greater or less extent, their external sovereignty. Their personality in international law is not destroyed." Examples are the Germanic Confederation (1815-1866), the United Netherlands (1580-1795), the United States (1781-1789), and the Swiss Confederacy (1815-1848). Finally, the federal union exists when states "are united under a central government, which is supreme within its sphere and which possesses and exercises in internal affairs the powers of national sovereignty. . . ." and the composite state alone is a person of international law.

The act by which the union is effected, is called, not a compact, but a constitution. In its external relations, the federal union resembles a real union rather than a confederation. It differs from the former in possessing still greater centralized powers, power which, in their relation to foreign affairs, can, in the case of some federal states, scarcely be distinguished from those of a simple state. It has the exclusive right to enter into general treaties and to make war and conclude peace, although, by its constitution, the component states may exercise certain powers of foreign intercourse, subject to the control of the central government. Its inhabitants have a common citizenship or nationality. If war breaks out between the component states it is civil war, not international.

Examples are Switzerland, the United States beginning in 1789, the German Empire (1871-1918), and the German Republic (1919-1934), the Soviet Union (1923), Argentina since 1860, Brazil since 1891, Mexico since 1857, Venezuela since 1893, and Canada since 1919.—*"Elements of International Relations," by Frederick A. Middlebush, Professor of Political Science and Public Law, University of Missouri, and Chesney Hill, Assistant Professor of Political Science and Public Law, University of Missouri. p. 53-4. McGraw-Hill Book Company, Inc. New York.* '40. *Quotations are from J. B. Moore. "A Digest of International Law." Vol.* 1. '06. *p.* 22-4.

No one familiar with the history of the past twenty years can believe that it would be possible, at the end of the war, to restore in Europe the *status quo* of August 1939. The choice for Europe is not between Hitler's totalitarian new order and return to the kind of anarchy, superficially modified by the League of Nations, that existed before the outbreak of the war. The choice is between Hitler's totalitarian "new order," and a "newer" order that Britain, with the aid of the United States and the British Dominions, might conceivably forge not only for Europe, but for the world. That choice exists only as long as Britain is undefeated. Should Britain be forced to yield, Europe would have no alternative but to bow to Hitler's terms. The passive resistance of conquered countries, notably Holland and Norway, is posited on hope of British victory. To expect that this resistance would continue if Britain were defeated is to indulge in a dangerous illusion.

Yet in retrospect it may well appear that Hitler—if he is not victorious—has performed a useful wrecker's job, although at tremendous cost. For he has destroyed many of the institutions and practices, some of them feudal in origin, which in the past had blocked not only federation, but even the most primitive forms of collaboration in Europe. Under the hammer-blows of Nazi invasion and domination, the European peoples are painfully acquiring a common political experience which may ultimately provide a basis for peacetime cooperation. The Nazis, taking a leaf out of the Communist book, effectively transformed what might have been international war into civil war. Today some of their opponents recognize that this war is not merely a conflict between nations—or, as the Communists would say, between "rival imperialisms"—but a civil war, between supporters of conflicting ideologies within all nations. This, in itself, tends to undermine national barriers on both sides, and reduce the hypnotic effect formerly exercised by the concept of national sovereignty. Similarly, the idea of some form of supranational political organization, which would correspond to the growing internationalization of trade and communications, is no longer a monopoly of those whom the Nazis have contemptuously described as "pluto-democratic internationalists." Today the Nazis, as a corollary to the fiercely nationalistic ideas on which they rode to victory in Germany, advocate the formation of vast continental units—developed, in their plans, not on the basis of free collaboration, but of domination by a self-appointed master race.—*Vera Micheles Dean, Editor, Foreign Policy Bulletin. Foreign Policy Bulletin. Mr.* 14, '41. *p.* 1-2.

The League of Nations was the latest of attempts since the *Pax Romana* and the Roman Empire to unite the peoples of Europe, or the greater number of them, in a single system. It differed from its forerunners in that it did not aim at complete political unity, but only at joint and corporate action in certain spheres of political, social and intellectual interest; it went outside the geographical boundaries of Europe and appealed for the cooperation of peoples of European civilization; and, most significant of all its differences from previous systems, it was based upon the voluntary principle and a degree of abrogation of sovereignty, and not upon force. It is, therefore, perhaps no matter for surprise that its most conspicuous success was precisely in those fields of activity in which before the first world war, interest, activities and joint action had been international and the barriers of national interests had been least operative—the field of the arts, sciences and social reform. In this respect it came near to reconstituting the international position of learning and the arts in Europe before the Reformation.

The fate of the League of Nations was a clear indication that the times were not yet ripe for so great a break away from the nationalist tradition. It has required the shock of a second world war and the imminent peril of free institutions throughout the world to bring once more into the field of practicable discussion the possibility of finding a basis of corporate action between nations which will ensure conditions of enduring peace. We may learn this lesson not only from America, where the President of the United States is urging upon peoples of very different civilizations in North, Central and South America, the necessity of a measure of common action in the interests of their common devotion to the ideal of political liberty, but also from the aims of our adversaries. They too, Germany in Europe, Japan in the East, are formulating a political system which transcends national distinctions, but under the dominance of a ruling caste—a reversion, it is to be noted, to the system of barbarism which in European history followed on the period of migrations rather than a step forward along the line of what has been noted as evolutionary social development. German dominance, however, in the occupied territories and in the countries subordinate to the Axis contrasts, to its disadvantage, with even the darker period of the Middle Ages in the complete repression of things of the spirit and the eradication of all freedom of thought by the suppression of universities, schools and centres of learning which are not prepared to follow the paths marked out by political expediency.—*Nature. D.* 21, '40. *p.* 788-9.

We come to the conclusion that the real reason why that embryo of world government called the League of Nations has failed to achieve world peace is due to the fact that it has been thinking of nothing else but world peace, in the puerile sense of "prevention of war," while leaving entirely fallow the real fields in which its activities ought to have fertilized the world, namely those of friendly and positive collaboration toward the general welfare of all the nations and men of the earth.

And so it happens that while, at one end, gold has been buried away in the entrails of the earth in Kentucky—thus reversing the process which at great cost extracted this gold from the entrails of the earth in South Africa, Siberia or California—at the other end of the world currency is disintegrated for the lack of gold. In some parts of the world corn and ewe lambs are burned for lack of markets, while in still other parts of the world thousands of men, women and children go hungry for lack of food. And while states cannot afford to provide houses for the houseless and clothes for the naked and food for the hungry, they are spending $10,000,000,000 in building armaments to destroy each other for no purpose which can be defined in world terms.

An organization known as the World Foundation has been formed precisely to bring these lamentable facts before the enlightened public opinion of all the nations. It is hoped to make the peoples realize that there are no longer any "foreign affairs," but only world affairs, and that such affairs can only be solved if they are understood from the world point of view.

The World Foundation aims to be a league of political education for world citizens. It is advocated by the following persons:

Allen of Hurtwood	G. Ferrerro
Norman Angell	W. E. Hocking
W. Arnold-Forster	Thomas Mann
M. J. Bonn	F. Maurette

Gilbert Murray	Stephen King-Hall
E. J. Phelan	Lytton
H. S. L. Polak	Arthur Salter
Jules Romains	Arthur Toynbee
G. A. Johnston	Ray Lyman Wilbur

S. de Madariaga

All of these men have considerable experience of the human ways and most of them have had long, direct experience of national and international administration. None of them can be said to be empty dreamers, vapid ideologists; all are men who realize the difficulties of practical life; and it is precisely because they do so that they now put forward what, in their minds, is the only way of obtaining permanent peace: the fostering of world citizenship as an indispensable preliminary to the success of world government, itself an indispensable instrument for what is becoming today the main—indeed, the only—problem of world life: the intelligent organization of life on the planet.—*Salvador de Madariaga, Spanish Author and Statesman. Christian Science Monitor Weekly Magazine Section. My.* 12, '37. *p.* 2.

One other proposal which deserves serious consideration is the product of the joint effort of two women, Lola Maverick Lloyd, who is the aunt of the fighting Texan, Maury Maverick, and Rosika Schwimmer, Hungarian-born stateswoman and feminist, who has been in the forefront of international peace movements for twenty-five years. Briefly their plan calls for a World Constitutional Convention to consist of democratically elected delegates from those countries willing to participate officially at this time and with unofficial delegates for the others. A World Federal Constitution would be drafted regardless of the attitude of present governments; it would be published in all parts of the world, and presented to all governments in the hope that the people themselves would eventually act.

Whether or not the procedure proposed is feasible, there is no doubt that the outline of a World Constitution is sound. It contains these minimum essentials of any adequate World Union: first, democratic procedure; second, total disarmament; third, world planning, for the control of backward regions, for the distribution of raw materials, for international public works, for migration of populations, etc.

Democratic procedure requires that no organized sovereign state at present existing shall be excluded from participation in the World Union, and that there shall be but one class of membership (no separation of large and small nations). It requires that the representatives in the World Union parliament shall be elected by popular vote in each member state, and shall not be appointees of the government of the member state. And it requires that voting in the World Union parliament shall be by individual representatives, and not by states; majority vote, and not unanimous vote, of the individual representatives being necessary to enact legislation.

Is there any actually visible, organized movement for a World Federal Union?

Last year the Federal Council of Churches of America in cooperation with the Foreign Missions Conference of North America authorized a joint committee to prepare a statement of the Christian conception of a political world order. The statement was presented at the International Missionary Conference at Madras, India, in December last year, and is now being distributed in pamphlet form to church members throughout the United States and Canada. The authors of this pamphlet very definitely take a stand for world government, and call for work on tentative drafts of a world constitution by qualified experts, preliminary to the calling of a world constitutional convention.

In this country there has recently been established an organization called the Campaign for World Government which has its main headquarters at Chicago, and is under the capable direction of William B. Lloyd, Jr. The American Section of the Women's International League for Peace and Freedom has come out in support of this campaign.

In England the powerful Peace Pledge Union, of which George Lansbury, M.P., is president, is now beginning to think along these lines. In Canada two members of Parliament, Mr. Rowe and Mr. Needham, are preparing to introduce resolutions endorsing the movement for a world constitutional convention Efforts are now being made to introduce a similar resolution in Congress.—*Robert Heckert, Lecturer on Politics. Common Sense. Jl.* '39. *p.* 13-15.

Is there a way of escape from the paralyzing grip of power economy now stealing over the world? There is only one, in a world as close together and as integrated as ours. There has always been one way of escape, and thus far we have refused to use it effectively enough to meet our ever growing needs. That is the way of world organization, political and economic. We citizens of the modern world, facing the problems raised by a recently acquired interdependence, are having to develop new social and political institutions on a world-wide base.

Our problem is in some ways like that which faced the citizens of the rapidly growing towns that, after the industrial revolution, were becoming great cities. You may recall that New York City had no paid fire department until about 1870. In London at the end of the eighteenth century there was no such thing as a metropolitan police force. Perhaps there had been no great need for such an institution in the past, and recognition of a new need for a central police system doubtless had to develop gradually, just as recognition of the need for a world police authority is gradually developing now. Under those circumstances there was a period when anarchy, in the worst sense of the term, held sway in the streets of London. If my historical information is correct, there was a long series of riots, associated with the name of John Wilkes, in which gangs went about avenging grievances under a ritual of shouted slogans. Wilkes saw the movement he had started grow completely out of hand, and the "fearful thing," the London mob, spread destruction.

It was in those days, while arguments for a metropolitan police were being rejected on the ground that such a body would imperil "rights and liberties," that a citizen of London was threatened with death by some persons with whom he had a quarrel. They announced that they would come to his house with their gang the next day. The citizen, in alarm, sought aid from a justice of the peace, only to get the answer, "We can act only after a crime has been committed, we cannot offer protection. That would be outside our sphere." The citizen finally rounded up a number of friends who agreed to stay in his house to help fight off the invaders—a sort of alliance system. The rioters arrived, and a pitched battle began. As the first shots were fired, white candles appeared in the windows of houses all along the street. That was the accepted sign, developed under the anarchic mob rule of the time, that inhabitants of those houses were not taking sides—nonintervention!

Such incidents are parables that have a direct bearing on the fundamental troubles of the world today. Nonintervention, the white candle in the window, has got to be supplanted, not by alliances or by taking sides in the quarrels of others, but by uniting all the law-abiding citizens into a community organization which will undertake, by the use of police power, to resist any resort to force. It is becoming increasingly clear that nothing less than a world federation with police authority is the *sine qua non* of a return to the economics of welfare and an abandonment of the economics of power in the modern world.—*Eugene Staley, Ph.D., Associate Professor of International Economic Relations, Fletcher School of Law and Diplomacy, Medford, Mass. Annals of the American Academy. Jl.* '38. *p.* 13-14.

For I dipt into the future, far as human eye could see,
Saw the Vision of the world, and all the wonder that would be;
Saw the heavens fill with commerce, argosies of magic sails,
Pilots of the purple twilight, dropping down with costly bales;
Heard the heavens fill with shouting, and there rain'd a ghastly dew
From the nations' airy navies grappling in the central blue;
Far along the world-wide whisper of the southwind rushing warm,
With the standards of the peoples plunging thro' the thunder-storm
Till the war-drum throbb'd no longer, and the battle-flags were furled
In the Parliament of man, the Federation of the world.

—*Alfred Tennyson* (1809-1892) *in* "*Locksley Hall written in* 1842.

FEDERATION OF DEMOCRACIES

UNION NOW[1]

The way through is Union now of the democracies that the North Atlantic and a thousand other things already unite—Union of these few peoples in a great federal republic built on and for the thing they share most, their common democratic principle of government for the sake of individual freedom.

This Union would be designed (a) to provide effective common government in our democratic world in those fields where such common government will clearly serve man's freedom better than separate government, (b) to maintain independent national governments in all other fields where such government will best serve man's freedom, and (c) to create by its constitution a nucleus world government capable of growing into universal world government peacefully and as rapidly as such growth will best serve man's freedom.

By (a) I mean the Union of the North Atlantic democracies in these five fields:

a union government and citizenship
a union defense force
a union customs-free economy
a union money
a union postal and communications system

By (b) I mean the Union government shall guarantee against all enemies, foreign and domestic, not only those rights of man that are common to all democracies, but every existing national or local right that is not clearly incompatible with effective union government in the five named fields. The Union would guarantee the right of each democracy in it to govern

[1] From book by Clarence K. Streit, National Chairman of Federal Union, Inc. New York; formerly correspondent, *New York Times*. Harper & Bros. N.Y. 1940. Copyright. Published by permission.

independently all its home affairs and practise democracy at home in its own tongue, according to its own customs and in its own way, whether by republic or kingdom, presidential, cabinet or other form of government, capitalist, socialist or other economic system.

By (c) I mean the founder democracies shall so constitute the Union as to encourage the nations outside it and the colonies inside it to seek to unite with it instead of against it. Admission to the Union and to all its tremendous advantages for the individual man and woman would from the outset be open equally to every democracy, now or to come, that guarantees its citizens the Union's minimum Bill of Rights.

The Great Republic would be organized with a view to its spreading peacefully round the earth as nations grow ripe for it. Its Constitution would aim clearly at achieving eventually by this peaceful, ripening, natural method the goal millions have dreamed of individually, but never sought to get by deliberately planning and patiently working together to achieve it. That goal would be achieved by the Union when every individual of our species would be a citizen of it, a citizen of a disarmed world enjoying world free trade, a world money and a world communications system. Then Man's vast future would begin.

One hundred and fifty years ago a few American democracies opened this Union way through. The dangers of depression, dictatorship and war, and the persuasiveness of clear thinking and courageous leadership, led them then to abandon the heresy into which they had fallen. That heresy converted the sovereignty of the state from a means of individual freedom into the supreme end itself, and produced the wretched "League of Friendship" of the Articles of Confederation. Abandoning all this the democrats of America turned back to their Declaration of Independence—of the independence of Man from the State and of the dependence of free men on each other for their freedom, the Declaration:

> That all men are created equal, that they are endowed by their creator with certain unalienable rights, that among these are life, liberty and the persuit of happiness, that to secure these rights governments are instituted among men, deriving their just powers from the consent of the governed, that whenever any form of government becomes destructive of these ends it is the right of the people to alter or to abolish it, and to institute new government, laying its foundations on such principles and organizing its powers in such form as to them shall seem most likely to effect their safety and happiness.

Finding they had wrongly applied this philosophy to establish Thirteen "free and independent States" and organize them as the League of Friendship so that "each State retains its sovereignty, freedom and independence," they applied it next as "We the people of the United States" to "secure the blessings of liberty to ourselves and our posterity." To do this they invented and set up a new kind of interstate government. It has worked ever since as the other, league, type has never worked. It has proved to be an "astonishing and unexampled success," as Lord Acton said, not only in America but whereever democracies have tried it regardless of conditions,—among the Germans, French and Italians of Switzerland, the English and French of Canada, the Dutch and English of the Union of South Africa. It is the kind of interstate government that Lincoln, to distinguish it from the opposing type of government of, by and for states, called "government of the people, by the people, for the people." It is the way that I call Union.

To follow this way through now our Atlantic democracies—and first of all the American Union—have only to abandon in their turn the same heresy into which they have fallen, the heresy of absolute national sovereignty and its vain alternatives, neutrality, balance of power, alliance or League of Nations. We the people of the Atlantic have only to cease sacrificing needlessly our individual freedom to the freedom of our nations, be true to our democratic philosophy and establish that "more perfect Union" toward which all our existing unions explicitly or implicitly aim.

Can we hope to find a safer, surer, more successful way than this? What democrat among us does not hope that this Union will be made some day? What practical man believes it will ever be made by mere dreaming, or that the longer we delay starting to make it the sooner we shall have it? All it will take to make this Union—whether in a thousand years or now, whether long after catastrophe or just in time to prevent it,—is agreement by a majority to do it, and which we can not possibly ever do except by agreeing to do it. Why, then, can we not do it now in time for us to benefit by it and save millions of lives? . . .

Union to me is a democracy composed of democracies—an interstate government organized on the same basic principle, by the same basic method, and for the same basic purpose as the democracies in it, and with the powers of government divided between the union and the states the better to advance this common purpose, individual freedom. . . .

Clearly prudence dictates that we should lay our new government's foundations on such principles and organize its powers in such form as have stood the test of experience. Clearly democracy bids us now unite our unions of free men and women in the Union of the Free.

Fantastic? Visionary? What are the alternatives? There are only these: Either the democracies must try to stand separately, or they must try to stand together on some other basis than Union; that is, they must organize themselves as a league or an alliance.

Suppose we try to organize as a league. That means seeking salvation from what Alexander Hamilton called "the political monster of an *imperium in imperio.*" We adopt a method which has just failed in the League of Nations, which before that led the original thirteen American democracies to a similar failure, and failed the Swiss democracies, the Dutch democracies, and the democracies of ancient Greece. We adopt a method which has been tried time and again in history and has never worked, whether limited to few members or extended to many; a method, which, we shall see, when we analyze it later, is thoroughly undemocratic, untrustworthy, unsound, unable either to make or to enforce its law in time. Is it not fantastic to expect to get the American people, after 150 years of successful experience with union and after their rejection of the League of Nations, to enter any league?

Suppose we try to organize instead an alliance of the democracies. But an alliance is simply a looser, more primitive form of league, one that operates secretly through diplomatic tunnels rather than openly through regular assemblies. It is based on the same unit as a league,—the state,—and on the same principle,—that the maintenance of the freedom of the state is the be-all and the end-all of political economic policy. It is at most an association (instead of a government) of governments, by governments, for governments. It has all the faults of a league with most of them intensified and with some more of its own added.

Though possible as a temporary stopgap, an alliance, as a permanent organization, has never been achieved and is practically impossible to achieve among as many as fifteen states.

The best way to prevent war is to make attack hopeless. It will not be hopeless while the autocrats, who by their nature are gamblers with abnormal confidence in themselves and their luck, have any ground left to gamble either that the democracies can be divided or that the inter-democracy organization is too cumbersome and loose to resist surprise attack. An alliance can not long make this gamble hopeless.

The Worst Alternative

Only one thing could be more visionary and fantastic, and that is the third possible alternative to Union, the one that would seek salvation in rejecting every type of interstate organization and in pursuing a policy of pure nationalism,—the policy of isolationism, neutrality, of each trusting to his own armaments, military and economic. For if the democracies are not to try to stand together by union or league or alliance, the only thing left for them is to try to stand alone.

The experience of the United States shows that even the most powerful nations can not get what they want by isolationism. The United States sought through the nineteen-twenties to preserve its peace and prosperity by isolationism. It did remain in peace, but isolationism can not be given credit for this since Britain and France followed the opposite policy of cooperation through the League of Nations and they, too, kept out of war. As for prosperity, isolationism failed to preserve it; depression struck the United States hardest.

Hard times led to war dangers which the United States in 1935 sought to lessen by the neutrality variation of isolationism. It adopted the policy of advising potential aggressors and victims that it not merely would not attempt to distinguish between them but would furnish supplies only to the belligerent who could come, get and pay cash for them. What has happened since this policy was adopted? Italy invaded Ethiopia. Japan invaded a huge part of China. Germany violated the Locarno treaty, and seized Austria, Czechoslovakia, Poland. The naval limitation treaties broke down. The League broke down. The Peace Pact and the Nine Power Pact broke down. All the world's peaceful machinery broke down, "recovery" sagged into "recession" and "peace" into war.

The United States has never armed in peace time as it has since it adopted this policy. And the end is not near. In proposing, Jan. 4, 1938, that Congress spend $990,000,000 on armaments, President Roosevelt referred "specifically to the possibility that, due to world conditions over which this nation has no control, I may find it necessary to request additional appropriations for national defense."

Balance Or Unbalance of Power?

The balance of power theory that prepared catastrophe now as then—there is no more sterile, illusory, fantastic, exploded and explosive peace policy than the balance of power. Look at it. Take it apart. What does it mean in common words? It means seeking to get stability by seeking to equalize the weight on both sides of the balance. One can conceive of reaching stability this way—but for how long and at the cost of what violent ups and downs before? And when the scales do hang in perfect balance it takes but a breath, only the wind that goes with a word spoken or shrieked in the Hitlerian manner, to end at once the stability, the peace that was achieved. Stability can never be more in danger, more at the mercy of the slighest mistake, accident or act of ill will than at the very moment when the ideal of the balance of power is finally achieved.

To try to start with all the world at once increases the number on whose consent agreement on a constitution depends, while inevitably lowering the average of political culture and experience available to meet the difficulty it heightens. Universality must be the goal of any plan for world government, but one can not advance when one tries to make the last step the first step, too.

The failures of the universalist method have led to various attempts to find some half-way ground by restricting numbers. Examples are the Pan America school, Briand's European Federation plan, and the post-war spectre of the old Concert of Powers. They all base their restriction of members on some factor, such as position on a certain continent or posession of great armed power, which keeps their membership forever restricted and excludes the possibility of growth into universal government. None has made a dent in our problem.

There remains what I call the method of the nucleus. It alone combines the truth in the restricted method with the truth in the universal method, and combines them in their common sense order. It alone seeks to achieve world government through the normal principle of growth, through taking care at the start to select the best seed and then planting it well and cultivating it.

This method would have a nucleus world state organized by the peoples best qualified to organize its government soundly on a basis favorable to its peaceful extension round the world, and it would count thereafter on the vitality of this nucleus and the character of its principles for its growth to universality. The nucleus method would turn to the leaders in inter-state government for leadership toward universal government. The rearguard may become the leader when a mass reverses its movement, but if the mass is to continue forward, the vanguard must lead.

Some sixty nations make the world political mass, and to count more than fifteen or twenty of them as the vanguard is to confuse the vanguard with the body and the rearguard, and deprive either one's terms of all meaning or the mass of all movement. The political character of the problem, the magnitude of the object and the need of early, sound solution all favor organizing the smallest practical number of the nations most advanced politically into a nucleus world government.

The Nucleus Needs To Be Democratic

What states shall compose the nucleus, the autocracies, the democracies, or a combination of the two? It can not be composed of autocracies alone. They are not strong enough. Their basic political theory is opposed to organizing law and order in the world except by the method of one conquering all.

Nor can the nucleus be composed of democracies and autocracies together. We organize a tug of war, not a government, when we arrange for those who believe that government is made for the people to pull together with those who believe the opposite.

The nucleus must be composed exclusively of democracies. To start to make a world government pre-supposes belief in the democratic principle that government is made by the people. To organize world government soundly we must turn to the peoples most advanced and experienced politically, and this too turns us to the democracies. Peoples that accept dictatorships must be classified, politically, among the immature, or retarded, or inexperienced, high as they may rank otherwise. While men accept being governed as children they must be rated as immature.

As the world must turn to the democracies for world government, the democracies must turn to their vanguard. To begin this task in a constituent assembly composed of all the peoples that call themselves democratic is to burden the most experienced nations with those least experienced. It is as well-intentioned and foolish as trying to preserve the Bill of Rights for our children by giving children the vote.

The essential, it is worth repeating, is to get government constituted soundly and without delay. One can be sure then that those left out at the start will not be left out long.

Universality the Ultimate Goal

We come to the second essential, that no limit whatever be placed on the growth of this nucleus, that its constitution make explicitly clear that it is meant to grow peacefully into universal government. If it is in the interest of the freedom of the individuals of fifteen countries to unite, it can not be in their interest to bar themselves in advance for any reason whatsoever from uniting with other men whenever it seems wise to them to do so, and when these others desire it too. Any exclusivity would run counter to the freedom for which the government would be made and would fatally turn against the nucleus those excluded and thus, at best, expose it to unnecessary dangers.

The admission of new members from time to time would keep this world government a powerful stimulus to democracy everywhere; it would need no propaganda bureau. Would not the establishment of genuine freedom of the press in, say, Soviet Russia, be hastened by the wish to join this world organization?

The provision for ultimate universality would be particularly useful in rousing within the autocracies the active force needed to replace their present regimes with democracy. The repressive measures in Italy, Japan, Germany and Russia are proof enough that the autocrats governing these countries—with all their secret information regarding public or, rather, private opinion in them—remain afraid of their democrats.

Investing in Union

When democracies form a union what really happens is this: The citizens of each withdraw certain powers they had invested in their national state and reinvest them, or part of them, in the union state. The operation involves loss of power by their national states but no loss of power by the citizens. They give the union state no more rights than they gave the national state. They simply shift certain rights from one to another.

The reason why there is no loss but merely a shift is that the citizens base their union government on the same unit that each of their national governments is based on, namely, individual man. Each man consequently remains in precisely the same relation to the new government as to the old.

Far from losing, the citizen gains power by union. While his power to decide action remains unchanged, the power of the union whose action he decides becomes much greater as the population increases. If a man must depend on himself alone for his security he must be on guard 24 hours daily. When he unites with five other men democratically for mutual security he needs stand guard only four hours. He gets 24 hours security for an investment of four hours. He gets six times more freedom, six times more defensive power. The more men with whom he unites the more freedom and power he has for less investment of them.

When the citizens of several democracies form a union they create a new state but, as we have said, this creates no new rights or powers for the state as State. If they have invested a total of, say, 15 rights in each national government, and they shift five of these rights to the union and leave the others untouched, the total rights of government remain precisely what they were, 15. The citizens divide them between two governments, instead of centering them in one, but lose none of their own power over government.

On the contrary they gain power and government loses power as regards the citizen. By dividing the rights of government between two governments the citizen leaves each of them incomplete. The national state loses supreme right to the union state, but the latter is not the complete State the former was, for the union's supreme right is limited by all the rights that remain reserved entirely to its member states. By this division and by the fact that both governments equally and independently originate in him, the citizen gains the power of balancing two governments to his own advantage, of shifting rights or appealing from one to the other as circumstances may suggest. The citizen of a complete national state has no such check-and-balance power over government. He is in the exposed position of one with all his eggs in one basket, all his investments in one company.

How a union extends the individual's effective freedom from the State,—whether the national, the union, or the foreign state,—may be seen by considering the state rights that he completely transfers to the union. These usually are:

1. The right to grant citizenship.
2. The right to make war and peace, to deal by force or treaty with foreign states.

3. The right to regulate inter-state and foreign trade.
4. The right to control the value of money.
5. The right to control postal and other means of communication.

(The union also has the right to tax individuals and enforce its laws on individuals, but these rights are not transferred to it from the national state, for the latter retains these rights equally. These are really enabling rights required by both governments to govern effectively in their fields. They are inherent in democracy's choice of individual man as the unit.)

Why Unions Can Act Swiftly

Because it takes man for unit a union can put any important proposal directly before all its principals simultaneously, as in an election or plebiscite. Even if a league could assemble in conference the whole executive and legislative branches of each government instead of a small delegation, it would not be equalling the direct action possible in a union. It would still be dealing with agents, not with the sources of power, the men and women, the citizens, who elect the state executives and legislatures.

When a union proceeds indirectly, through agents or representatives of its units, it can still act more rapidly and easily than a league. In a league no agent ever represents more than one unit. In a union every agent must represent many units. His power is always delegated to him by several hundred or thousand of the union's units. A league inevitably makes the delegate a puppet depending on the instructions of his government; a union inevitably keeps its representatives from being rigidly tied to instructions and makes them freer to respond quickly to new facts or arguments.

The representative in a union may be advised by different units in his district to do this or that on a given issue; the advice may be contradictory; he must use his own judgment and strike a balance between the conflicting instructions he thus gets-and guess what all the silent units in his district want him to do. Presumably he will try to follow the wishes of the majority of units in his district, but he is free to decide (under penalty of being defeated at the next election) what these wishes are. He is free, too, to vote against the wishes of the articulate majority in his district, presumably in the belief that the inarticulate are with him, or that time will justify him, or that he can persuade a majority at the next election that he was right. The delegate to a league can not possibly do this; he would be recalled at once by his government. Because a union acts by majority it can act much more quickly than a league.

Once there is agreement in a union to act, action can follow at once. There is no need in it to wait for its units to ratify the decision of their agents; the vote of these representatives suffices for law to take effect. Here again union has a tremendous advantage over a league.

Finally, the greater the emergency in a union the greater is the popular pressure for action—that is, the greater is the pressure of the units on their agents—and the faster the union machinery moves. The difficulty and danger in a union are that it can and may act too swiftly. Where the problem in a league is to get up enough steam to turn the wheels, in a union it is to control the speed, to arrange safety valves, governors, brakes, such as the American Union has in the powers reserved to the people and the states, the two-house Congress, the presidential veto, the Supreme Court, and the time required to amend the Constitution.

The knife edge is removed from disputes between states in a union because the citizens of each state are also citizens of the union, have the same control over both, and inevitably rate higher the citizenship that opens the wider field to them, lets them move freely from state to state, and gives them their standing in the world. When a man is equally sovereign in two governments as he is in a union, disputes between these two agents of his tend to make him an arbiter instead of a partisan.

History is even more reassuring than reason in these regards. For example, there were many disputes—including eleven territorial ones—among the Thirteen American States during their league period. War threatened to result from some of these disputes, and this danger was one of the reasons that led them to shift from league to union. All these disputes lost in explosiveness after union, none of them threatened war thereafter. Supreme Court decisions settled them without the theoretical danger of a state defying the Court ever actually arising.

There is no example in the history of the American Union of a state refusing to accept the Court's decision in an inter-state dispute, of seriously threatening to use force against another state. A state that contemplated such action in the American Union could not gamble on being left to fight it out with the other state as could Italy with Ethiopia, and Japan with China in the League of Nations. Each state government knows that, should it resort to force, it would change its conflict from one with another state to one with the government of the United States, which is required by the Constitution to "protect each of them against invasion" and "domestic violence," which has enough armed power at hand to overwhelm at once the strongest single state and which can draw immediately, directly and without limit on the Union's whole potential power. The Union, moreover, can aim its coercive power at the Governor and other responsible members of such a state government as individual offenders. It can act against them personally on the ground that they, and not the people, are to blame, and that as American citizens who are waging war against the Union they are committing treason.

By establishing the Union the democracies can gain much more security for less armaments than by any other method. They need only admit other nations to the Union to increase that security while reducing armaments.

Armaments, however, are only one measure of power. Our Union, we have seen, would be even more powerful in other respects. It would enjoy almost monopoly world control of such war essentials as rubber, nickel, iron, oil, gold and credit. This, with the invulnerability from surprise attack its decentralized strength would confer and the prestige its centralized general staff and its swiftly effective Union government would give, would enable it to reduce its armaments safely below even the two-power standard it could easily enjoy. The Union would have nothing to fear from most of the peoples left outside at the start; it could count on their support even before they entered it. Except for police work the Union's only need to keep armaments would be as a temporary precaution against the militant absolutist powers—Japan, Germany, Italy and Russia.

Economic Disarmament: We come to the second great problem, economic disarmament. Production and trade, unlike armaments and money, are not the monopoly of any democratic government. They are instead in the hands of tens of millions of individuals, operating alone or through great collectivities called corporations. When democracy deals as a unit with democracy in this field, where not the state but the individual is in fact the governing unit, its negotiations are unimaginably complicated by the multiplicity of conflicting and connecting independent interests involved. Mixed with these are strategic considerations arising from the failure to settle the military disarmament-security problem. The result is again failure, and the failure induces in turn a trend to make production and trade as much a weapon of the state as the army is.

Union is not, like a league, an improved means for solving this problem: here again it is itself the solution. There is no other way than Union to solve this problem, if only because *Union alone allows this tangle of private property interests to be tackled by its own common denominator, the individual.* Where under the best of leagues trade barriers remain and any reduction in them is not only temporary but precarious, exposed to the sudden exercise by any nation of its sovereign right to denounce them because of a national emergency, these barriers vanish completely and forever when states form a union.

Since the democracies do two-thirds of the world's trade, mostly among themselves, their abolition of trade barriers among themselves would solve the economic disarmament problem not only for themselves but practically for all the world. No serious foreign trade problem would remain for The Union and no outside country would withstand the bargaining power of this rich market with its monopoly control of essential raw materials. The Union would not need tariffs to protect any industries as strategic or subsidies to agriculture as preparation for a blockade. Here again the Union of only fifteen democracies provides a base big enough to solve practically the whole world problem.

The Union promises to reduce unemployment to where it would be no grave problem. The Union would do this by freeing trade, stabilizing money, lowering costs, reducing armaments, guaranteeing political security, eliminating the war danger, diverting into healthy channels the billions now being wasted, cheapening and speeding communications and making the worker and his product far more mobile, restoring confidence and opening vast new enterprises. If the problem of unemployment cannot be solved along these lines it would seem indeed insoluble.

Then there is the pressing problem of reducing taxes, economizing on government, avoiding centralization's danger of dictatorship. Under national sovereignty taxation and governmental powers have been growing everywhere like weeds. Only the Union seriously tackles the problem of how the democracies are to recover from the taxation and borrowing and bureaucracy and unnecessary government with which nationalism has afflicted them.

The Great Federal Problem

What shall be the division of rights or powers or fields of government between the Union and the national governments?

If to each field of government we apply the test, *Which will serve our individual freedom best, to give the Union or leave the Nation the right to govern in this field?* we find five main rights that we need to give to the Union. They are:

1. The right to grant citizenship.
2. The right to make peace and war, to negotiate treaties and otherwise deal with the outside world, to raise and maintain a defense force.
3. The right to regulate interstate and foreign trade.
4. The right to coin and issue money, and fix other measures.
5. The right to govern communications: To operate the postal service, and regulate, control or operate other interstate communication services.

Manifestly, the Union must provide citizenship in the Union. Obviously this brings each of us an enormous gain in individual freedom. Since we remain citizens of our nations in becoming citizens of the Union we lose nothing and only gain. Union citizenship must involve interstate citizenship in the sense that a citizen in moving from one state to another retains all his Union rights and can change his state citizenship easily. The case for giving the other four rights to the Union is no less clear. We are seeing every day in all these fields that the rights we have granted our national governments to maintain separate armed forces, separate customs areas, separate currencies and separate communication systems have become not simply unnecessary to individual freedom but increasingly dangerous interferences with it.

HOW SHALL WE UNITE? [2]

We come to the problem of method: How, concretely, shall we unite our democracies to this desired degree? We can

[2] From *Union Now* by Clarence K. Streit, National Chairman of Federal Union, Inc. p. 138-47. Harper & Bros. N.Y. 1940.

divide this problem in two. There is, primarily, the underlying political problem of putting these general principles into constitutional form, establishing the Union and its governmental machinery. There is, secondarily, the practical problem of meeting the various transitional and technical difficulties raised by transfer of each of the five rights to the Union.

The Constitution of the Union

The only detailed or concrete plan that the Union can need is a draft constitution. For the establishment of the Union eliminates many of the problems for which we now think we need plans and planned management, and it provides itself the mechanism—government—for solving the various problems of transition.

The Convention that framed the Constitution uniting the Thirteen American democracies not only framed no plan except the Constitution, but it had no draft even of a constitution when it began, nothing but the broad outline of the Virginia plan for one—and New Jersey and Hamilton soon produced opposing plans. Unlike us they had no existing federal constitution on which to base their planning.

Those who would constitute unions can turn now to many time-tested successes. For reasons that will be seen when we study carefully the American Union I believe that we should turn particularly to the American Constitution and experience for guidance.

The Union Legislature

The chief technical problem in drafting the Union Constitution is the organization of its governmental machinery, its legislative, executive and judicial departments, and its mechanism for amending the constitution.

Practice is strongly in favor of a two-house Union legislature with one house based completely on the population and the other modifying this principle of equal men in favor of equal states. If the Constitution allows one representative for every half million or million citizens, the result would be roughly:

Australia	13	7
Belgium	16	8
Canada	21	11
Denmark	7	4
Finland	7	4
France	84	42
Ireland	6	3
Netherlands	16	8
New Zealand	3	2
Norway	6	3
Sweden	12	6
Switzerland	8	4
Union of South Africa*	4	2
United Kingdom	93	47
United States	258	129
Totals	554	280

Those who fear this would give Americans too much weight in the House need to remember two things. One is that this weight would diminish with every new democracy that entered the Union. The other is that there is no more danger of the American deputies or those from any other nation voting as a bloc when elected individually by the people of separate election districts than there is of the New York members of the Congress or the Scottish members of Parliament voting as a unit now. Party lines would immediately cut across national ones in this Union as in all others.

As for the Senate, its main purposes are to safeguard the less populous against the more populous states, the state governments against the Union government, and the people of the Union against over-centralization. In the American Union the method of achieving this purpose consists partly in allowing two senators to the people—not the government—of each state, no

* Based on the white population since Negroes there lack the right to vote.

matter what the number of people in it may be. This might be copied in our Union. The difference in population between the United States and New Zealand, the most and the least populous democracies in our Union, is proportionately about the same as the difference between New York and Nevada.

For my part, however, I would favor a slight modification of this part of the American system. I would allow two senators to every self-governing nation of 25,000,000 or less population, two additional senators for every additional 25,000,000 or major fraction thereof up to a total population of 100,000,000, and thereafter two more senators for each 50,000,000 or major fraction thereof. This would give two senators to each of the fifteen democracies except France, the United Kingdom and the United States, the first two of which would have four and the third would have eight. The results of the two systems may be seen below:

Australia	2	2
Belgium	2	2
Canada	2	2
Denmark	2	2
Finland	2	2
France	2	4
Ireland	2	2
Netherlands	2	2
New Zealand	2	2
Norway	2	2
Sweden	2	2
Switzerland	2	2
Union of South Africa	2	2
United Kingdom	2	4
United States	2	8
Totals	30	40

The American method would give the small democracies a preponderance of five-sixths. The other would give them three-fifths of the Senate at the start, and these proportions would grow with the admission of new member nations since nearly all potential members have less than 25,000,000 population. It would seem wise to allow the government of so vast a Union as ours to draw more than the American system permits on the experience of the democracies most accustomed to government on a big scale, so long as the Senate's function of safeguarding the small democracies and decentralization is not thereby endangered. Either way the senators would be elected at large by each nation, and each senator would have one vote.

Parliamentary Or Presidential Government?

There are obvious arguments for the parliamentary and for the presidential system of government. The former is more responsive, the latter more stable. One can argue that in this new venture of establishing union on a world scale, and among so many historic nations, the first aim must be stability. Once the Union is firmly established its government can be made more responsive when the need becomes insistent, whereas if the Union is so responsive at the start as to be unstable it may be too late to remedy this defect and keep the Union together. It is safer to cut cloth too long than too short. Moreover, the establishment of the Union eliminates so much of the work of government today as to make responsiveness less necessary.

On the other hand, one can argue that by eliminating all the burden and waste of unnecessary government and by generally freeing the individual we stimulate enormously the most powerful sources of change. The drafters of the American Constitution had no way of knowing how rapidly the United States would grow under the free conditions they provided. We know now from this experience how conducive individual freedom is to rapid growth, invention, discovery, change in everything. We need only look back to see how the tempo of change has been accelerating every generation since government began to be made on the principle of the equality of man and for the Rights of Man. We cannot make this Union without speeding proportionately the tempo of change. Prudence once required for freedom stable rather than responsive government. Now prudence demands greater provision for adaptability.

My own view favors a combination of the responsive and the stable, of the parliamentary and presidential systems,—a combination aimed at keeping the advantages of each, meeting the peculiar needs of our Union, and insuring that its government will not seem too strange to any of the democracies. This brings us to the problem of the executive power. Only here do I think that we need to invent or innovate in making this Constitution, though not very much even here.

The Executive

My suggestion is that instead of establishing a single executive we vest executive authority in a Board of five persons, each selected for five years, one each year, or each elected for ten years, one every other year. This would assure constant change in the Board and constant stability. I would have three elected by direct popular vote. I think it highly essential that there be some officer or officers in the Union elected by and responsible to the people of the Union as a whole, as is the American President. The other two members of the Board I would have elected in between the popular elections, one by the House of Deputies, the other by the Senate. This should assure a more representative Board. The Board would establish a rotation whereby each member would preside over it one or two years. Three should form a quorum of the Board and it should act normally by the majority of those voting.

The Board, I would further suggest, should delegate most of its executive authority to a Premier who would exercise this power with the help of a Cabinet of his own choosing until he lost the confidence of either the House or the Senate, whereupon the Board would name another Premier. I would give the Board power to dissolve either house or both of them in order to call new elections, and I believe it should also have a power of veto somewhat similar to that which the American

President has. I would make the Board commander-in-chief of the Union's armed forces, and empower it with the consent of the Senate to conclude treaties and name all the Union judges.

I would also have it report to the people and the Legislature from time to time on the state of human freedom and of the Union, and on the effects and need of change, and to recommend broadly measures and policies. In short, I would entrust the more general and long term duties of the executive to the Board, and leave the more detailed and short term duties to the Premier and Cabinet.

The aim of this system is threefold: First, to assure the supremacy of the people and to provide strength, continuity, stability and foresight in the executive while keeping it responsible to and representative of the people. Second, to reassure all those who would be fearful of any one man having too much power in the Union, or of all executive authority being in the hands of, say, an American, or an Englishman, or a Frenchman. Third, to avoid the unhealthy burden now placed on one man by the American system, while enabling the head of the Union to fulfill the liaison functions which the British royal family do to some extent in the smaller British Commonwealth, and which would be much more necessary in the Union. All members of the Board would be expected to travel through the Union. It would be easy for the Board to arrange rotation whereby one would be visiting the more distant parts of the Union while another was visiting the less distant parts and the other three were at the capital. Such, broadly, are the aims of the system I suggest. I believe few will object to these aims, and certainly I would not object to any other system that promised to secure them better than mine, or nearly as well.

The Judiciary

The essentials to me here are that there be an independent Supreme Court, that no controversies among member states be excluded from its jurisdiction, and that the Constitution be made explicitly the supreme law of the Union. To attain these ends I would favor copying broadly the method followed in the American Constitution. No doubt there would be controversy over whether the Supreme Court should have the right to invalidate laws as unconstitutional. I believe it should have this right. The essential purpose of this right is, however, to keep the Constitution supreme—to keep intact the division between the more fundamental law which can be changed relatively slowly, the Constitution, and the less fundamental law which can be changed relatively quickly, the statutes. It would seem wiser to accept any system that gives reasonable promise of attaining this purpose than to delay or sacrifice the Union by controversy over the question of method.

The Amending Machinery

Connected with the problem of the judiciary is the problem of how the Constitution shall be amended. Many of the objections made to the American Supreme Court would be more justly aimed at the American Constitution's amending mechanism. It makes that Constitution too hard to change, too rigid, and it has for me the further disadvantages of being based too much on the states as corporate bodies. All that has been said of our Union's need to adapt itself more quickly to change than the American Union needed to do when it began applies with special force to the present problem. I would suggest that the constitution be amended by majority vote of the voting citizens on proposals that had gone through some preliminary scrutiny, with several choices open as to the kind of scrutiny.

It would be expressly stipulated in the Constitution, however, that certain constitutional guarantees, such as the right of each nation to conduct its own affairs in its own language and the right of each citizen to freedom of speech and of the press, could not be lessened without the consent of each nation.

Such are the main lines on which the Union could be constituted. Those who desire to see how these proposals look when actually applied will find in the annexes an illustrative draft constitution containing them. It may give a better idea of them as a whole, and it provides an easy means of indicating how various minor constitutional problems not treated here might be solved.

THE MEANING OF DEMOCRACY [3]

Since the fifth century B.C. men have taken the name "democracy" and applied it to a certain type of political system. They have disagreed about its features and still more about its merits. But there has been no serious disagreement concerning the broad type of political system to which the name belongs. It has generally been attached to states in which a fairly inclusive citizen body elected its rulers or leaders by choosing between opposing candidates, after free discussion of their respective proposals or qualifications for office. The more inclusive the citizen body that participated in these activities the more democratic was the state. The system named democracy could be realized in greater or less degree. But wherever, on the coasts of Greece or in the valleys of Switzerland, among Germanic tribes or in mediaeval cities, in England, France, or the United States, in China or India, citizens or subjects have demanded a voice in the affairs of state, wherever they have resisted controls imposed on them from above, wherever they have refused to be taxed without being represented, wherever they have claimed the right to criticize the policies of those who governed them, wherever they have developed an articulate and responsible public opinion, there, according to universal usage, the movement has been named democratic.

So, when the question is raised, we can all point at democracy, for we all recognize certain signs that denote its presence. . . .

[3] By Robert Morrison MacIver, Professor of Social Science, Barnard University. *New Europe*. 1:3-4. December 1, 1940.

The value of democracy is maintained by the difference between it and its alternatives. If we defend democracy it is not because it is free from defects or in itself an ideal or absolute thing, but because we find it more desirable than any practicable alternatives. What has this political system to offer that the others lack? What does it lack that the others offer? Often, because we do not define at all or because we define badly, the alternatives are not fairly stated. For example, the alternatives are not, as many apologists have claimed, the rule of the many and the rule of "the mass" and the rule of the few. The mass, in the sense of Ortega y Gasset, has effective unity only when the social organization is shaken by a major crisis. It is the crowd swollen to national dimensions, an interstitial phenomenon breaking its bounds. And when that happens the mass demands not democracy but its Fuehrer. It is the condition of dictatorship. For thus only can the leader become the pied piper, playing such cunning notes on his propaganda pipes that he leads them blindly whither he wills.

These pseudo-alternatives take many forms. We are told, for example, that democracy is incompatible with socio-economic planning, whereas planning is of the very essence of dictatorship. Neither statement is in accord with the facts. Dictatorship offers us a quickly constructed and quickly executed plan of some sort, superimposed and shielded from criticism. Democracy offers us the kind and degree of planning that public opinion will support, always subject to the criticism of opposing forces. Dictatorship includes the cultural scheme in its planning range. Democracy is incompatible with the direct control of the cultural life. These differences by no means sum up to the contrast between a planned order and an unplanned drift. Nor do they imply that the scheme of order in a dictatorship is more stable or more secure than in a democracy, or even that a dictatorship solves the problem or a crisis more completely than does a democracy. Dictatorships arise during grave crises because they are congenial to distracted or desperate men, not because they have demonstrated their superiority. As Karl Mannheim says, "to wish to cure a society in a state of crisis by establishing a dictatorship over it is like the physician who believes he is curing a sick child by forbidding it to cry."

When we look at democracy in the light of its alternatives its meaning is not far from us. What does it offer us that no alternatives can provide? The answer is not a matter of opinion but of fact. It is written in the record. Democracy is the only political scheme that makes government constitutionally responsive to the free tides of public opinion. Its constitution is the only one that rests on the right of all citizens to have an opinion about their government and to organize that opinion so that they determine, or at least control, the policies of government. It is the only political scheme that allows men to differ freely in opinion, drawing the line, if at all, only at the point where groups threaten to establish a system that would deny the same right to others. Free criticism is essential to the life of democracy while it is fatal to dictatorship. Democracy is the only political scheme that is inherently precluded from the direct control of the faiths, the aspirations, the life principles of its citizens, and that must leave culture free to follow its own creative way. For it could not control the motions of culture without repudiating the primary right of opinion. Finally, democracy is the only political system that makes the state the changing ever-responsive agency of the community, instead of imposing on the community the sheer stamp of the state.

Whatever organization, planning, direction, leadership, may be compatible with these principles, democracy admits; whatever is incompatible with them, democracy rejects. We have defined democracy as the institutional embodiment of certain principles. We have not defined it as being any particular set of institutions, nor on the other hand have we defined it as being merely a set of principles. We do not identify it with a parliamentary system or a representative system or any sort of economic system or any specific mechanism of government, no matter how closely associated with the history of democracy. These systems change; they must change if they are to adapt themselves to changing conditions and to changing needs. Why, for example, should we imagine that a senate and a house of representatives constitute the eternal sacred form in which the public business of a democratic society must be transacted? They were created to meet a situation that was not sacred and is certainly not eternal. Still less do we identify democracy with majority-rule. That would be a loose and utterly misleading identification, since a majority can crush the democratic rights of a minority and give itself up to dictatorship. On the other hand we do not identify democracy with unembodied principles, such as the self-realization of a people, the solidarity of the nation, or the liberty of the individual. Vague principles of this sort provide no clear ground for distinguishing democracy from alternative political schemes, and indeed the proponents of these opposing schemes often proclaim that they satisfy these principles better than does democracy. We can find no criterion of democracy in principles without institutional embodiment or in institutions apart from principles.

The meaning of democracy is given in the relation of the two. Democracy abides wherever political institutions ensure the free role of a public opinion that extends its own freedom into the future. To define it thus is one thing; to evaluate it another. Men evaluate it differently; there seems to be no reason why they should not define it alike. For the value lies in the profound difference that it makes to human destiny and to human well-being according as men choose one system or the other.

AN ENGLISH-SPEAKING UNION? [4]

Although the idea of a commonwealth of English-speaking countries is not new, it has never before come so close to

[4] By Mallory Browne, Chief of the European Bureau of the *Christian Science Monitor*. *Christian Science Monitor Weekly Magazine Section*. p. 7, 15. October 12, 1940.

actuality. The agreement between Canada and the United States to set up a joint defense board, as well as the recent Anglo-American accord on the leasing of naval bases, are substantial straws in a wind that is by no means a mere passing breeze.

Despite these signs of unmistakable progress, union of the United States and Great Britain can not yet be considered practical politics. It certainly has advanced, however, from the realm of abstract sentiment. Indeed, it has lately attained the status of a serious, if still essentially vague, and indeterminate, project.

Something not far short of official recognition was, in fact, given to the idea of a union between Britain and America when it was proposed in the British parliament recently. A former cabinet minister, Mr. Leslie Hore Belisha, National Liberal M.P., for Davenport, indirectly launched the proposal in the House of Commons. During a debate that followed Premier Winston Churchill's announcement of the agreement to lease British naval bases to the United States, Mr. Hore Belisha declared that if the accord "should lead to the same kind of relationship as we hoped for in the case of France, and to eventual common citizenship, the evils of this war will have been almost worth-while."

If these words were simply an allusion by a single M.P., they might not be of any particular moment. But they are the expression of a view which I have heard put forward recently by many people in Britain.

Just before the final collapse of France in the middle of June this year, the British government suddenly sent its dramatic offer of union to the tottering French cabinet then at Bordeaux. When this news became known in England it was already too late. Mr. Reynaud had resigned and his successor, Marshall Petain, had appealed publicly for an armistice. Britain's offer accordingly lapsed.

At the moment it was issued, conditions were so crucial that it was not hard to understand why Prime Minister Churchill

—for the initiative in this historic move came from him—has launched this unheralded offer of union. It was a case of leaving nothing undone, however drastic and revolutionary, to avert the impending collapse of France. But even at that time, not a few people in Britain felt the move was a mistake. More than one Englishman objected vigorously, startled at how close he had come to waking up one morning and finding himself a citizen of France. And there were many who said then: "If only it had been a question of union with America, it would have been all right."

Since that time the idea that the offer made in that hour of stress to France should be applied to Great Britain and the United States has made definite progress. The parliamentary statement by Mr. Hore Belisha is in fact in the nature of an implicit acknowledgment that the project is now on record and that sooner or later it will come up for official action.

Naturally this does not mean that such action is imminent—far from it. If there is one thing that the present British government is being careful about, it is precisely the matter of relations with the United States. There is no attempt in London to deny that Britain needs urgently all the aid it can get from America in this war. But there is also a sharp recognition of the need to "make haste slowly"—very slowly. Washington and London have long since learned by experience that the progress of Anglo-American cooperation cannot be forced. It must be allowed to unfold.

Nevertheless, it is undoubtedly true today that the idea of establishing a greater measure of unity between the British Commonwealth and the United States of America is viewed with favor, not only by a large section of the British public, but by influential people and what are currently called government circles, to an extent that a short time ago would have seemed almost fantastic.

It must be re-emphasized that there is no intention, in what has been said, to imply that anything official is being or will be done along these lines. The idea has, it is quite true, advanced beyond the realm of fantasy. It is no longer an idle notion, but a definite project, supported by a great many serious thinkers in both countries. But it is still a long way from being a matter of practical politics.

When these qualifications are kept in view, the whole thing falls into its proper perspective. Once this is done, however, there is still ample room for considering the project more fully in relation to its future potentialities.

At the moment, the version of an English-speaking commonwealth most in vogue is that of a union based on the essential points of Britain's offer to France. The argument is that although the fact may be a little less apparent, in reality democracy today is hardly less threatened in Britain and America than it was in Britain and France last June. In support of this, Ambassador William Bullitt's recent statement is recalled: "It is my conviction, drawn from my own experience and information in the hands of our government in Washington, that the United States is in as great a peril today as was France a year ago."

This being so, it is asked, why should not the preamble of the draft declaration submitted to the French government last June apply equally to America and Britain today?

These points [of the declaration of June 16] are a startling indication of how far the British government was prepared to go in that moment of crisis, in throwing over orthodox notions of national sovereignty and indeed of nationality itself. Britain was ready to abolish all barriers between the two countries and to declare that they should no longer be two nations, Britain and France, but one Franco-British union. It was ready to give instantly full British citizenship to all Frenchmen, and to make all British subjects citizens of France. It was ready to establish a constitution providing that matters of defense, foreign policy, finance, and economics should be organized jointly under the union. It offered finally to merge, to a large extent at least, not only the cabinets of the two countries but their two parliaments as well.

There is no doubt that this far-reaching offer will prove to be a major milestone in the history of mankind's progress toward the poet's dream of "the Parliament of man, the federation of the world." For nearly all these points, significantly enough, are emphasized in Federal Union.

But Britain's offer was made, of course, not to a group of nations, as Federal Union proposes, but to a single country, and to England's chief ally at that time. It is precisely the argument of many who favor an Anglo-American union that wider forms of federation must begin by closer unity between those peoples who already possess a certain fundamental similarity of background, of ideals, and of language. The British Commonwealth of Nations is the simplest form of such a free association of free peoples, all speaking the same language.

If it was possible to envisage and actually to propose unity between this Commonwealth—or at least its keystone country, the United Kingdom—and France, how much more natural should seem the idea of union between the British Commonwealth and that other great English-speaking nation, the United States of America?

There are of course tremendous obstacles and difficulties to overcome before any such plan reaches the point where it may be practicable. In fact, there is little doubt that most people would today be inclined to dismiss it as frankly impossible. Surely, however, that is a case to which those wise words of Fridtjof Nansen are particularly applicable: "The difficult is that which we can do today; the impossible takes a little longer!"

UNION: OCEANIC OR CONTINENTAL[5]

The two contrasted themes concerning potential membership are ideological on the one hand and geographical or cultural on the other. There is much to be said for each. The ideological approach led Mr. Streit to propose a union consisting of sixteen

[5] *Round Table.* 29:741-4. September, 1939.

democracies. The geographical and cultural approach led Count Coudenhove-Kalergi—whose ideas have experienced a popular revival under this new stimulus—to propose a series of unions, each based on continental solidarity. It will be well to consider these two proposals on their merits as contrasting possible bases for international federal union. From the point of view of Great Britain, they present themselves as a choice between participation in an oceanic union and participation in a United States of Europe.

The major merits of the former concept are fourfold. In the first place, it would unite a group of peoples having long experience of parliamentary democracy, of the responsibilities of freedom, and of respect for minorities. In the second place, it would link constitutionally countries that are already closely linked economically and ideologically, through their situation on the world's oceans. Contiguity by land is not the only kind of bond that geography provides: the sea joins as well as separates, and in cheapness and ease of transport France, for example, is much closer to the United States than she is to Rumania. Their situation on the oceans—Switzerland excepted—has also given to the members of Mr. Streit's projected union a common outlook on world affairs, free of the myopia and claustrophobia that sometimes afflict continental peoples. In the third place, oceanic union would enable the greatest of all existing international institutions, the British Commonwealth of Nations, to remain intact, within a wider federation. It would relieve rather than accentuate the present conflict of motives in United Kingdom policy, the conflict between responsibilities to Europe and responsibilities to the Commonwealth. Finally, the oceanic union, being confined to no single continent, would be capable of solving within itself, as indeed the British Commonwealth is capable of solving within itself on a smaller scale, the vital and growing problems of relations between continents and races—provided, that is to say, Mr. Streit's project were modified to allow non-white countries like India, which fulfil the basic democratic condition, to enter the union on equal terms with other members.

On all these points the alternative project of European union (associated with a Pan American federation and other continental unions) is open to criticism. It has, first, to surmount the obstacle of different forms of government, some of which are the reverse of democratic. Secondly, it lays, perhaps, undue weight upon mere geographical contiguity. New Zealand is certainly in the economic and social orbit of the United Kingdom; equally certainly, Rumania is not. The most that can be said is that there are degrees of economic connection, just as there are degrees of democracy or dictatorship; and that regarded as a whole a continent like Europe is closely knit in economic and social intercourse—Great Britain, for example, having intimate relations with the Scandinavian countries, they with Germany, and Germany with the Danubian basin. A chain is no less strong because its terminal links do not touch each other.

Thirdly, the continental concept of union would present the United Kingdom, and Ireland also, with a very difficult choice between their European and their extra-European ties. It might mean the virtual dissolution of the British Commonwealth, leaving it as scarcely more than an informal means of technical and administrative cooperation between certain special members of different continental groups. Supporters of the project could argue, of course, that this sacrifice would be worth while, in compensation for the great advantages implied in European unity; or that the importance of the British Commonwealth would actually be enhanced, because it would become the main bridge between the several continental units.

A purely continental union, fourthly, would have no chance of providing, within its own boundaries, a solution of those inter-racial problems which threaten to become more difficult and dangerous than mere international problems within the next few generations. That would have to remain a task for a second stage, when the relations between the several continental federations themselves were reorganized on a new footing.

On the other hand, two arguments of great weight can be advanced in favor of the continental basis of union. In Europe, if it could ever be brought about, it would solve automatically and permanently the problems that threaten to set the whole world ablaze with war, problems of frontiers and *Lebensraum*, problems of rabid and excessive nationalism. These troubles the project of oceanic union, unless and until it led to something wider, would not abolish but would only hold in check by creating an "unbalance of power." It would be an enormous combination of the undoubted "Haves" against the self-styled "Have-Nots." The lesson of "unbalance" in the past is that sooner or later it inevitably turns into a balance of power, because the dominant side lacks resolution to retain its advantage, while the subordinate side imposes stern sacrifices on itself in order to throw off its inferiority. The continental form of union is capable, in theory, of abolishing forever both balance and unbalance of power within each continent. The second great argument for that form is its cultural basis. There is a unity of European civilization which it will take more than an interlude of National-Socialist barbarism to destroy. This unity is deeply grounded in history and religion, and even some of the apostles of aggression draw inspiration from the concept of a Europe re-united under a Pax Romana or a Holy German Empire. Democratic policy is indeed handicapped today by its comparative lack of the unifying motive in its approach to the problems of European order. Certainly it would be unwise to base a permanent organization of human society on a division in Europe resulting from a peculiar politico-economic conjuncture which may prove only temporary.

None of these arguments, in one cause or the other, is final. They are not indeed advanced here in order to show conclusively the superiority of one type of federal union over the other; for the likelihood is that if and when international union becomes practicable it will borrow from both forms. The point to which this article has been addressed is the need to base any political superstructure on a foundation of common interest and common sentiment which will give rise to a common loyalty. This groundwork of unity in the lives and thought of men must be strong enough and lasting enough to endure as long as the union itself, that is to say, far beyond the horizon even of our dreams.

PLAN FOR UNION [6]

It is my conviction that the strongest, sanest and most durable guarantee for this new world is a union of the United States of America and the six independent units of the British Commonwealth: the United Kingdom, Ireland, Canada, Union of South Africa, Australia, New Zealand.

This may appear, to the suspicious, another start on another blueprint for utopia, another Wilsonian vision. It isn't. It is the practical realization of the destiny for new world leadership which, whether we admit it or not, or whether we like it or not, is now being thrust upon us.

It is my belief that we Americans are ready to admit this and accept it. I believe that we are conscious of our responsibility for keeping the peace in that largely moist half of the world in which we are fortunate enough to live. If we were alone in a totalitarian world—a world in which the term "cut-throat competition" would mean just that—we might manage to isolate ourselves behind a wall of steel. But we should do so at the expense of our standard of living and, before long, of our faith in our own democratic processes. We wouldn't like that. We wouldn't stand for it. We'd soon be pushing all those ships and planes and guns and men on to the offensive.

But the English-speaking world is big enough for all con-

[6] From article by Robert E. Sherwood, Playwright. *Life*. 9:98-102. October 7, 1940.

ceivable purposes. It's a world bounded on the northeast by the British Isles, on the southeast by the Union of South Africa, on the northwest by Alaska, on the southwest by Australia and New Zealand. Its center is in the U. S. and that would be the center of its foreign and military policy. It would have no involvements whatever in the continent of Europe. It would constitute a power of unassailable magnitude, dominating all the oceans; and this power would be in the hands of 200,000,000 people who speak the same language and believe in the same three fundamental things—liberty and justice and peace.

The political mechanics of an English-speaking union have been set down, simply and clearly, by Clarence K. Streit. The supreme government would be organized on the basis of proportional representation, so that the United States would have a majority in the ratio of about eight to five over all the other states put together. Each state would, of course, continue independently to fly its own flag, choose its own rulers, apply its own taxes, enact and enforce its own laws, chew its own gum. It would even be free to dislike all the other states to its heart's content. (This clause is inserted out of respect for the Irish.) But all uniting states would have in common the same immovable constitutional cornerstone: the Bill of Rights.

This is the practical, workable, easily attainable plan for a new world. It is logical, it is inevitable, as an evolutionary development in human progress. It is based, to begin with, on sound economic fact: the British Commonwealth is our best customer and we are its best customer. But there are considerations much more important than that. I don't propose to insult the reader by handing him or her any of the old, pompous bunk which is always repeated by white-tied orators at Pilgrim dinners—the routine patter about how "the futures of our two great nations are indissolubly linked because we both talk the language of Shakespeare and Shelley and Keats." Americans are inclined to remark on that, truthfully, "Nuts! *We* don't talk the language of Shakespeare!" But, in a recent issue of *Life* I read a letter from an English girl in which she said that America's greatest contribution to Britain's defense was the expression, "So what!" And when recently the Germans boasted that they were shelling London from a range of 99 miles, the official British comment on this claim was "Hooey!" And day after day, during the terror of the blitzkrieg, we have heard the voice of the whole British people, expressing themselves in those inspiring monosyllables, "We can take it!" The British don't talk the language of Shakespeare, either. They talk the language of Damon Runyon.

In the Victorian era, when England was proud and mighty, the suggestion of a union such as this would have failed to disturb a single cobweb in the halls of Westminster. But in the past quarter of a century, the sun of empire has resumed its progress westward. The old British policy of maintaining control over the balance of power in Europe has brought the entire commonwealth too close to the ragged edge of destruction. This has been recognized by that far-seeing statesman, Winston Churchill. On August 20, last, he concluded a long speech in the House of Commons with two paragraphs of extraordinary significance. Speaking of the negotiations then in progress between Washington, Ottawa and London for the leasing of bases in the Western Hemisphere, he said:

> Undoubtedly this process means that these two great organizations of the English-speaking democracies, the British Empire and the United States, will have to be somewhat mixed up together in some of their affairs for mutual and general advantage.
>
> For my own part, looking out upon the future, I do not view the process with any misgivings. No one can stop it. Like the Mississippi, it just keeps rolling along. Let it roll. Let it roll on in full flood, inexorable, irresistible, to broader lands and better days.

(Note that Mr. Churchill picked his analogy from *Show Boat* by Edna Ferber, Oscar Hammerstein II and Jerome Kern.)

We Americans should consider this remarkable statement with the utmost care. It was the head of the British government, speaking to the elected representatives of the British people.

Mr. Churchill is himself half American. He is a historian and a student of history. (He is also a prophet.) He is as familiar with Washington's Farewell Address as is any of our isolationist Senators. He knows that among Americans there can be no answer but assent to Washington's famous question: "Why, by interweaving our destiny with that of any part of Europe, entangle our peace and prosperity in the toils of European ambition, rivalship, interest, humor or caprice?"

Mr. Churchill was saying that the destiny of Britain must be away from Europe. It must center in the New World. The destiny of all parts of the British Commonwealth must eventually be interwoven with that of the United States, as Canada's destiny most certainly is today. Mr. Churchill was talking not about an impossible alliance but a possible union.

Mr. Churchill, like Mr. Roosevelt and Mr. Willkie and Senator Burton K. Wheeler and John L. Lewis, is a leader who gained leadership only with popular consent. He is the product of a system which has been developing for more than 700 years, since the Anglo-Saxon tradition of civil liberty began. In the darkness of the twelfth century, when feudalism was forcing the people of Europe to crawl upon their hands and knees and beg for the favors of their overlords, individual Britons rose up and demanded for themselves an essential right—the right of trial by jury. They gained it and they have never relinquished it. Magna Charta followed, and after it a long and ever more positive assertion of rights, leading to the institution of parliamentary government. In the seventeenth century the poet John Milton first asserted the rights of freedom of speech. In the eighteenth century came the Declaration of Independence.

The American Revolution created not only the United States. It made possible the free British Commonwealth as it exists today. As David Cort has said in his stirring article, "Democracy, Unlimited," published in the August 19 issue of *Life*: "It is not often remembered now that English members of Parliament said then in the House of Commons that the Americans were fighting for English liberties as well as for their own."

The enemies of freedom have been able to cite many cases of the most arrant injustice by both Britons and Americans. They can advertise effectively the treatment of the Irish and of the American Indians. They can point to plenty of ugly splotches on the record. But there is one important fact which they can not deny: in every part of the English-speaking world where liberty has been established, it has never been renounced, as it was renounced in Germany when Hitler came to power. It has been fought for and bled for; but it has never been surrendered. It has spread all over the earth and has been extended to many races. Consider the French in Canada. They left France when that nation was under Bourbon tyranny. They were deeply religious people, far removed from the influence of Voltaire and the effects of the French Revolution. But, after nearly two centuries under the British flag, they have developed and maintained a passionate spirit of independence.

The progress of the cause of freedom may have been slow, but, like Ol' Man River, it has been inexorable. It has broadened with the spread of education. It has deepened with experience. The Nazis, Fascists and Communists may say that all the prating about liberty in the English-speaking democracies is hypocritical as long as India and the Philippines remain under British and American sovereignty. But how long would such leaders as Gandhi and Quezon be permitted to live if India and the Philippines came under Nazi, Fascist or Communist rule? Would any component parts of Hitler's proposed empire have complete autonomy, including even the right to secede, as the British Dominions do now? Certainly not! That autonomy, the Nazis would say, is just another evidence of democratic weakness. In the "Master State" there will be no "rights" of any kind whatsoever.

There have been threats of a "Master State" before in central Europe. During the Napoleonic wars, when it seemed that the conqueror was to extend his influence to this hemisphere, Thomas Jefferson proposed a "union" with Great Britain (he even went so far as to propose a "marriage"). And when the Monroe Doctrine was promulgated by the United States in agreement with the British Government, James Madison said: "With the British power and Navy combined with our own, we have nothing to fear from the rest of the world; and in the great struggle of the epoch between liberty and despotism, we owe it to ourselves to sustain the former, in this hemisphere at least."

Forty years after Madison's time his hopes for Anglo-American cooperation were subjected to severe tests in our own Civil War. The diplomacy of Abraham Lincoln, supported by Queen Victoria and the sentiments of the common people in England, averted calamity.

There is still a tendency among Americans to believe that our statesmanship in world affairs has been hopelessly inept—that, in all international relationships, we have consistently been suckers. This is the assumption that all Americans are unsophisticated hicks and easy marks for foreign city slickers. That kind of American thinking can best be described with the expressive adjective "corny." Since the activities in Europe of the father of our diplomacy, Benjamin Franklin, we have done pretty well for ourselves. Franklin had a broadly international mind. He said: "God grant that not only the love of liberty but a thorough knowledge of the rights of man may pervade all the nations of the earth, so that a philosopher may set his foot anywhere on its surface and say: 'This is my country.' "

Franklin's dream was the exact negation of the old feudal European conception of chauvinistic nationalism. It was the American dream of "a more perfect union." And that has been the proper inspiration of all American foreign policy, from Franklin through Jefferson, Madison, Monroe and Lincoln, down to the Secretaries of State of the present century, John Hay, Elihu Root, Charles Evans Hughes, Henry L. Stimson and Cordell Hull. In only one great world crisis have we failed utterly to convert immediate emergency into historic opportunity. That was in 1919, when our policy hurtled from the visionary and impractical extreme of Woodrow Wilson's plan for world cooperation to the equally visionary and impractical plan of the isolationists to keep us out of everything.

That one failure was a bitter experience for us Americans. One hope was shot from under us. We found a substitute hope but that one has been shot away too. Hitler has destroyed our isolationism as decisively as he circumvented the Maginot Line. Today, because Britain is engaged in a war to the death, we are in it too. I don't think many Americans are kidding themselves about that. Even though they believed that the sending of 50 of our destroyers was an act of war against Germany, they were for it. Americans know that if Hitler conquers Britain, he has conquered a part of ourselves and is directly threatening the rest of ourselves.

The British may, by a miracle of heroism and endurance, hold out long enough to give us a chance to prepare adequate defenses for this one continent. We can then say: "Thanks, and goodby. We're no longer concerned with your fate." But we shall have large problems to face, even then. If the British seapower is gone, we shall be compelled to build our own empire, establishing our outposts farther and farther from our own shores. Our sense of insecurity will grow as the range of bombing planes increases. We shall have to plant the American flag perilously close to Europe, Africa, Asia. Conscription of our youth and billions annually for defense will be our permanent policy.

Such a future for us is unthinkable. Imperialism is simply not our game. We have no relish for it and no natural aptitude for it. Our genius is for union. The successful experiment of the union of 13 sovereign states—13 which have since become

48—is the greatest American contribution to human progress.

By a union with the British Commonwealth, we cannot hope to reform the world, either with moral preachments or at the point of a gun. We cannot expect to redraw the map of Europe at another Versailles. But we can promote our own future security—for 100 years, 200 years—and how much permanent progress of civilization may not have been made in that time?

We can, moreover, achieve these immediate gains:

We can prove that the power of collaborative organization is not all on the totalitarian side.

We can end Hitler's dream of world domination through world revolution. All of the alliances he may make with the other totalitarian states of Europe and Asia—alliances based on nothing but mutual greed—will be ultimately profitless while control of the seas and of world trade remains with us.

Most important of all, we can give to the oppressed people of the captive nations the proof that at last there is dynamism in the democratic faith; there is alive on earth a mighty unified force ready to negotiate a just peace—not on the suicidal terms of appeasement and not on the suicidal terms of the provedly rotten status quo.

And let us not forget that an all-important factor in that status quo was our own policy of escapist isolationism. We have cast that off now; we must also cast out any thought that we can go back to hopeful isolationism whenever the present terror is ended. And let us not imagine that we can postpone our plans for the future until the future has arrived. It is not alarmism, it is not hysteria, to say that tomorrow may be forever too late. The world may soon achieve co-ordination which is founded not on the Bill of Rights but on *Mein Kampf*. There is nothing now that can stop this but the collective force and spirit of the British and American peoples.

I believe that the spirit of the British and American peoples is now as never before right for the bold, constructive step toward union. Our common faith, which has been tested on a thousand battlefields from Waterloo to Gettysburg, is now meeting its supreme test on the white cliffs of Dover and within the gray walls of London. We are in a mood for great, historic accomplishment. We have statesmen on both sides with the necessary intelligence and imagination and courage.

We know that the old world has run down, like a clock that has been shaken by too many alarms. We can and must build a new world, to ring out a future which will be fit for decent people to live in, together, at peace.

THIS CHALLENGE TO WORLD DEMOCRACY [7]

The times in which we live are a test of the good will and intelligence of the American people. What report does intelligence convey to us about our position in the world today? We see that the world, apart from ourselves, is divided into three camps. In one camp stand the totalitarian powers, joined together in a working union in their effort to barbarize the world and to reduce it to a condition in which power would have no other law than its own say-so. Their so-called new world is dedicated to the principles that all men are created unfree and unequal, and that government must, under no circumstances, rest on the consent of the governed, or promote the welfare of any group except the insolent masters of the state, ruling the masses of mankind by terrorism and corruption.

In the second camp stand the nations that have already been enslaved by the totalitarian powers; and that have either accepted their barbarous aims, like the supine and treacherous Vichy government, or who bravely endure the totalitarian yoke, while they plan at the earliest possible moment to throw it off.

These nations have been enslaved, partly by external misfortune, but even more by their own unwillingness to face the kind of world in which they live, and to make the necessary

[7] From article by Lewis Mumford, Author of *Design for Living*. *Federal Union World*. 3:1, 8. January, 1941.

sacrifices of political sovereignty to make that world secure for a peaceful and democratic scheme of living. Together, the now-enslaved states of Europe were superior in man-power, in industrial wealth, in natural resources, to Nazi Germany; and even without England's help they might have prevented both Germany and Italy from menacing their freedom. But these passive countries failed to arm themselves sufficiently, and they failed to stand together in a close union: hence they fell like a row of ninepins when the Nazi ball zoomed down their alley.

In the last camp stand the people of the British Commonwealth of Nations, the English, Scotch, Welsh, Irish, New Zealanders, Canadians, Australians. In Europe and Asia the British government made the same mistakes as the other democracies: they sought first to maintain their isolation and independence, at the price of justice for China, Abyssinia, Spain, Austria, and Czechoslovakia, the countries that were being wantonly overrun by the totalitarian powers. As a result, the British eventually found themselves alone, fighting with their back to the wall.

England's errors and sins were grave ones; but since the awakening that came at the rescue of Dunkirk the people of England have atoned for the stupidity and cowardice and muddle-headedness of their Hoares and Chamberlains by one of the most superb exhibitions of national unity and collective courage that history has ever witnessed. Today the valor of the British is all that stands in the Western world between civilization and totalitarian darkness, between the path of continued development and that Nazi-Fascist scheme which, in the name of peace, would widen the empire of slavery, misery, and death.

Now where do the American people stand? By everything sacred in our history, in our way of living, we stand at the opposite pole from the totalitarian states. We cannot be neutral about the totalitarian challenge to world democracy; it is a challenge to us and to our democratic institutions; it is aimed against everything that we hold dear. We know that despotism and barbarism belong to the slimy past, and that we belong to the future. If fascism is a wave, as Mrs. Lindbergh would have it, it is a wave of corruption; and our duty is not to ride on it, but to resist it and circumvent it and combat it, as we would any other natural evil, like a plague.

The men with mechanical hearts may warn us against being true to our own traditions. Those who have received compliments from Hitler or medals from Goering may urge us not to antagonize the totalitarian states. But the antagonism is not of our creation; it exists by reason of their nature and our nature. We know that we cannot live as a free people in a world dominated by the atrocious sadists who have created the Axis governments. Such a life would be such a long hell of insecurity and anxiety that outright slavery might seem preferable.

What, then, is the alternative? The alternative is a simple one. We must unite our forces at once to the only forces that are resisting Hitler—the forces of the great English-speaking peoples whose domains spread around the globe. Alone, the odds are against us, as they are against the British people. But in a free and equal partnership with the other English-speaking peoples, we would still be the most powerful bloc of nations on the planet: powerful in man power, powerful in command of the seas, powerful in industrial resources and production, and powerful—this is no less important—in the possession of common ideals, the ideals of liberty and fair play.

Not merely would the major resources of the world be at our command, whatever the temporary victories of the Axis powers in the Near East. But we would still have the far from negligible support of the peoples of India and South America, and not least, of China. In short, the United States and Great Britain, combined, stand for the world, whereas Germany and Italy and Japan stand for only a small part of the world; and even if Stalin's Russia joins them more actively, their assets will still be more real on paper than they are in fact, for their starved and discouraged populations are no match for us free peoples.

What I am pleading for here is nothing so temporary and infirm as a military alliance. What I am pleading for is a permanent federal union, first between the two great groups of English-speaking peoples, to serve as the nucleus of a world federation. The immediate advantage of this union would be to secure the downfall of the Nazi-Fascist regimes; the permanent benefit would be the constitutional union of mankind. For a union between the peoples of Great Britain and the United States would serve as the core of a world-wide organization to which all democratic peoples would in time adhere, as partners in a common task, as builders of a common order.

Such a union would be the most effective war measure that could be taken against the Fascist threat; indeed, without it our purely physical rearmament will lack both energy and purpose. For we are not making these vast expenditures of money, we are not demanding the services of millions of young men, merely to defend the status quo. Nothing can be defended, nothing can be saved, unless at the same time we save the whole fabric of civilization, and establish it on firmer and broader foundations than the small-minded and jealous nations of the past were willing to build.

The military effect of such a union would be immense. It would ensure that the British people would go on fighting, in the face of unspeakable terrorism and misery, until we were sufficiently armed to take up our share of the burden. Such a union would give hope to the enslaved democracies of Europe and encourage them in acts of sabotage, violence, and reprisal that would hamper their savage Nazi masters. Such a union would give powerful aid to the valiant Chinese, our ancient friends in the East. Finally, such a union would become the natural starting point of a world order, the first center of peace and cooperation in an order that would eventually include every civilized people on the planet.

Plainly, this union will not be effected easily; for nothing that is worth doing today can be done easily. The working out of such a world-wide federation will take time, patience, political sagacity; and it will demand economic sacrifices no less than political ones. Union Now is not an easy prescription; not a patent medicine with a pleasant taste that will immediately give one the illusion of peace and security and freedom. Like our own American union, the new order will be hammered out by trial and error, by conflicts, contests, judicial decisions; possibly even by war. But there is no alternative. The only question is whether the American people have the intelligence and the good will to take this step before it is too late.

Will we take the risks? Will we make the sacrifices? Will we assume the responsibilities? Will we become again the leaders and pioneers in a new world?

If we fail to rise to this challenge, our failure may help to usher in the Dark Ages. If we meet it promptly and gallantly, we may well lay the foundations for a great epoch of human development.

CAN ANY NATION LONG ENDURE ALONE? [8]

It is time we asked ourselves why . . . this great counter-revolution against freedom and equality is sweeping the world. It has not happened because three or four bad men have captured great states. That's too easy! These men and the movements they incorporate have risen because of democracy's failures to solve outstanding social, economic and political questions. *Twenty-two years ago the United States, England and France, having just won a world war, held in their hands the power to consolidate their victory and maintain peace and freedom on this planet for centuries.* That they were not able to maintain it for

[8] Address by Dorothy Thompson, Newspaper Columnist, at the Federal Union's "United States of the World" dinner. *Federal Union World.* 3:1, 8, 9. March, 1941.

even a quarter of a century is a worse indictment of our blindness than anything that Hitler can say.

Now we are engaged in a great civil war, testing far more than whether a nation so conceived and so dedicated as all the democracies have been, can long endure. It is a test of whether *any* nation can long endure. For what we are seeing in Europe is the *pulverization* of nations. We are seeing nations turned into feudal fiefs, ruled over by satraps from Berlin, ruling not in the name of a nation but of a secular religion.

This apocalyptic course of events has been possible only because nationalism had reached such lengths that it had become its own invitation to death! We are confronted with the extraordinary spectacle of sixty-five million people threatening to subdue 250 million in a few months' time,—people who do not belong to jungle tribes, but who are members of highly organized, civilized, and armed states. And these people have been subjected for only one reason: their concept of nationalism produced the idea of neutrality, and forbade them to make a union for genuine collective action.

They have been picked off, not by arithmetical, but by geometrical progression. Czechoslovakia subdued, was not out of the game, but became an arsenal for a new step—against Poland; and Poland subdued, was not out of the game, but became a labor supply for Germany's fields; and France subdued, was not out of the game, but became another arsenal for Germany and the base for her invasion of England. And England subdued, would not be out of the game, but would become the base for the domination of the Atlantic Ocean and the encirclement of the Americas.

A nation does not have to be invaded in order to lose a war, and it does not have to fight a war in order to lose a war. It needs only to be put in a position where it cannot possibly make a successful war in defense of its vital interests.

If the British Empire falls, that will be the position of America. There will be systematic blackmail against this country.

We shall have a toll bridge at the exits of the Atlantic Ocean, and we shall have to pay tribute on everything that passes it. We shall have emissaries in this country, not only from the German Nazis, but from English Nazis. If we want to sell corn to Europe, the price asked will be the muzzling of our press, and the removal from public life of the people speaking on this platform tonight and the President sitting in the White House tonight. We shall have lost the freedom of our citizens to move on this planet, and of our ships to move,—except on other people's terms. Japan will close in on us,—and if we resist Japan, Germany will close in on us. And as I have said, we shall have lost a war without ever having moved a weapon.

After the last war, the center of financial, economic, and political power for the whole Atlantic world had passed to the United States. For a century previous to 1914, there had been no world war, because the British Empire was strong enough to keep the peace. Yes, there were minor wars; but there was no war involving whole continents. But in 1918 the British Empire was no longer strong enough to maintain this role. Great Britain and the United States could have maintained it, and by collaborative integrated action could have guaranteed peace to this world for 500 years. The very same people who now are in Washington counselling isolation are the people who have torpedoed every essential action. The war answers them; the war that Woodrow Wilson predicted would occur within a generation, unless this country accepted its responsibilities.

For over a hundred years, the British Empire, with all its faults, with all its injustices,—faults and injustices which Englishmen themselves have denounced,—kept open the seas for freedom of trade. After the last war a role was assigned us by history. It was to be co-partner with the other free Atlantic States in carrying on that role. . . . What did we do? We encouraged economic nationalism by our own example. We had become the greatest creditor nation in all the world; and we were at the same time the greatest producers in the world of wheat, corn, cotton, iron and steel, motor cars and typewriters. We had a choice. We could have insisted on the debts being paid and succeeded the British as the greatest free trade nation. Or, we could have liquidated the debts, and maintained a protected economy. Instead, out of blindness, stupidity and greed, we insisted on having incompatible things: we insisted on the debts being paid, we raised our tariffs, we created new debts by lending new money abroad to the tune of billions; and with this new money, we subsidized our own exports, and thus contributed to the bankruptcy of Europe and to our own bankruptcy, because there is an ethical law in the world, as well as an economic law. We left the protection of victory in the hands of an empire no longer strong enough to protect it, and today we are appalled by the results.

The destruction of freedom did not begin with Mr. Hitler. It's been going on progressively ever since the last war. People's memories are short. They do not realize that when the last war began an American could travel anywhere in the civilized world without a passport. There was no such thing as a work-permit from one end of Europe to the other. A German student could transfer his credits to the Sorbonne, to Louvain, or to Oxford. The United States could sell her goods in free markets throughout the entire civilized world. All of these freedoms have been progressively destroyed. Every nation has attempted to be a self-contained unit, and we now have the spectacle of Germany trying to exercise a monopoly over the whole continent and as much of the world as possible.

This cannot be counteracted by our attempting to set up a rival monopoly in the Western Hemisphere. That program will fail because it is economically idiotic. The whole of the Western Hemisphere contains only 270 million consumers, one-ninth the population of the Eastern Hemisphere; and the problem of the Western Hemisphere is a problem of over-production and lack of markets. Our agricultural and industrial plants are larger than our own needs. We cannot buy the produce of South

America and dump it in the Atlantic Ocean. It has to be sold to the people of the Eastern Hemisphere who need it. *We* don't. Power follows economics. And the economics of South America tie it up to Europe and not to us. Argentine beef goes to the British Isles, not to us; and a few tins of corned beef cause a crisis in Congress. Look at the facts and let them speak, and speak sense.

In 1938,—before this war began,—76.7 per cent of the total exports of the United States went to the British Isles and the British Empire. In the same year, 79.5 per cent of the total imports of the United States came *from* the British Isles and the British Empire. We are not economically tied to South America. We are economically tied to the English-speaking world—to the little island of forty-two million people off the coast of Europe, which is fed from our fields, and at this moment must be armed, if it is to survive, from our factories. The sources of those raw materials in which we are deficient lie either within the British Empire, or else inside the radius which the British fleet helps defend—along with our own fleet, and the fleets of the Atlantic powers now fighting with the British, especially the fleet of the Netherlands.

I doubt if there was ever another occasion in history, except one, when the logic of economic and political facts pressed peoples toward the forming of a more perfect union. There *was* one previous example: that was the thirteen States of the American Continent. If you will take down the *Federalist* papers today and read the arguments advanced by Hamilton, Madison and Jay for the American federation,—the American Union,—you will find those arguments as applicable to a federation of the English-speaking world right now as they were to the states then. I ask you to read the third and fourth papers of the *Federalist* on the dangers from foreign wars and foreign influences to an inadequately large union of states. You will find in the third paper the word "appease," used in exactly the sense that we use it today—namely that unless a federation of states is large enough and represents a strong enough power vis-à-vis the rest of the world, those states will have to "appease" stronger powers: that is to say, they will have to relinquish basic interests in order to avoid conflicts which they are not strong enough to win.

We are now in this situation. The whole world is drawing together. Great Britain was strong vis-à-vis a divided world. *We* were strong vis-à-vis a divided world. But neither Great Britain nor we are separately strong enough to defend our interests against a united Eurasia. The only constructive idea that can be advanced as a synthesis of both unity *and* diversity is the idea that first found birth on this American Continent, —the concept of federation. That concept means unity in the things that demand unity and diversity in the things where diversity is an advantage. What the English-speaking world needs now and what it has needed ever since the last war is unity in the following things: 1. Defense,—naval and air defense; 2. A unity of money,—one currency and an integrated banking system; 3. Free trade between all its parts; and free movement of its citizens; 4. A labor office that will see that in relation to the general index wages are equal throughout the parts of the union, so that a Lancashire worker cannot be exploited to undercut a Detroit worker.

Achieve these things (union) in the English-speaking world, and you will have set a model for at least Europe and Western civilization. Establish one federation and you will attract others to it and suggest other federations which can some day again be integrated. On such a basis alone could we make a peace that would restore freedom in this world, and allow Germany to have that position which her powers and talents demand. And since we are the most powerful of the English-speaking peoples, the move must come from us.

A FEDERATED EUROPE? [9]

[The sentiment in England for federation] is hampered in my opinion by its tendency to interpret federation in the sense that Mr. Clarence Streit gave to it in a book that awakened keen interest even before the outbreak of this war. This able treatise lacked the sense for history. The analogy of the thirteen original American states on which Mr. Streit builds his entire argument is wholly misleading. These states had no immemorial past of independence to surrender and no pride in their world-wide power; they had, moreover, a common political and cultural heritage and a common language. The eighteenth century thinking that underlies the American Constitution is not a mold into which the political systems of contemporary Europe could be fitted. If ever Europe federates, it will be with less regard to abstract logic and more to practical convenience. Certainly it will shun any rigid constitution. Local interests, moreover, are far too strong to allow of more than a gradual and partial lowering of tariff barriers.

But it is conceivable that the logic of security will drive all or some of the European states to create a common defense force for air, sea and land. If they do this, they must reduce their own national forces to the level of a militia or police. Common defense implies a common foreign policy under a single ministry or council, which would have to manage all the foreign relations of its members, and undertake the protection of the lives and interests of all their citizens beyond its frontiers. It is axiomatic that dependent colonies must come under the ultimate control of the federation, and that their former rulers must abandon all the privileges of ownership and monopoly. The control of communications and of currencies should fall to the federation. The requirement of a common foreign policy would oblige it to control foreign investment.

[9] From article "The End of Small Nations," by H. N. Brailsford, British Journalist. *American Mercury*. 50:281-4. July, 1940.

In a common system for the control of credit and investment, it would have a leverage that might enable it to attempt economic planning on an international scale. Through a federal university and through a federal wireless station it might work for cultural solidarity.

The difficulties are obvious. One need not dwell on the obstacle of language, on the inertia of mankind, nor on the tyrannous strength of traditional nationalism. The chief difficulty is that while every citizen would gain safety, an enhancement of prosperity and a sense that civilization had returned to this earth, on a short view many entrenched interests would suffer—the ruling class that looks on the empire as its entailed estate and on the army and navy as a field for its sons' careers; the captains of "big business" who wield in a national capital an influence which would be very much feebler at the federal center. Federation, on this showing, could come about only if progressive ministries, based on the masses, were in office in London and Paris at or soon after the end of the war. The French are likely to favor the idea, for they wished to endow the League with a common army, and saw the economic advantages of M. Briand's abortive proposal for a United States of Europe. The smaller states will certainly prefer a federation to a Grand Alliance.

To my thinking, the fundamental difficulty, the superstition of national sovereignty, can be overcome only in one way. The federation must repose authority in a Congress that represents its peoples. The curse of the Genevan Assembly was that its national delegations voted as solid units. The result was that every decision was a trial of strength between the great powers, with the little states skirmishing round them. What really voted was the British Navy and the Bank of England. On this plan one could never escape from power-politics. If, however, the delegates to Congress voted as individuals, decisions would follow the normal dividing lines of opinion and class interest, rather than those of nationality. Only in this way can we hope to reach democratic government by majority vote.

The mention of democracy raises the most thorny question of all. Would the federation admit only states that satisfied the Western conception of democracy? Must it exclude not merely the defiantly Fascist powers, like Italy and Spain, but Russia also, and the hermaphrodites, Poland as she was or Rumania as she is? The dilemma seems insoluble. On the one hand it is certain that some measure of ideological sympathy is essential for cordial cooperation. Representatives of the British and French Left would not sit quietly on the same bench with Spanish Fascists. Again, it is clear that Fascists, who aim solely at the advancement of their national state, could not cooperate sincerely in a European federation. Finally, without freedom of the press in all its member states, there could be no useful discussion of its common affairs. On the other hand, this ideological argument cuts clean across the realistic requirements of defense. The federation ought to control a continuous stretch of territory. It must throw its shield over the weaker European states, however disreputable their internal politics may be, for if it fails to do so, they will again tempt an aggressor. It ought to take over the narrow waterways, notably the Straits of Gibraltar, the Suez Canal and the Dardanelles—a difficult requirement, unless Egypt and Turkey were members.

What, finally, do we mean by "Europe?" For the purpose of defending Western civilization, Europe begins with Britain and France. But both of them have overseas empires. It might not be difficult to include their dependent colonies. But what shall we say of the British Dominions, or of a self-governing India? To include Canada and New Zealand would be to make nonsense of the European idea. To exclude them would be to smash the British Commonwealth. Safety would demand the inclusion of the whole Mediterranean area. Russia raises peculiar difficulties. Every exclusion seems invidious, yet one prime cause of the League's failure was that it took the world for its parish. Western and Central Europe is, on the other hand, a natural unit, with a common culture, a common history and a manageable area. But it cannot federate until the Germans have returned to the morals of Western civilization. I have not discussed Mr. Streit's rival proposal of an Atlantic Federation, for the simple reason that I cannot conceive as possible the entry of the United States.

The logic of history and every argument of self-preservation make for Europe's federation. If we consent to make two optimistic assumptions—that the West wins and that progressives come into office—it is probable that an attempt will be made to create it. It would be a grave mistake to repeat the procedure of Versailles by including the federal plan in the treaty that ends the war. A year or two of peace should be spent in preparing the way. My own conception of how to do it would be to inaugurate with the armistice a vast international scheme of public works. That would mean salvation to the soldiers and workers of both sides, as they faced the terrors of unemployment beside cold forges and silent guns. The aim should be to employ Englishmen, Frenchmen and Germans to make for the backward peoples, white and colored, in the colonies and the client states, the equipment that in time may lift the level of life of the primary producers up to that of the industrial workers. In no better way could that consciousness of solidarity be promoted which is the moral foundation of federation. If for this purpose, after the ruin and hate of war, Europeans could combine for mutual aid, there might arise from their cooperation a call for unity so imperious that it would compel their governments to federate. But it is easier to see such visions than to bring to power the men who might give them reality.

STREIT'S FEDERAL UNION [10]

We are uplifted by Streit's assertion that there are fifteen all-powerful democracies in the world today—possessing "overwhelming world power in every field". . ."almighty on this planet." But after reading Streit's 178,000 words, in which he repeatedly states that these fifteen democracies are to be formed into a Federal Union, we are surprised by the "ten little words" which provide that the Union may be established by three nations only—Great Britain, France and the United States—and that immediately these three nations shall have formed this Union, they—and they alone—are given sole power to admit or bar any or all other nations; and that no other nation may join this Union unless its ideas and mode of government are like those of the three nations.

It seems evident that as soon as a Federal Union were formed of these three democracies, Great Britain would at once vote to admit Australia, Canada, Ireland, New Zealand and South Africa. And certainly the United States would not object to their admission, because their peoples are democratic and self-governing.

In line with Streit's ideal, that the individual should be the unit in democracy, he proposes a House of Deputies, to be composed of representatives chosen directly by peoples of all member nations. Then we are amazed—for Streit's plan next provides that no act of this democratic House of Deputies can become law until it is approved by the Senate of the Union; and his provisions for representation in the Senate give Great Britain, and her colonies and associates, absolute control of the Senate—forever, according to Streit's plan!

This is how it is done: Each nation of the Federal Union is allowed one senator for each 12½ million of its people, up to

[10] From pamphlet "Which Road to Permanent Peace" by Brown Landone, Editor-in-Chief of *History of Civilization*. p. 11-19. Landone Foundation. Orlando, Florida. 1940.

a population of 100 million. By this plan, the United States would be allowed eight [or ten] Senators. But, all the self-governing colonies or dominions of Great Britain are allowed two Senators each, even though not one of them has a population equal to that of Chicago and New York City. By this means, Great Britain—with its Australia, Canada, Ireland, New Zealand and South Africa—has two votes more than the combined votes of France and the United States.

Even if the seven other minor democracies of the fifteen which Streit designates, are immediately admitted to the Union, the result would—because of obligations soon to be considered—be still worse for the United States.

Streit's plan of creating a democratic House of Deputies; then depriving it of power and centering the power in the Senate, reminds us of the Preamble and Covenant of the League of Nations. Its Preamble gives power to member nations and to its Assembly; and then the Covenant annuls all such powers and centers all power in the Council.

There is another similarity: Each member of the Council of the League, by its right of one veto vote, is given absolute power to annul all acts of the Assembly or member nations. So also, by Streit's plan of the Federal Union, one nation—Great Britain, with her associates—is given absolute control of the Senate of the Federal Union.

This also reminds us of what one great nation was able to do, and did do, in the League of Nations, in stopping movements for the peace of the world, by use of her veto power in the Council. When smaller nations led by Czechoslovakia insisted on presenting a plan for disarmament, Chamberlain, on March 12, 1925, by the absolute power of his own veto vote, killed that effort toward peace, and opened the way for the greatest peacetime armament race in history. These facts make us wish carefully to consider the wisdom of any plan which would give such power to any one nation—whether it be Great Britain, France, or the United States.

Next consider four obligations which would greatly affect the United States if it joined the Federal Union.

First, each member nation at once transfers all its non-self governing territories to the Union.

Second, the Union is immediately obligated to protect all of these territories against all invasion! These territories include the gigantic colonial empires of Great Britain and France; and it is conceivable that Russia might sometime invade India; Japan invade Australia; and Italy invade France's colonies in Africa.

Three great factors are needed to protect these immense colonial areas against invasion. They are: gold-credit, resources and man power. Britain and France are lacking in all of these. The United States can, and would be obligated to, provide all three!

Great Britain and France would, according to Streit's plan, have absolute power in the Senate of the Federal Union, and—if the United States were a member—they would have the moral right to demand that we fulfill our pledged obligation. If we declined, then we would realize that we had previously surrendered all our gold, and our navy and war aircraft, when we entered the Union.

If the seven other small democracies should immediately become members, then our obligations would be greatly increased. We would then be pledged to protect two other colonial empires—Holland's East Indian colonies and Belgium's African empire.

With our own modest little outlying islands, it is difficult for us to conceive the immensity of all these colonial empires, which we would be obligated to protect against all invasion. Their areas equal all of Canada, plus all of Mexico, plus all the nations of South America, plus all of Europe; and then three other areas added—each equal to all of the United States east of the Mississippi River! All in all, almost half the land area of the earth—far flung, world-wide—on all continents and in all oceans—something to defend!

Third, the nations of Streit's Union are to accept a common budget, and to turn over all gold to the Union.

Fourth, the Union—with a common budget and our gold—is to assume payment of all debts of Great Britain and France incurred by them in building up all their armies and navies, and air forces, and also to assume payment of all the century-old debt which Great Britain and France have incurred in acquiring their vast colonial empires. Streit states, "It is only fair that the Union should assume such debt."

Such obligations make us think!

We want world peace; but we are beginning to realize that there is a plan, hidden within the wish-ideal of Streit's proposal.

We can not believe that Streit—so sincerely idealistic—consciously realized the significance of this plan. It may be that his many-year contact with European diplomats in Geneva led him unconsciously to accept ideas which were very tactfully suggested by skilful diplomats. Whatever the source, the result is a clever plan, clothed with Streit's high idealism.

Streit's Tables of Data make us wonder. We, too, would like to believe that democracies are all powerful, and that totalitarian powers are mere weaklings—but we cannot accept Streit's data that the total of trained effectives of the army of the United States is 74.1 per cent greater than all the well-trained soldiers of the German army; or that the number of war aircraft of Great Britain and France is greater than the combined war air fleets of Italy and Germany and Japan. Moreover, Streit's admission in his footnotes, that the data he uses in his tables are different from what he knows to be true present data, does not restore our confidence.

We find that Streit's so-called powers of democracies are not powers at all, but lists of the possessions of the democracies—the very wealth which the totalitarian powers desire and are determined to take. As suggested in the title to this section, the mere possession of a barrel of emeralds is not a power which keeps robbers away.

Streit adds that his Federal Union is to be formed in exactly the same way that our own thirteen colonies were formed into our national union.

All the colonies, no matter what their differences, united to form their union; while Streit proposes that only a few nations shall unite to form his Union, and that no others shall be admitted until they give up all ideas of government in which they differ from the original few.

The colonies practiced the democracy in which they believed, that all men are created equal in the right to determine for themselves the kind of government they shall have. Hence, no matter how different the political and religious and economic ideas of the thirteen colonies, each gave up something of its ideas, so that all could unite to form a national union—Catholics of Maryland, Pilgrims of New England, commoners of Pennsylvania, and cavaliers of the South!

But Streit's plan is different! He proposes that a very few nations shall form a Union, and then say to the rest of the world —you may join us if you adopt our ideas, and change yourselves enough so that we can approve of you. . . . Chapter by chapter, he tells truly what the colonies did, and the reader accepts it, because it is true. Then he repeatedly asserts that his method of forming a Federal Union is like the method the colonies followed.

If Streit's plan had been tried by the colonies, then the rigid commoners of Massachusetts and Connecticut and Pennsylvania might have formed a union and said to the other colonies— "Our ideas are the only right ideas, and you can not join our union until you give up your ideas and accept ours; you of Maryland must give up your obedience to the Catholic Church, and you of the South must give up your great landed estates and your ideas of cavalierist superiority over people who work for you. Only after you have done this, will we consider whether or not we think you are fit to become one of us."

If Streit's method had been used by the colonies, there would have been years of inter-colonial wars, and no union.

So also today, if Streit's plan is attempted, and the fifteen democracies—owning half the earth and most of its natural resources—should form themselves into a Union with definite intent not to let the totalitarian powers share in the wealth, until those autocracies become democracies, then the great armed and starved powers of Germany-Italy-Japan-Russia will start the greatest of all wars, to obtain some of the resources and territories of the democracies.

In Streit's proposed Federal Union, we find three basic essentials: first, his own high ideal of individual man as the sovereign unit of true democratic government; second, what seems to be the creation of other minds—a very clever plan which strips the proposed democratic House of Deputies of all its power, and turns that power over to a Senate, which Senate is so constituted that one nation and its dependencies and associates are given absolute power; then third, there is a conflict of purposes.

Important as are the obligations of this amazing plan, we are not now concerned with the provisions that we should surrender our sovereignty as a nation; accept a common budget; obligate ourselves—because of our gold credit, available resources and man power—to provide most of the means of defending the titanic territorial empires of Belgium, France, Holland and Great Britain; surrender our gold; and assume the part of the one creditor able to pay all the unpaid debts which the four great colonial nations have incurred in generations past, in acquiring one-half the world as their colonial empires.

Important as these obligations are to us, it is still more important now to decide whether or not Streit's Federal Union would, if established, tend to maintain peace or lead to the greatest war of all wars.

To make our decision justly, we must first recognize the power of the armed forces of the four great totalitarian nations, and their starved condition. Although Russia has resources, they are not yet easily available, and will not be for twenty years. Hence all four of the great dictatorships are starved nations. Streit recognizes this condition—stating that these powers—with all their masses of people—possess only from 1 per cent to 10 per cent of the essential resources of the world.

Then second, we must recognize that the great democratic nations which Streit proposes to form into a Union, possess one-half the territory of earth, 50 per cent to 90 per cent of the twenty-three most essential resources, and 90 per cent of the world's gold.

Third, we must next recognize that these democracies—as armed powers—are not as strong as are the dictatorships, and never can be, unless they also become dictatorships.

Fourth, we should recognize that the possessions of the democracies are not powers.

Fifth, that the autocracies have openly avowed that they intend to secure—take by war and conquest—some of the territorial wealth and resources of the democracies, even if it is necessary to completely destroy such a power as Great Britain in order to obtain what they want.

Sixth, when we view facts clearly, without letting our wishful thinking run away with us, we realize how weak mere possessions are as means of protection; and that—in the present economic setup of the world—they may be weakening dangers instead of powers of defense.

So, seventh, it seems evident that Streit's Federal Union, if formed, would result in greater wars than man has yet known. You can not loudly tell a strong and powerful and poverty-stricken man that you have millions of ten-dollar bills lying around loose on your front porch, without his trying to get them—particularly if he has already declared that he will, if necessary, use force to get some of them.

THERE IS A PRACTICAL MEANS [11]

We need a Super State consecrated to one purpose, given but one power, to attain but one result. Then man shall be able to enforce a permanent peace on earth which will solve most inter-nation problems.

But any league or union, trying to meddle in and solve all minor problems, will do naught but create more friction.

The League of Nations, for example, has had power for twenty years to consider "any circumstance whatever." That is one reason why it has made a mess of its attempt to use its powers—war in Ethiopia and Japan and China; milk for babies in Poland; the puzzle of which nations should be blamed when the Chinese attack Japanese troops with airplanes supplied by France, and the Japanese—using bombs made in Germany and airplanes from Italy—bomb the Chinese hidden in the building of a United States missionary! Then also, disagreements over profits of inter-nation railway tickets have led to months of discussion. So many powers and so many problems, means much talk and little done.

Similarly, the senate of the Federal Union, as proposed by Streit, would be given a multitude of powers to handle a host of problems—imposing taxes on us to pay the colonial debts of Great Britain and France; preventing South Africa from abrogating contracts between a white and black; determining the value of a Japanese yen in Bombay; using our gold to pay for England's mandate over Palestine; sending our young men to Borneo or Indo-China to prevent invasion by Japan, or to Sudan to prevent invasion by Italy—so many powers, so many problems. It is amazing. Streit seriously proposes that his Federal Union shall have power to take over absolute sovereignty of each nation and to determine the weight of a pound of

[11] From pamphlet "Which Road to Permanent Peace," by Brown Landone, Editor-in-Chief of *History of Civilization*. p. 30-40. Landone Foundation. Orlando, Fla. 1940.

butter in Arizona! Try to do everything, and nothing will be done.

Super State shall have no such power! Each nation will retain its sovereignty. In this plan, the nations will do but one thing new—create a Super State as their Police Force of the World. With but one purpose and one power—and with no discussion to create friction—the one aim can be attained!

Super State will be a unity of nations.

The League of Nations is nothing but a list of non-unified nations. And Streit's Federal Union demands that there shall be no more real nations—that each nation shall surrender its national sovereignty to form his proposed union. In fact, the proposed Federal Union would create dis-unity—for it would be a bloc of democratic nations, opposed to a group of totalitarian nations—a house divided within itself—ripe for continuous dissension.

The Super State will be honest in living up to its ideal of the individual freedom and right of all men and nations to choose their own form of government. In contrast, the Preamble of the League promises democracy, and then its Covenant changes it to absolute autocracy. And although the Federal Union professes to proclaim freedom of all men and their inherent right to govern themselves, still it insists that 428,000,000 peoples of four great nations shall not have the inherent right to be considered equals, unless they give up their right as free men to determine their own respective forms of government, and change their ideas to agree with those of the Federal Union.

The Super State will not be formed of nations of one ideology only, because peoples and their ideologies can not be killed off. Democracy means the freedom of individuals to determine their own mode of government. Leaders may be deposed or assassinated; but peoples and ideologies live on. So the Super State will be formed of all nations—not a union, but a unity of all. Only thus can future wars be avoided.

Super State will exist by itself. In contrast the League of Nations has been enmeshed in the midst of powerful and quarreling nations, and tied to them. Streit's Federal Union would be located everywhere! Streit proposes that its House of Deputies shall hold its sessions—as one-night stands—in New Zealand or Algiers, British Columbia or South Africa.

Super State will own oceanic islands as territories of its own, so that it shall be apart from all nations, and all nations free of it! Super State shall at all times keep its armed forces—armies, navies, aircraft—at its own oceanic island bases, except when necessary to use such forces temporarily to maintain peace.

Super State shall possess no power, encroaching on the rights of nations; it shall have no power whatever, except to preserve the peace of the world—power to prevent any nation taking aggressive action against any other nation, to maintain the freedom of all seas, and to lessen age-long causes of war.

This last shall include no power to take or even allot any raw materials of the world. Super State shall, however, have power to prevent any one nation from withholding sales of raw materials to any one nation, if it is selling such materials. That is, to preserve world peace, the Super State shall have police power, not to control materials, but to prevent international hi-jacking of raw materials and blackmail by world trade!

Super State will have no assembly or congress of any kind—to talk and create differences and dissension.

The Assembly of the League has spent twenty years in talk! It has created more differences and dissension than any other world organization in history. No matter what its sincerity, it has never been able to agree upon any one thing—not even on its action regarding Russia's invasion of Finland.

And Streit's proposed Federal Union—with its common budget and use of resources of the United States to meet age-old debts of Great Britain, its plans for our defense of titanic colonial territories of other nations—all these matters would lead to endless talk, and greater dissension than even the League has created.

Super State's one purpose shall be to preserve peace. On the question of whether we want peace, or whether nations shall be allowed to murder each other, there is nothing to discuss. Hence, as stated, Super State shall have no talking assembly or congress. To enforce peace, discussion is no more needed than a city police force needs a congress to discuss which gang of boys shall be allowed the largest rocks to hurl at one another.

Super State will be independent.

The League of Nations is subservient to its autocratic Council. The Federal Union—as proposed by Streit—would be under absolute control of one nation and its associates, because of that nation's control of the Senate of the Union.

The Super State can never be controlled by any great populous nation or group of such nations, because there is no representation according to population. (Proportioned representation is essential only when there are problems to be settled by discussion.) Needing no discussion to maintain peace, the Super State shall be composed of an equal number of representatives from every nation. This is just, for peace is as important to a Finland or a Latvia as to Great Britain or France.

The Super State will not be financially dependent on any nation or group of nations. The League, for its expenses, is dependent on the whims of its prosperous member nations. The Federal Union would take over all gold and all money of its nations, and this gold and money would be controlled by the one nation controlling its Senate. In contrast, the Super State financially will be made permanently independent by means which are also financially beneficial to all nations. (See Section Sixth of Draft.)

The Super State can never become a super-militaristic power, because its Supreme Peace Council shall not itself have control of producing the means and processes used by its armed forces. That is, although the Supreme Peace Council shall have right to use the army and navy and aircraft of the Super State to maintain peace—it shall have no power to increase armament production or perfect any new discovery of destructive gases or rays. These functions shall be under the control of a Peace Armament Board, which shall be composed of experienced executives of prominent religious movements of the world.

It has been objected that such men are idealists. This is true; and idealism is needed for control of the means of war. Executive idealists are practical—everything worth while ever done on earth, has been done by idealists. No group of men, except religious leaders who have also been experienced executives for twenty years, will possess both the idealism and capacity needed in the work of this board.

Since all nations shall surrender their armies and armament, the armed force of the Super State will gradually be reduced to a minimum. With all nations disarmed, only an insignificant force will be needed!

Simplicity, directness, limitless results.

Once all nations are disarmed, neither national industry nor world trade will be limited as in the past by armed control of ports or seas or fear of forever preparing for war. With peace enforced, nations will produce wealth which will not be used up in costs of armaments and war. Then, man can forge ahead, fulfilling his demands for the ultra-comforts and luxuries he desires, because—with the wealth previously spent for armaments and wars—man will be able to pay for the things he wants. This is a gigantic factor. If the Super State had been in operation as of August 1939, the $216,000,000,000 of destruction and spending of a subsequent twelve months of war could have been spent for man's needs—18 billion dollars a month!

Simplicity, directness, limitless results!

With a Super State there could be no problem of Russia and Finland—for, with all nations disarmed, including Russia—Russia, with no navy, would not even desire naval bases to protect its Leningrad seaport or control the Baltic Sea; Finland could not have been invaded by armed forces; and there would be no problem of the Dardenelles; no problem of Italy and Great Britain over the Suez, et cetera. And when resources of the world can no longer be held in bondage by armed forces of great powers, all the major causes of friction over resources and living space will disappear.

With a Super State consecrated to one purpose, having but one power, to be used to attain but one result—and with no World Congress to talk and create disagreement—permanent peace can be attained, and the prophesied good will to men on earth can become a reality.

The Draft which follows [had] its genesis in work done in Europe from 1911 to 1914 by officials and private citizens working to create a United States of Europe. The work was interrupted by the war, and later put aside by advent of the League of Nations.

During the Peace Conference of 1918-1919, the hope that a world organization would be effected and given power to enforce permanent peace, took on the fervor of spiritual expectancy. Then the Constitution of the League of Nations was made public.

Today, again, it is evident that nothing but power to enforce peace can establish permanent world peace. Its author is cognizant of its crudeness of form and inept phraseology; but holds (1) that a Super State must not be a talking international congress; (2) that it must be limited to the one function of enforcing peace; (3) that it must be financially independent of all nations; (4) that provision against dominance of the Super State is essential; and (5) that it must own all major instruments of war, to the end that no nation or group of nations shall ever again be able to make war.

Then we shall have peace!

A Super State Which Shall Have Power to Enforce Permanent World Peace

Tentative Draft

Cognizant of the failure of attempts to maintain world peace by talking federations or leagues or unions of nations, we consecrate ourselves to the ideal of a Super State which shall have power to enforce permanent world peace. The essentials of the Super State shall be:

First, all nations shall surrender to the Super State all their war equipment and armaments of all kinds,—to the end that no nation or group of nations shall ever again possess the means of making war.

Second, with formation of the Super State, every nation shall lose its right to choose whether it shall or shall not surrender its armed forces.

(As a policeman has the right to compel any unlawfully armed maurauder to surrender his gun and as the maurauder has no right of choice in the matter, so also the Super State shall have power to compel any unwilling nation to surrender its means of making war, and the nation shall have no choice in the matter.)

Third, the Super State shall have power to prevent any nation or people from taking any aggressive war action against any other nation or people, and power to enforce peace if any nation or leader or group of nations or leaders shall have started aggressive war action.

Fourth, the territories of the Super State shall be Oceanic Islands, separate and apart from the mainlands of all nations.

Fifth, the Super State shall not be initiated until great powers shall be willing to join in its formation; and it shall not be organized by any group of nations of but one ideology of government.

Sixth, the financial stability of the Super State shall never be impaired by any nation decreasing its financial support for any reason whatsoever; therefore, each nation shall surrender to the Super State permanent ownership of one-tenth of the bonds of its national debt, with provision that (1) the principal of said bonds shall never be paid, and that (2) the interest of said bonds shall be paid semi-annually to the Super State for so long as the nation shall exist.

Seventh, to preserve the impartiality of the Super State, no nation shall have any representation in the Super State, either because of or in proportion to, its area or population or wealth,—to the end that no one nation or group of nations shall ever unduly influence or obtain control of the Super State.

Eighth, to prevent any possible future development of Machiavellian power in the Super State, the executive power of said Super State shall be vested in a Supreme Peace Power Council which shall be composed of not less nor more than two life members from each nation; and the Super State shall have no right or power to station any part of its army at any time on the territory of any nation, except when preventing attempted aggression against that nation; and all ships of the navy and aircraft of the airforce of the Super State, shall be kept at its oceanic island bases, except when being used to enforce world peace; and the Supreme Peace Power Council shall have no control of Peace Armament Board.

Ninth, to preserve the powers of individual nations, the Super State shall possess no power other than its right to preserve the peace of the world, maintain freedom of the seas, and lessen the age-long causes of war; it shall possess no power to regulate or control the activities of the citizens of any nation; it shall possess no power to interfere with the policy or ideology or form of government of any nation; and it shall possess no power to interpret the laws of any nation.

Tenth, the Super State shall maintain its army and navy and aircorps bases only on or at its Oceanic Island Bases and Territories; said armed power of the Super State to consist of (1) a Super State Army composed of 5 per cent of the regulars of the present armies of the nations of the world; and (2) a Super State Navy of all naval ships of all kinds surrendered to the Super State, and sufficient naval personnel; (3) a Super State Air Force of all war aircraft surrendered to the Super State, and sufficient personnel; and (4) a Super State Armament and Equipment Works of which a Peace Armament Board shall have absolute control.

Eleventh, the Super State's Armament and Equipment Works shall be established on one or more Oceanic Island Bases separate from all other activities under control of the Executive Supreme Peace Power Council; and said Armament and Equipment Works shall be under absolute and secret control of the Peace Armament Board, which Board shall own and control all secret formulae, processes, inventories and scientific discoveries—of rays or substances—of a destructive nature.

Said Board shall be composed of leaders of religions of peace; each member of said Board shall be elected for life by a religious organization in which he shall have served as an executive twenty years in consecrated work for the welfare of man; there shall be one member of said Board for each nation; said Board shall have autocratic power in employment of scientists to work in its research and production laboratories; and the Supreme Peace Power Council shall have no power whatsoever, to regulate or limit, or in any way control the activities and work of the Peace Armament Board.

Twelfth, the Super State shall possess special powers of governing by decree, its Oceanic Island Bases and Territories and all its armed forces and all inhabitants living within the boundaries of its bases and territories; and the Super State shall have power to issue decrees of international law, limited (1) to maintaining equal freedom of all seas for all nations and their nationals, and (2) to preventing the economic starvation of any individual nation.

Thirteenth, the Super State shall establish a world citizenship based on the ideal of the brotherhood of man—to the end that each such world citizen shall have the right to citizenship in each nation in the world, in the same way that each citizen of the United States now has right to citizenship in any State of the United States.

UNION NOW? NO [12]

Proponents of the scheme at first vigorously and somewhat indignantly denied that the chief result of such an alliance would be to bind us to take part in the quarrels, intrigues, and conflicts of European nations. Then came the war. Soon after the capitulation of France, the true nature of Union Now was frankly admitted. It was made quite clear in Mr. Streit's proposals for union with Britain. In a full-page advertisement, which ran in several large American daily newspapers recently, he made it abundantly plain that union with Britain would permit the United States to defend Britain with American arms.

"The Union will at once control the sea," said Mr. Streit. "The Union defends us from a separate peace. . . . Defense now needs Union Now. . . ."

Then this plea: "We now have an age-making opportunity to carry our constitutional principles across the seas, as our fathers carried them across this continent."

Have Americans reached the day when the only way they can carry their constitutional principles to a Europe torn and ravaged by war is with fire and sword? By battleships, tanks, planes, and flame throwers, spread democracy! By union with a belligerent, plan a peaceful world!

"The Union defends us from a separate peace—." There you have the heart of the matter. America must not permit

[12] From article by Bennett Champ Clark, United States Senator from Missouri. *Rotarian.* 57:14-15, 57. October, 1940. This article represents the negative of a debate, the affirmative of which, represented by Clarence K. Streit, was published in the same issue. Copyright by Rotary International; not to be produced in whole or part without permission of *The Rotarian.*

this war to end without getting into it, must not allow a peace to be written without helping dictate, as a belligerent, its terms!

On the very face of it, union with Britain means union with Britain's present war. But, say the advocates, this war is America's war. Who gave them authority to say that? Have the American people declared themselves into this war? Their whole attitude and desire, their overwhelming sentiment, has been to maintain their neutrality, to seek to bring this war to an honorable end, and to help write a peace, as a great neutral nation and democracy, which will prevent such great tragedies in the future.

Union would mean not only joining the present war, but also all Britain's future wars. It would mean joining the unholy intrigues, the play of imperialistic power, the frictions and conflicts, that have plagued Europe for hundreds of years.

Union with Britain is to be followed, we learn, as rapidly as possible, by union with the other "democracies." The combination would control one-half the earth, rule all the oceans, govern half the people, own nearly all the materials essential to war, and completely dominate the trade of the world. Unlimited military and economic pressure, it is said, could be put upon the outcast nations, to make them be good. And how would peace be preserved? By force of arms! "Thus we could keep the peace by sheer overwhelming preponderance of strength," says Mr. Streit.

But such a concept is repugnant to every lover of democracy and peace. We do not believe peace can be kept by "sheer preponderance of strength." We are witnessing the tragic failure of the age-old method of keeping the peace by oppression, force, and fear. If the "democracies" are so anxious for the spread of democracy, why did their statesmen not lend greater aid to rehabilitating the German people, a condition requisite to popular sovereignty, after 1918? Why was not the Wiemar Republic encouraged to live? Why were the traditional practices of "to the victors belong the spoils" followed in the postwar settlement?

Peace will never come to the world by any ganging up of the more favored nations, who control territory, resources, and trade, against the less favored nations, democratic or totalitarian. Greatly as we who love liberty dislike totalitarianism, we know that our way of life and government cannot be forced upon other people by clubs or guns.

But, we are told, Union would guarantee, to the nations joining the scheme, three rights:

First, individual rights, such as freedom of religion, speech, and press.

Second, the right to practice democracy.

Third, the right to travel, trade, study, work, play, and live freely "in all that half of the world that would be Union territory."

But we of the United States have all these rights already! How could union with other nations secure us any new rights? Americans pulled away from Britain, back in 1776, in order to secure these very rights.

What, then, would America gain by Union Now? Nothing! The loss, on the other hand, would be the security now enjoyed in these rights. Union with Britain would make the United States no longer master of these rights. Americans would relinquish the guardianship of their most priceless treasure, the heritage of human liberty. They would be sharing this guardianship with the peoples of empires, monarchies, and other government forms.

But, it is argued, the United States could have a "good influence" upon other nations joining the Union, in winning them to accept the democratic way of life and government. Very well. But why should the United States relinquish its sovereignty to do this? Do not the ideals and practices of freedom impress these other nations sufficiently as worth adopting, without merging governments? If the United States is to set up as a model democracy, can it not continue to furnish an example of how a democracy ought to function, of how beneficial are the practices of freedom, without allowing its hands to be tied by nations not yet in accord with the concepts of democracy?

The Federal Union of the United States rests upon a common ideal—human liberty under law; upon a common purpose, to make government function for the welfare of all, upon a common tradition of peace and goodwill toward all other peoples of the world. Could one stroke brush aside the traditions of imperialism, of "balance of power" politics, of authority based upon force?

It is unthinkable. The United States has a great rôle to play—but it is not to go backward—backward into the practices of nations that have written history in the blood of wars fought to maintain the *status quo.* It is to hold aloof from military alliances, from balances of power based upon force, from the intrigues of military leaders who lead their people periodically into slaughter.

Rather, America's rôle is to maintain its traditional attitude of cooperation and goodwill toward all other peoples of the earth. To do this, the United States must be kept at peace during these mad days of bloodshed and destruction, ready to bind up the wounds of war—an example of a democracy, strong and well defended, but untrammelled and free, functioning for the welfare of its citizens and the world.

WORLD UNION [13]

In considering the plan of World Union proposed by the Streit movement, under the slogan "Union Now," the first question is that of the method of representation of the component nations. Mr. Streit bases his plan on representation by population and allots some 24 representatives to the British Commonwealth of Nations, some 27 to America, and does not at all

[13] *Conscience* (India). 2: Special Supplement. October 31, 1940.

consider admitting China or India, as India, for example, would be entitled to some 70 representatives and China 80.

Any system of World Union which fails to take into account India and China is ignoring the very heart of two great racial civilizations and shows an intolerable bias.

Since the world is a measurable and spatial unit, and since nations are related and interrelated by those very spatial boundaries, it would seem that a representation by geographical areas would be more fair. . . . World Union must envisage the idea of regional leagues within greater regional leagues until the final League of the World is reached in a Central World Government.

However, it would surely not be fair to ignore the factor of population, so this representation by geographical areas would be weighted by the consideration as to whether the area-unit was sparsely, moderately, heavily or over-populated. Imagine, for example, that a sparsely populated territory the size of a small European or American state would be entitled to one representative. A moderately populated territory the same size would be entitled to two representatives, a heavily populated area the same size to three representatives, and an over-populated area the same size to four representatives. Under such a system, a small over-populated European state like Belgium might be entitled to four representatives, while a country like Iceland would rate perhaps only one representative. Such weighting would keep down the proportionate representation of large sparsely populated countries like Asian Russia, but the geographical area system would make possible the admitting of countries like China and India without giving them a preponderance of influence due to their tremendous populations.

It is the "one man one vote" idea slightly modified according to the size of the man, the "man" in this instance being a geographical area-unit.

There might or might not need to be actual divisions within this World-State into set geographical areas wherein Councils would consider all problems arising within their respective territorial jurisdiction. But at least any problem that arises should first be considered and decided within the geographical area in which it arises. If the problem arises within the boundaries of a nation it will thus be decided within that nation, for such a form of representation will give absolute sovereignty to every nation within its own borders, *provided* that what a nation did within its borders concerned itself alone. But when there comes oppression, automatically there is an exodus from the nation where tyranny dwells—refugees go forth, and with the flight of the first refugee, or even with an appeal from within the nation to external aid, the problem ceases to be an internal national problem and becomes one that needs a wider jurisdiction for consideration. This is self-evident in all dealings between the family and the state, and needs only to be applied between the various nation-families and a World State.

If a problem concerns one or more nations, the nations concerned can decide what and how large a geographical area they mutually feel can best consider their problem. If no decision can be reached which satisfies both litigants, appeal can be made to wider and wider geographical areas, until one can quite well imagine an intractable problem finally coming before the World Council itself for consideration. But this is exactly what happens in the body—itself a model state. Problems are first treated in the local areas in which they arise. They may finally involve greater and greater geographical areas, in the end needing the attention of the Man himself. However, there would be an advantage in composing differences within the smallest area possible, for in the area immediately surrounding each litigant its vote would be proportionately high, while in the World Council the individual nation would find itself with only a small vote as regards the ultimate decision of its own vital problems.

The type of union above envisaged would no more interfere with the internal sovereignty of the uniting parties than the present unions of the British Commonwealth of Nations or the United States of America interfere with the sovereignties of their component elements. Such a union would make possible the admittance of any worthy nation regardless of its geographical area of population. Such a union is fair.

Granted to any given geographical area the right to vote for a certain number of members of the World Council, shall we stick in the mud of the old-fashioned communal type of representation—that is, that the representatives for any given area must be chosen from within the area, regardless of whether or not there are great men within the area? Or shall we permit each area to choose from the whole world those members of the World Council which it feels will best serve the world?

This privilege granted, there would be no question that the interests of a locality would be subserved, for where narrowness still inhered in a community it would vote for its own people whether or not they were great people. But at least they would have the privilege of voting for greatness even if they did not utilize it. The narrow American would always vote for an American candidate and the narrow Briton for the British candidate. But there would be a growing liberal element in both countries which would vote independent of and uninfluenced by the origin of the candidate.

To ensure one native spokesman, a rule might be made that at least one representative should be a citizen of the area itself.

Since each nation is to be supreme within its own boundaries on the matter of its internal administration, it is perhaps too much to hope that graded franchise will be the rule within the nation, that is, that a man will have the right of vote in an area no wider than he can comprehend and understand. According to the ancient Indian system, the simple villager can vote in village affairs only; the man whose interests are wider than the village can take part in the next larger unit of administration, and so on up to the largest unit of all—the nation itself. But a point must be noted here: the intelligence of a man to administer civic affairs cannot be determined by the crude measure of literacy. A blind man who cannot obtain braille books is "illiterate," but he may be the wisest man in a city. The foreigner in India who cannot read the mother language scripts is "illiterate." Many "self-made" men have hidden from all but their most intimates the fact that they cannot read or write, and while it is undoubtedly a handicap it has not prevented them from successfully administering huge undertakings of various kinds.

But whether or not the graded system of electorate is adopted within the nation, the larger geographical areas must surely see to it that only those men be in their Council Chambers who have a vision of the area as a whole, with, as is natural, an emphasis on a special locality. With the privilege of voting for greatness regardless of race, nation, creed, sex or caste, there would be a possibility of this being achieved.

To ensure that every brother, whether of a minority or a majority, has his due, the majority must never be permitted to dominate. Within any given area no 51 per cent majority should be able to elect 100 per cent of their allotted representatives, but rather every vote should have its say. For many years in the City of New York graft ruled, for, with the majority system of election, a minority literally by hook and by crook could swing itself into a small majority and thereby elect 100 per cent of its candidates, thereafter controlling that great American city.

A few years ago proportional representation was introduced by a determined drive on the part of New York's great hard-working and honest majority and the graft machine crashed. This type of voting provides that the voter name not only the candidate which he most favors, but several others in their order of preference. If his favorite candidate has already been elected by a sufficient majority, or has so few votes there is no possibility of his being elected, his vote is shifted to the next name, and so on, until his vote at last fulfils its purpose—helps to elect a candidate of which the voter approves. Thus a majority of 51 per cent will elect only 51 per cent of the candidates. The minority of 49 per cent will have its vote fulfilled in 49 per cent of the candidates finally chosen, and there will be a strong opposition where there is a strong minority. Only through such a type of voting will the Council Chamber mirror the actual conditions inherent in the area it is supposed to represent.

With the triple ensurance of the privilege of voting for greatness wheresoever it was revealed; with a graded system of candidature, even if this could not yet be achieved as to the voter himself; with a system whereby each minority receives its just and fair proportion of spokesmen without having to resort to the unfair and hatred-breeding systems of communal representation; there can be envisioned the foundations of a mighty Council Chamber wherein Greatness would dominate all less than itself, and in the fire of Understanding all sense of separateness would fuse into a mighty World Unity.

EXCERPTS

When the war is over I hope we can all remain joined in a great confederacy of democratic states so that this curse will never occur again.—*Wendell L. Willkie, Presidential Candidate,* 1940, *in address in Montreal. New York Times. Mr.* 26, '41. *p.* 18.

In the world of business the need for unions of this kind has long been recognized. What, after all, is an international industrial agreement but an undertaking by men of imagination to step over their national boundaries and form a union?—*British Industries. Ag.* '39. *p.* 209.

As I wrote to him [Streit] after reading his book: "Universality, or quasi-universality, may be attained when the union has made good, and the politically backward nations have qualified for admission to it. For the present, universality is a hindrance, not a help; a counsel of perfection, not practical wisdom."—*Wickham Steed, British Journalist. English-Speaking World. Je. '39. p.* 261.

[Federal Union] is not advanced as a hard and fast plan, complete, final, and perfect, but rather as a possible way to achieve the goal all free people desire, a peaceful, prosperous world.

We Federal Unionists believe this is the best plan yet set forth. We seek to put it before our people. Let it be discussed, studied, criticized, modified, improved. Let it be abandoned for something better if something better can be found.

The important thing is that we in America find the best way to a real peace and follow it.—*"Let's Not Make the Same Mistake Twice." Federal Union, Inc. N.Y. '*41. *p.* 2.

It is worth recalling that democracy reached its widest extent in human history in the years after the first World War. The failure of democracy to retain the position it had achieved was due less to the peace than to the failure of the democracies to realize the implications of their increased interdependence. Democracy under present conditions implies effective world organization, and while it is not certain that the United States and the other democracies will understand this after the present war, any more than they did after the first World War, there is always the hope that lessons may be learned through experience.—*Quincy Wright, Author. Asia. Jl.* '40. *p.* 392.

However desirable a closer union in the Western Hemisphere may be, the fact is and remains that our fate is closely bound up with Western Europe—historically, racially, politically and economically. Whether this is "geographically logical" or not, is historically irrelevant. It is *politically* logical, and the existence of the British Empire proves that common interests have a logic that can overcome geography. Incidentally, London, Paris and Berlin are considerably nearer to New York than the capitals of Brazil and Argentina. Our formula of federation cannot leave out the European democracies without endangering the values by which we live.—*Harry D. Gideonse, President, Brooklyn College. Asia. Je.* '40. *p.* 294.

[Federal Union] is an organization which was established some months before the war to advocate federation and to study its problems. Not only has it established research committees to deal with particular aspects of federation, with colonies, with economics, with the federal constitution and federal law, committees which are manned by experts, but it has seriously tackled the job of converting public opinion to federal ideas. In recent months it has explored and advertised the potentialities of federation as a war-winning weapon and given detailed consideration to the problems involved in the transition from national to federal sovereignty in the conditions that are likely to arise at the end of the war.—*C. E. M. Joad, Professor of Philosophy and Psychology, University of London. New Statesman and Nation. Ag.* 31, '40. *p.* 208.

Within less than two years of the publication of the book [*Union Now*], we find press correspondents reporting from Tokio that Japanese authorities are much worried over the possible imminent "federation" of the United States and the British Empire. This is followed within ten days by a parliamentary query in London concerning negotiations between British and American authorities looking toward immediate union. These questionings would never have arisen if there had not been clear evidence that such union was being most seriously considered by responsible persons in official positions. Thus, something well known to many (but "in confidence," so that no convincing proof of it could be offered) begins to reach the public.

The Washington Merry-Go-Round revealed the fact quite specifically in mid-summer, but its significance apparently was not sufficiently credited then.—*Federal Union World. O.* '40. *p.* 2.

John G. Winant, American Ambassador to the Court of Saint James and formerly director of the International Labor Office at Geneva, was asked by reporters on February 7th whether he favored union between the United States and Great Britain, according to a special wire to *The New York Times.* The question itself was very significant. So was the new Ambassador's reply, despite its diplomatic caution:

> I think some day collaboration will have to reach much farther than the United States and Great Britain. . . . I would rather not discuss now what form I think this collaboration should take; it is a complicated subject.

Mr. Winant had been quoted previously as approving of union, at least by implication.—*Federal Union World. Mr.* '41. *p.* 9.

What Federal Union does not mean:

Not a league, like the one at Geneva or the one our thirteen original American states once formed before they adopted the Constitution.

Not an alliance, forever in danger of falling apart when most needed, like the British-French alliance.

Not a super-state—no more than is our American Union.

Not any form of a super-state government of governments.

There are only two ways of organizing interstate relations. One way is to make the state the basic unit: that is the league-alliance—bloc method. The result is government of, by, and for governments. It has never worked.

The other way is to make man the basic unit: that is the *federal union* method. The result is government of, by, and for the people. It has never failed to work. It has worked here for us for over 150 years. It has worked in Australia,

Canada (two languages), South Africa (two languages), and Switzerland (four languages).—*"Let's Not Make the Same Mistake Twice," Federal Union, Inc. N.Y. p.* 11.

What shall we have gained if we can realize anything resembling this project of federation? Firstly and chiefly we shall abolish internecine war in Europe, the homeland of our civilization. That is a negative statement. In the positive sense we shall achieve vastly more: we shall rescue the priceless values of this civilization itself. It cannot survive the totalitarian corruption that assails all it prizes—truth and mercy, honest dealing and intellectual integrity. If the peoples of Europe can be led to erect this structure, it will be because they demand a political framework within which they may lead a social life governed by reason and humanity. If we abandon the old concept of the sovereign state, it will not be because we have changed our views about a legal theory. It will be because we have reached an ideal of human fraternity that embraces our neighbors, who in other languages think the same civilized thoughts. We can end war only by widening patriotism. If that is what we intend, the rest follows inevitably. Our Federation will organize the democratic discussion and decision of our common affairs. It will respect the rich variety of a continent, that has preserved many stocks, many cultures, many tongues, through all the vicissitudes of its history. It will end the anarchy of our economic life by orderly planning for the common good. In so far as it still must arm, it will arm for the common safety alone.—*H. N. Brailsford, British Journalist, Writer for the Manchester Guardian. "The Federal Idea." Federal Union. Lond. p.* 15-16.

In less than six months events swung us from a point where we were quarreling over mail censorship at Bermuda to one where this island had become, by friendly agreement, a common outpost of the censors and the censored. While we Americans talked generalities at Havana, we put teeth in President Roosevelt's Kingston pledge by setting up at Ottawa a Defense Board with belligerent Canada, and called it a "*Permanent* Defense Board," without even that adjective's rousing the wrath of the isolationists. This Board began at once what Europeans would consider the "staff talks" of a military alliance—without any public mourning of the neutralism that had been forcing the British to tow across the Canadian line the war planes they bought from us.

Vast quantities of arms have found their way from the arsenals of the United States Army to the British firing line. The latest American war planes have been put at the disposal of the British. Events have even persuaded our government to reverse itself and find it legal to transfer fifty destroyers to belligerent Britain. And the idea of making this transfer has developed in a few weeks from a sale to an agreement whereby our "neutral" country leased from belligerent Britain naval bases for 99 years, from Newfoundland to South America. If we take all that has happened in the past nine months as a measure of how much may happen in 99 years, we shall see that Anglo-American affairs are already mixed far more than those of any other Great Powers. The Axis has not gone in for 99-year agreements or "permanent" boards. Even its alliance with Japan against us is for only ten years.—*Clarence K. Streit, Author of "Union Now." Atlantic Monthly. N. '40. p.* 532.

At this most fateful moment in the history of the modern world, the Government of the United Kingdom and the French Republic make this declaration of indisoluble union and unyielding resolution in their common defense of justice and freedom against subjection to a system which reduces mankind to a life of robots and slaves.

The two governments declare that France and Great Britain shall no longer be two but one Franco-British Union.

The Constitution of the Union will provide for joint organs of defense, foreign, financial and economic policies.

Every citizen of France will enjoy immediately citizenship of Great Britain, every British subject will become a citizen of France.

Both countries will share responsibility for the repair of the devastation of war wherever it occurs in their territories, and the resources of both shall be equally and as one applied to that purpose.

During the war there shall be a single War Cabinet and all the forces of Britain and France, whether on land, sea or in the air, will be placed under its direction. It will govern from wherever it best can. The two Parliaments will be formally associated.

The nations of the British Empire are already forming new armies. France will keep her available forces in the field, on the sea and in the air. The Union appeals to the United States to fortify the economic resources of the Allies and to bring her powerful material aid to the common cause.

The Union will concentrate its whole energy against the power of the enemy no matter where the battle may be.

And thus we shall conquer.—*Text of declaration issued June 16, 1940 by the British Foreign Office on the proposal for the merging of the British and French Empires. New York Times. Je.* 18, '40. *p.* 9.

Miss Dorothy Detzer wonders whether England or Great Britain or the British Commonwealth is a democracy; or whether we are not a sort of Empire, and therefore not ripe or fit for union with the great American democracy.

Only this evening I heard someone speak about the "American Empire of the Pacific." He may be right or wrong, but he said it. Miss Detzer has the same kind of thought when she looks upon Britain as an "imperialism"—whatever that may mean. I am afraid her ideas are somewhat out of date.

Now, I attach a very special meaning to the term, "democracy." To my mind, it means a system, or systems, designed to insure the greatest possible measure of individual freedom among the sovereign communities of responsible citizens. It means fundamental respect for the human personality as the touchstone and safeguard of true civilization.

The late Pope Pius XI was an upholder of democracy. Many may think he was not. I think he was a great and gallant Christian gentleman, who used all the power of his spiritual authority to withstand the sorry passions of blood and hate that serve the anti-democratic dictatorships which deny human rights and carry on their infernal offensive against the freedom of human minds and souls. In this sense, Pius XI was a true democrat.

At the end of the first quarter of the eighteenth century, Voltaire wrote that "England, and the English, are the freest country and the freest people in the world, the country where men are free to say or to publish what they like, where there is no torture or arbitrary imprisonment, where religious sects of all kinds are allowed to flourish, to denounce war as un-Christian, and where a man goes to heaven by what road he pleases." The picture that Voltaire drew then may have been overdrawn, but was not substantially untrue. Today we have all the essentials of freedom he enumerated then, and they exist throughout the British Commonwealth in whose charter it is written that free institutions are its lifeblood.—*Wickham Steed, British Journalist, former Editor of London Times. Town Meeting (Bulletin of America's Town Meeting of the Air) Vol. 4. no. 18. Published by Columbia University Press,* 2960 *Broadway. N.Y. Speakers: Clarence K. Streit, Dorothy Detzer, Wickham Steed, and George E. Sokolsky.*

Sovereignty over the dependent colonies of member-states must pass to the Federation. This does not, of course, affect the Dominions or India, which ought to become a Dominion within the briefest interval after the end of the war. One or two of the Crown colonies which should soon be ripe for full self-government might also be excepted. In what follows I am thinking mainly of tropical Africa.

The former empires must begin by renouncing all the economic privileges that flowed from their political connection with these colonies. As in the mandated territories under the League, any form of tariff preference would be forbidden. There must be no discrimination in the investment of capital: nor should the natives be used as a source of man-power. The Federation should declare its intention of educating these populations as rapidly as possible for self-government.

In the meantime, should the Federation attempt to administer these colonies directly? Certainly it must exercise the ultimate control over them. But it might be wise to leave the present administrations in charge in most cases under a mandate and subject to inspection. A democratic Germany might receive one or more mandates.

But the former Imperial Powers should not reserve to their subjects a monopoly of posts as administrators, officers, scientists and technicians. An international service open to qualified citizens of all the member-states, both colored and white, should be trained in an international college. Men who have been educated together will be able to work together. Its graduates would eventually serve all over tropical Africa, so long as white administrators are required.

The future material development of Africa, the building and running of railways, motor roads, harbors, power stations and other public works might be entrusted to a disinterested corporation, which should raise its capital internationally. It should pay only fixed interest charges, and return all profits to the natives, for cultural development. Disinterested trading corporations might in the same way handle the agricultural produce of the natives and sell to them imported goods. Possibly mines and plantations could be managed in the same way. The object would be to end profiteering at the expense of the natives, and create a fund for educational and health services.—*H. N. Brailsford, British Journalist and Writer. "The Federal Idea." Federal Union. Lond. p.* 11-12.

Perhaps the major contribution the United States has to offer in the field of world organization is our form of government—the federal union plan. Our heritage in this field, plus the later development of the British Commonwealth of Nations, would seem to prove the feasibility of federal union of nations with similar background and culture, with the minimum curtailment of national sovereignty.

The United States can, if public opinion will permit, return to that position of leadership in international cooperation that we as a nation held from 1899 to 1919. During that period, the United States led in every form of world cooperation, including the first and second Hague conferences, the adoption of the Open Door Policy and its corollary, the proposals for a world court, a league of nations, and an international police force. In order to return to this type of leadership, which we voluntarily relinquished during the period following the World War, it will be necessary for the American people again to abandon narrow isolationism.

The leadership of America is needed now as never before, particularly as the other major democracies are fighting a life-and-death struggle. We have a responsibility to make the maximum contribution toward world organization, because we are the most powerful nation in the world from the standpoint of economic resources, political prestige, and moral influence. Because of our geographic position and because we are the most important neutral power, we can make a contribution toward world organization such as no other nation is in a position to make. No other nation in the world has less to lose and more to gain by helping to build world organization than the United States. Our future destiny as a free people depends on the kind of a world we now build for our children. We can leave them a heritage in a world of peace and security, ruled by law and order; or by inaction and isolation we can leave them a world of chaos and disorder with wars, anarchy, and social disintegration. It is to our interest and the interest of our posterity that the world be organized for peace and that we make an appropriate contribution to that end.

Francis B. Sayre, former Assistant Secretary of State, recently said:

> The United States cannot afford to be a cipher at this critical moment of world history. . . . To the cause of right above might and of law over anarchy, our interests and our civilization commit us. In no other way can lasting peace be made secure. To this great end our country's foreign policy is dedicated.

At the beginning of the present European War, on September 3, 1939, President Roosevelt, in a radio address to the American people, said:

> It seems to me clear, even at the outbreak of this great war, that the influence of America should be consistent in seeking for humanity a final peace, which will eliminate, as far as it is possible to do so, the continued use of force between nations.

—E. Guy Talbot. Regional Director, National Council for the Prevention of War. World Affairs Interpreter. Autumn, 1940. *p.* 294-5.

The British are stronger than ever in the magnificent morale that has enabled them to endure all the dark days and the shattered nights of the past ten months. They have the full support and help of Canada, of the other dominions, of the rest of their Empire, and the full aid and support of non-British people throughout the world who still think in terms of the great freedoms.

The British people are braced for invasion whenever such attempt may come—tomorrow—next week—next month.

In this historic crisis, Britain is blessed with a brilliant and great leader in Winston Churchill. But . . . no one knows better than Mr. Churchill himself that it is not alone his stirring words and valiant deeds that give the British their superb morale.

The essence of that morale is in the masses of plain people who are completely clear in their minds about the one essential fact—that they would rather die as free men than live as slaves.

These plain people—civilians as well as soldiers and sailors and airmen—women and girls as well as men and boys—they are fighting in the front line of civilization at this moment, and they are holding that line with a fortitude that will forever be the pride and the inspiration of all free men on every continent, on every isle of the sea.

The British people and their Grecian Allies need ships. From America, they will get ships.

They need planes. From America, they will get planes.

Yes, from America they need food, and from America, they will get food.

They need tanks and guns and ammunition and supplies of all kinds. From America, they will get tanks and guns and ammunition and supplies of all kinds.

China likewise expresses the magnificent will of millions of plain people to resist the dismemberment of their historic nation. China, through the Generalissimo Chiang Kai-shek, asks our help. America has said that China shall have our help.

And so our country is going to be what our people have proclaimed it must be—the arsenal of democracy.

Our country is going to play its full part.

And when dictatorships—no I didn't say if, I said when dictatorships disintegrate—and pray God that will be sooner than any of us now dare to hope—then our country must continue to play its great part in the period of world reconstruction for the good of humanity.—*President Franklin D. Roosevelt. Radio Address. New York Times. Mr.* 16, '41. *p.* 42.

It is possible here to suggest only an outline of the division of economic functions in a federation of states designed to achieve the aims outlined in President Roosevelt's declaration [message to Congress, January 6, 1941]. The first care of the federal government of such a union will be the regulation of interstate commerce. Some writers on this subject have suggested that existing barriers will have to be removed gradually so as to ease the strain on protected producer groups. But Hitler's methods have already made nonsense of tariff systems in Europe and, although they have not freed trade in Europe, they have made clear the costly futility of selling without buying. Moreover, the end of the war will bring a tremendous demand for goods in famine-stricken Europe and it will be far easier to satisfy this efficiently if internal free trade is introduced immediately.

A second important federal function will be the provision of a reserve bank linking the central banks of the various states which, in Europe, are already state-owned or closely controlled. It would be the business of this federal institution to ensure an even distribution of credit to various parts of the union, making available the surplus savings of one area to meet excess demands in another. It will also be necessary to organize a federal investment bank for the purpose of financing long-term projects and in particular to promote the development of the more backward districts.

Another formidable task will be the reorganization of interstate communications. Parts of Europe are woefully deficient in transport facilities, and existing systems have all too often been inspired by strategic rather than economic considerations. Repairing the ravages of war in this field will be an enormous job, and one that will provide a unique opportunity to create a coordinated system of highways, railroads, waterways, and airways.

Other federal economic functions would include the interstate connection of public utilities, the control and eventual socialization of interstate monopolies, and the supervision of colonies. A federal constitution insuring peace and a federal economy for maintaining production near capacity would afford the participating countries a standard of living hitherto unknown. Consider how economic development has been throttled in the past twenty years: by armaments, which even in peacetime swallow from 10 to 50 per cent of national incomes; by drives for self-sufficiency, involving production of *ersatz* goods at three or four times the cost of imports in terms of labor effort; and by tariffs, which everywhere have undercut purchasing power by forcing it into dear markets.

There are those who gladly agree that federation would be a good thing for Europe but question the advantages of American membership. To such doubters I can only offer here two brief arguments. The inclusion of the United States in a postwar federal union with all or part of Europe would give this country moral leadership by virtue of its advanced political and economic development and it would remove for all time the danger of a clash should a United States of Europe, on which we had turned our back, struggle to maturity in isolation. From the economic angle it would mean the availability of a field of investment, politically safeguarded, which would bring new life to our capital goods industries. And the ensuing era of prosperity would enable the social and economic adjustments, which we must make under any circumstances, to be carried through with a minimum of strain. The opportunity awaits us if we have the imagination and daring to grasp it; we can take the lead in loosening the Gordian knot which is choking the life out of our civilization.—*Keith Hutchison, Associate Editor, The Nation. Nation. Mr.* 22, '41. *p.* 355-6.

I have never had much confidence in Mr. Streit's *Union Now,* composed exclusively of democracies. I have always believed it would simply result in two great combinations, one democratic and the other totalitarian, which would eventually come into conflict. I am strongly of the belief that the present condition of continental solidarity on the Western Hemisphere is the best form of *Union Now* and the only hopeful sign on the international horizon. No one, of course, can foretell what will happen to the present League of Nations, but there is no doubt in my mind that the splendid organization for technical investigation and diffusion will unquestionably remain.—*Stephen Duggan, Director, Institute of International Education. Asia. Jl.* '40. *p.* 392.

Space and time do not permit an adequate analysis of the Streit plan. A wide discussion of it may serve a useful educational purpose in stimulating thought as to the basic problems of cooperation for peace. The principal objections to the plan are: (1) that it diverts attention from a single world league for peace embracing all civilized nations; (2) that it would leave outside some 50 nations, including great states like Russia, Germany, Italy, and Japan, as well as the Latin American Republics, and would thus erect a new kind of balance of power or alliance; and (3) that it would cause non-imperialistic democracies like the United States, Switzerland, and the Scandinavian countries, to join in a partnership with imperialistic nations in perpetuating imperialism with its subjection of unwilling peoples. In this connection India is frequently mentioned. In view of the fact that the people of the United States are unwilling to join a World Court and voluntarily submit a legal case to it, if and when they desired, and in view of their past unwillingness to enter the League of Nations with its limited powers, it may well be questioned if they are ready to enter into a Federal Union with such strong powers as Mr. Streit proposes.

Nor is the Streit plan a regional plan such as the Pan American Union, which has proved itself to be of inestimable value in the Americas. Indeed this regional union for peace has recently received new support, and there is a feeling that it has abundantly proved its worth in a time of stress and strain.—*J. Eugene Harley, University of Southern California. American Society of International Law. Proceedings,* 1940. *p.* 107.

You will gather that I am somewhat skeptical about America's putting too much emphasis upon, let us say, "Union Now." Mr. Clarence Streit has done us a good service in helping us to realize that we shall not get enduring peace simply in terms of coercion. We should not have got a sound federal union by an agreement of thirteen American states to coerce one of their number who might do others a wrong. It is only action in common interest that makes for unity. So far, Mr. Clarence Streit has served us well. But today, his "Union Now" would turn out to be something like what I judge Professor Schuman meant when he spoke of a "grand alliance"; a military alliance; an alliance of the "virtuous" against the "wicked"; an alliance likely to mean indefinite war; an alliance to which I am opposed with all my heart and soul and mind and strength.

And even if this "Union Now" were to be effectuated after peace, so that it would not perforce be of military nature, I do not think its advocates have at all thought through the problems of colonial peoples and the European empires in Africa and Asia. I do not think they have at all thought through the economic basis of peace.

I hope the day will come when we can have a federation of the cooperative commonwealths of mankind, but I do not for a moment imagine that after this war we can set up a world government with power over nations analogous to the power of the federal government at Washington over the government of the state of Pennsylvania at Harrisburg. I do not even think that desirable, and I am quite sure that if it were achieved at all it would not be a real federation. It would be the work of a dictator; it would be a new Pax Romana backed by mightier legions than those of Rome.—*Norman Thomas, Socialist Candidate for President,* 1928-1940. *Annals of the American Academy. Jl.* '40. *p.*46.

It may be that no two nations, to say nothing of fifteen, would unite as closely as Mr. Streit demands, but if we believe that nations must push forward in the ways of international co-operation it is vain for us to say where the limits will be reached. The rate of progress depends on conditions, some of them psychological, that are subject to unpredictable change. Arising from the present war there may be catastrophic experiences in store for the world which may create revolutionary changes of temper and opinion.

It is more pertinent to consider whether we would be justified in proposing with Mr. Streit to limit the basis of union to democratic countries. He frankly admits that his list of fifteen founder nations is made with some arbitrariness. He excludes all the Latin American republics because if he admitted any it would be invidious to refuse others. He is not always sure whether a country is a democracy or not and he had doubts about Soviet Russia! He has no qualms about the exclusion of Germany, Italy and Spain because their forms of government are not democratic. If democratic countries are to adopt this position of untouchability is not democracy making itself something arrogant and intolerant? The services of Germany, Italy and Spain to the civilization of the world compare not unfavorably with those of the best three in Mr. Streit's list of the favored fifteen. The social conditions in some of the democratic countries are not exemplary in every respect and in some cases are a bitter mockery of democracy. The faith that Mr. Streit displays in "peoples" and his distrust of their governments, though democratically elected, making him insist on a union of peoples and not of governments, reflects unflatteringly on democratic practice, but of this he does not seem to be aware and he takes the sacredness and superiority of democracy for granted, as the one thing not to be questioned or criticized. With this attitude democracy may be the bringer of the sword and not of peace to the world.—*Henry Somerville, former Associate Editor, Catholic Register, Toronto. Catholic World. Jl.* '40. *p.*457.

I must confess that I find these proposals rather breath-taking. They would bring about a more profound revolution than that which took place when the American colonies abandoned the Articles of Confederation and accepted the Constitution. The proponents of these plans apparently expect the adoption of such revolutionary changes by a group of nations which have a consciousness of kind, a community of feeling, much less pronounced than that which prevailed among the American colonies. I consider these plans a bit too ambitious. I cannot see a large number of countries suddenly parting with their independence and agreeing to abide by the majority decisions of a federal legislature. Nor can I envisage them surrendering at once all control over tariffs, money, credit, and prices. No, any attempt to bring about such a sweeping and sharp departure from long-established and accepted ideas of national sovereignty and independence would only provoke an unwelcome reaction which might doom all international experiments to failure. Very likely a federation should have greater powers than the League, but none so great as those of the federal government at Washington. No doubt a federation should not be completely hamstrung by a rule requiring unanimity, but it might only succeed in provoking defiance if it proceeded to act by simple majority rule.

If there is to be a federation, I would prefer it to be on a geographical rather than an ideological basis as Clarence Streit proposes. True, there are several things to be said in favor of confining the union to democratic countries. The democratic nations share a certain community of spirit that is absent among other countries. They have somewhat the same conception of government and of the relationship of the individual to society. These factors might facilitate federation. Yet I doubt the practicability of a union of the scattered British dominions, the United States, Britain, France, Scandinavia, the Low countries, and Switzerland. There is no geographic or economic unity. The social and economic needs of such a country as the United States would differ markedly from those of Scandinavia. Any attempt to reduce them to a common denominator might fail.

Moreover, any union on a purely democratic basis would no doubt sharpen the ideological conflicts of the world. It so happens that the democratic countries are at the same time also the wealthiest. A union among them would be equivalent to a union among the wealthier states here in the east of the United States of America, to the exclusion and detriment of the poorer states of the south and west. Mr. Streit assumes apparently that all countries would hurry to adopt democratic institutions and bills of rights in order to be admitted into the select circle. I fear this is taking too much for granted. It presupposes that the natural historical evolution of every country is toward democracy. I can see no proof for such an assumption. Democracy, for instance, has never flourished east of the Rhine. There is little indication that it ever will take root there, but I would not, on that account, exclude the entire area from participation in organized international political life.

No, I would rather see the world evolve toward some form of regional federalism. Just as the Pan American Union exists for the Americas, another organization should have jurisdiction over all or most of Europe. The evolution toward a real federation, however, must be slow and painful. I would not attempt to give it too sweeping powers at first. At the same time I would try to preserve the League of Nations in some form in order to cap the regional organizations with an institution universal in scope. There are many problems which transcend regions, which concern all countries alike. Even a

League which has no powers of coercion but provides only for periodic consultation, would serve a useful purpose.—*John C. de Wilde, Foreign Policy Association. Middle States Association of History and Social Science Teachers. Proceedings.* 1939. *p.*14-15.

REGIONAL FEDERATION

MYTH OF THE CONTINENTS [1]

In earlier writings as well as in his latest book Charles A. Beard reads from (or into?) American history the lesson that "continentalism" represents the destined course of our foreign policy. Jerome Frank, writing a chapter of "Disintegrated Europe and Integrated America," argues that the basic issue in Europe, and the cause of unfortunate developments in Germany and Italy, has been "the absence of continental integration." In America, he continues, we have continental integration, "and therefore the possibility of relative self-sufficiency." Stuart Chase embroiders still further Frank's theme of "disintegrated Europe, integrated America," collects figures to explore the possibilities of various "continental economic units," and, in the last sentence of his book, urges the United States to avoid economic and political entanglements in the affairs of other nations which, "in the nature of their geographical deficiencies, must quarrel, until some day they too achieve continental unity."

The Western Hemisphere complex, so conspicuous in discussions of American foreign policy, has often been associated with ideas of "continental" unity and "continental" solidarity. A noteworthy instance occurred in a symposium at the meeting of the American Political Science Association a year ago where Clarence Streit's plan for Interdemocracy Federal Union was up for discussion. A distinguished political scientist—a student of municipal government—based his criticism on the view that the natural political and economic grouping is the "continental" one. He therefore favored solidarity with Latin American countries as against overseas countries.

[1] From article by Eugene Staley, Professor of International Economic Relations, Fletcher School of Law and Diplomacy. *Foreign Affairs.* 19:481-3. April, 1941.

There is, of course, a tremendous literature on the theme that "Europe" must unite. Coudenhove-Kalergi's *Pan Europe*; the efforts of practical statesmen like Briand, Herriot and others to promote European union; and more recently a new flood of books, articles, plans and speeches advocating a "United States of Europe" or some sort of European federation all carry a continental emphasis. Sometimes there is an explicit argument to explain why continents, as such, must be united. Thus, H. N. Brailsford writes, "Air power has made inevitable the unification of continents." More often than not, however, this point is simply taken for granted.

On the other hand, there are strong trends in current political action and thought, as well as existing economic and political connections, which cut directly across continental lines. Public opinion and official policy in the United States are today influenced very decidedly by the realization that our own ability to defend ourselves depends in no small measure on what happens in Europe and Asia. The British Commonwealth of Nations, so long as it stands, will continue to be a practical challenge to the thesis that continental units are the natural ones. The war emergency has publicized the fact that the economic affiliations of much of South America, as well as the cultural affiliations of Latin America in general, are with Europe—distinctly un-continental. In the realm of thought about the future, particularly in the discussion of war and peace aims, continental lines are being as regularly disregarded by some as they are being emphasized by others. Proposals like "Union Now," and the more moderate proposals of those who, while doubting the feasibility of complete federal union, nevertheless envisage some kind of a permanent bond between the United States and other democratic nations, reject the continental principles in favor of an ocean-linked unity.

One general theme runs like a red thread through most of these discussions, by continentalists and non-continentalists alike. That is the conviction that the day of the small, completely independent, sovereign national state is past. There will be in the future—and ought to be—*larger* politico-economic units of some kind. This, in the view of the present writer, has to be accepted as unquestionably sound. But is the natural progression from small, sovereign states to *continental* groupings? There is reason for making an examination of this question now, for the words "continental" seem to be acquiring strong emotional and symbolic values which may even affect policy. Is this a well-founded development, or have we here an instance of the fascination (not to say tyranny) of certain words? What are the general characteristics that mark off continental from non-continental, overseas, or maritime groupings? What is to be said for permanent supra-national groupings of a continental sort as compared with non-continental, maritime, or oceanic groupings? With respect to the defense problem of the United States, what are the relative virtues of a policy which stresses "continental" defense lines (admitting aid to Britain largely because it buys time for preparation), as against a policy which allies us with overseas friends in all-out resistance to the totalitarian challenge and in joint maintenance of dominant world sea-power?

THE PAN-EUROPEAN MOVEMENT [2]

Program of the Pan-European Union

1. A European League of States, with mutual guarantees of the equality, security and independence of all European states;
2. A European League Court for the amicable settlement of all conflicts between European states;
3. A European military alliance with a common air fleet to ensure peace and proportional disarmament;
4. Gradual creation of a European Customs Union;
5. Common access to European colonies;
6. A common European currency;

[2] By Count Richard N. Coudenhove-Kalergi, President, Pan-European Union. *Labour*. 1:9-13. February, 1939.

7. The fostering of the national cultures of all European nations as the basis of a common European culture;

8. The protection of all national and religious minorities in Europe against denationalisation and oppression;

9. The collaboration of Europe with other groups of nations within the framework of a world-wide League of Nations.

Technical progress has entirely altered the conditions of world policy. It takes less time to fly today from London to Rome than it took a century ago to travel from London to Glasgow.

Consequently Europe has become virtually smaller than the United Kingdom was during the 19th century.

This European continent has become still smaller since Russia, comprising about half the area of Europe, expanded into the Soviet Union, forming a single political body from the Baltic to the Japanese Sea and living under cultural, economic and political conditions quite different from the rest of Europe. Formerly Russia was a European country with Siberia as its Asiatic colony. Now Russia and Siberia form the Soviet Union, a link between Europe and the Far East, four times as large as its little European neighbor.

On the other hand, we see Pan-Americanism working to unite all republics of the New World into a huge federation under the leadership of the United States of America, itself larger than the whole of Europe.

We must consider as another important fact the efforts of Japan to unite the "yellow" races into a Far Eastern Federation, with a population of 600,000,000 of Chinese and Japanese. If this effort succeeds, this Far Eastern Block of Mongolians might become in two generations the greatest military and industrial power of the world.

So all over the extra-European world huge political and economic federations are being formed. The biggest of these groups is the British Empire. Canada is larger than Europe, and Australia nearly as large. India is about as large as Europe and nearly as densely populated as Europe.

Among these great groups of states the European continent remains split up into 32 sovereign states and economic units without any common link or organization. This part of the world is living in pure anarchy. One state tries to ruin another; they all are arming against each other, calumniating and blackmailing each other; and driving together towards a great war.

The League of Nations tried to create some kind of organization amongst the European states. It was a failure because it did not follow the laws of evolution, and tried to federate the whole world without beginning by federating Europe; because it set up an ideal of tomorrow before attempting the tasks of today.

A world-wide League of Nations remains our task for the future. But we must learn from failure that we can only organize the world after having succeeded in organizing those parts of the world which are still living under the law of the jungle: first of all Europe.

So the idea of European union can never be considered as separate from the greater idea of world union, but only as a first practical step to this highest political aim.

There is no doubt that European disunion is not eternal. Technical progress will prove itself stronger than national hatred. But it is very doubtful if this reorganization will be realised by war or by peaceful means or if it will be organized on the basis of national equality and personal liberty, or on the principles of national socialism under the rule of Germany.

If Great Britain retires from Europe, it is almost certain that the enormous German power will establish its hegemony first in Central Europe, and then in Western Europe, without any European power being able to prevent it from playing the same role in this European union that Prussia played in the German Federation of Bismarck.

The only power that can prevent a German dictatorship over Europe, and can establish a European federation based on the equality of nations and free populations is Great Britain. If

Great Britain decides to assume the moral leadership of Europe, three-quarters of the continent would follow such an initiative with enthusiasm. And I am sure that even the rest of Europe would join in the very near future this great European union, and help to overthrow all reactionary forces opposed to this great political and economic achievement.

Such a European federation would bring advantages to all nations without doing harm to any of them. It would secure permanent peace, and make possible a massive reduction of armaments. But it would also secure a higher standard of living for the working classes of the whole of Europe by creating a huge European market.

Nowadays, the industries of the different European states are competing with each other. They are forced to export their products more cheaply than their neighbors. For the sake of these exports, they reduce the standard of living of their working classes. Economic policy and social policy are opposed.

This difficulty will remain as long as Europe is divided up by customs barriers. No social reform in the interior of these states will be able to raise the standard of living. The only way to do so is to organize Europe as a great economic and monetary unit that will not be obliged to live on exports, but will be able to sell its productions, and the productions of Africa, in its own market.

As soon as such an organization is accomplished, social and economic policy will be allied: the higher the standard of living of the working classes, the greater their capacity for buying European industrial and agricultural products.

Therefore every social policy in Europe ought to demand first of all a European Commonwealth, rich and strong enough to compete with the United States of America, the Far East and the Soviet Union.

The Pan-European movement has been working for sixteen years for such a European Commonwealth. As soon as the United States of America decided definitely not to join the

League of Nations, the Pan-European movement started its activities. It set up its headquarters in Vienna, where it held its first congress in 1926. After having gained the support of a great number of political leaders of all democratic parties all over Europe, it invited Aristide Briand, in 1927, to accept its presidency. Briand accepted, and till his death in 1932, cooperated closely with this movement. In 1929, he invited all European governments to examine the Pan-European problem, and to constitute some form of European federation. On May 17, 1930, Briand published his famous "Memorandum," disclosing the main plan for a united Europe. On the same day the Pan-European Union held its second congress in Berlin.

Briand's initiative failed. At that time European misery and anarchy had not yet reached a state which proved the necessity of a European union. The Governments still thought that such a federation was not necessary. The strong movement of public opinion all over Europe did not induce them to follow Briand's suggestion. So this great statesman died without seeing the realization of the idea.

After Briand's death the Pan-European movement continued its work. It worked, without the cooperation of the great European powers, principally as a moral and economic movement. In 1932, it had its third congress in Basle, in 1935 its fourth congress in Vienna.

The worse conditions become in Europe, the more strongly the Pan-European ideal appeals to thinking people throughout the continent as the sole way of salvation. Its moral influence increases from year to year. A free plebiscite among the nations of the European continent would undoubtedly give a strong majority in favor of a United States of Europe, combining national independence with a common foreign policy, military policy, and economic policy.

But the key to the European problem does not lie on the continent: it lies in England. If Great Britain were willing to take the moral leadership of European unity and liberty, the continent would follow.

A serious obstacle to the assumption of this leadership by England is the inter-continental character of its Empire. Some British statesmen fear that a stronger link between England and the continent might disturb Imperial Unity.

I think this point of view is wrong. Great Britain needs a peaceful and prosperous Europe at its back to be able to continue its Imperial world-wide policy. It needs a peaceful continent, free from any hegemony, to be able to send its fleet and its air-force to other parts of the world.

If, on the other hand, Europe remains in a state of anarchy, Great Britain will be always obliged to concentrate its fleet and air-force in Europe, and will in the long run lose great parts of its Empire. If England retires from the continent, then there is no doubt that Germany will in less than a generation dominate Europe. Then Great Britain will be at the mercy of this continental power, just as it would have been if Napoleon had won his war and realized his European ambitions.

The invention of the aeroplane has the same consequences for the future of Great Britain as the invention of the cannon had in the history of Venice. The defense of Great Britain cannot be assured by armaments alone, but finally only by a European federation, under its own moral leadership.

There is no antagonism between its Imperial and its continental mission. During three centuries Austria was at the same time the leading power of the German federation, and on the other hand dominated its own Danubian Empire. Thus a policy is conceivable that would allow Great Britain to control with its right hand its children beyond the seas, and with its left hand its brothers and sisters on the European continent: securing for both of them peace, liberty and prosperity.

THE WORLD GERMANICA [3]

The Germans have a clear plan of what they intend to do in case of victory. I believe that I know the essential details of that

[3] By Dorothy Thompson, Columnist, New York *Herald Tribune*. New York *Herald Tribune*. p. 17. May 31, 1940.

plan. I have heard it from a sufficient number of important Germans and persons closely in touch with important Germans to credit its authenticity, the more so as previous information regarding military strategy which emanated from the same sources has been completely confirmed by the events.

Germany's plan is to make a customs union of Europe, with complete financial and economic control centered in Berlin. This will create at once the largest free trade area and the largest planned economy in the world. In western Europe alone—Russia is another chapter—there will be an economic unity of 400,000,000 persons, skilled, civilized, white men, with a high standard of living. To these will be added the resources of the British, French, Dutch and Belgian empires. These will be pooled, in the name of Europa Germanica.

The Germans count upon political power following economic power, and not vice versa. Territorial changes do not concern them, because there will be no "France" or "England," except as language groups. Little immediate concern is felt regarding political organizations. The Belgian King will remain on his throne, and may be rewarded with the throne of Holland. Mussolini will remain on his balcony and Victor Emanuel on his throne; other governments will be set up, but no nation will have the control of its own financial or economic system or of its customs.

The Nazification of all countries will be accomplished by economic pressure. In all countries contacts have been established long ago with sympathetic business men and industrialists, and those who have been openly hostile will be punished by boycott. The German occupation armies will fraternize with the Allied soldiers and persuade them that the great social revolution has occurred.

As far as the United States is concerned, the planners of the World Germanica laugh off the idea of any armed invasion. They say that it will be completely unnecessary to take military action against the United States in order to force it to play ball with this system. They point out that there will be no other foreign market for the raw materials and agricultural products of the United States, since these can hardly be sold in the Western Hemisphere.

Here, as in every other country, they have established relations with numerous industries and commercial organizations, to whom they will offer advantages in cooperation with Germany. Certain conditions will have to be met. No orders will be taken from or given to firms headed by personalities unfavorably regarded by the Nazis. No advertising contracts will be placed with newspapers directed by or publishing the work of pro-Ally or anti-Nazi editors or writers.

(This is exactly the way in which they have already swung into line the press of southeastern Europe.)

The immense gold reserve of the United States will be, obviously, worthless. The international currency will be a managed currency, the German mark, and all external trade will be based upon barter. This new world-wide complex will want raw materials, and will pay for them in manufactured goods. The United States will become an economic colony, for its economic independence will be lost. There will be immense demands upon the southern and middle western states for cotton, wheat, etc., and upon the mineral wealth of this country, which they will take at high prices measured in terms of manufactured articles. The German planners predict a stampede of the South to collaborate with this system. This stampede will be fostered and directed by their agents.

South America will be conquered by business agents, not by guns. The plantation owners will be asked by the Germans whether they want to sell their meat, cotton and raw materials to Germany in exchange for machinery, industrial material, automobiles, etc., or whether they want to be boycotted. Inasmuch as the chief market of South America is Europe—and obviously the United States cannot take these products, which compete with our own—they count on the complete breakdown of the

Western Hemisphere policy. "America," they say, "will be reduced to attempting to conquer these countries, while we have all the arts of economic persuasion at our command. We shall be the peace-makers and they the war-makers." The economic penetration has already been established in all South American countries and in Mexico, and will be accompanied by political ultimatums and propaganda activities.

German will be the industrial and financial dynamo at the center of all this, with special privileges. Reference is made to the American Civil War, to the conquest of the industrial North over the agricultural South. France will be kept to agriculture and the manufacture of quality goods. "She can still make dresses and women's handbags."

London is to cease to be a financial center, but will be the chief commercial center, under Nazi domination. When it is possible to find pro-Nazis of French, British or other nationality, they will be put into power in their own countries. Otherwise, German governors will be put in. In any case, all political activities will be quietly watched by the Gestapo.

To accomplish all this it is necessary to complete a total war against Britain and France. Original plans were to drive through to the Channel ports and offer a separate peace to France. The progress of the German armies, however, now leads the German generals to the belief that they can deal a knockout blow to both London and Paris.

The former is to be accomplished by the invasion of Britain at a time when her very meager army is decimated. The Nazis intend to blast a channel or channels across the Channel—corridors across the corridor—probably from Antwerp or Calais. They will sweep mines from a fairly narrow channel with speedboats and submarines and heavily mine both sides of it, transporting troops under the cross-Channel fire of heavy guns of a size and range not yet used in this war.

Nazi troops now concentrated in Norway will be used for the invasion, simultaneously, of Scotland. Invasion will be by giant submarines, boats and planes.

Assault troops will be landed at the same time at half a dozen points along the coast. The Nazis have speedboats which can carry 200 men and can cross several times a night.

They consider London the easiest city in the world to invade, once the troops have landed. The roads approaching it are undefended, many major highways and numerous small roads converge upon it and are connected with crossroads through which several units can approach at the same time and retain communication with one another.

All operations will be accompanied by terrific air attacks.

The British Isles will be held as hostage for the Empire and the fleet. It is contemplated that the fleet will be scuttled or will go to Canada. "But no new stand can be made in Egypt or in Canada or elsewhere in the Empire or among the commonwealths because we shall have the British Isles at our mercy, with the entire population. We will destroy the ports and cut them off from food. They can either sign on our terms or be systematically *ausgerotted* and starved."

The Nazis believe in the system of hostages. They now admit that they tried it first with the Jews to see whether world-Jewry would buy out its co-religionists. They thus demonstrated that the humanitarian impulses of the world are one of their own most useful weapons.

Russia will not be invaded. "We have no interest in the political system. Stalin will work with us. We are only interested in the organization of the Russian transport system, in increasing the production of the oil wells and exploiting minerals. Russia is full of our engineers and more of them will be welcome. The Russian system is all right, but it needs Nazi discipline and German technical skill to exploit it. Slavs cannot organize."

They do not believe that the proletarian workers in any country will seriously oppose them—even if they could. They argue that the tendency in all democracies demonstrates that workers only want to eat and have work, and care nothing for national matters or for individual liberty. What remnants are left of the pre-Hitlerian epoch myths will be terrorized out of the workers by the Gestapo. "And," they add, "there is nothing that capitalists will not do, if profitable. Democracies have taught their people, workers or corporation chiefs to believe only in money."

And, finally, only the master race, the Germans, will be allowed to bear arms. If, however, the United States wants to concur, all armaments can be radically reduced.

PAN AMERICA CONSULTS [4]

The system of consultation is nothing new for the nations of the Western Hemisphere. The Latin Americans have been consulting together ever since they achieved their independence from Spain and Portugal almost a century and a quarter ago. In conferences at Panama in 1826, at Lima in 1847, at Santiago in 1856, at Lima again in 1864, at Bogota in 1880, and in numerous other international gatherings they have sought to ward off interventions from outside, to settle disputes among themselves, and to devise machinery for the perpetuation of amicable relations. For the past fifty years the United States has been meeting with all the other independent republics of this hemisphere in periodic international conferences of the American states, the first of which assembled at Washington in 1889, the second at Mexico City in 1901-1902, the third at Rio de Janiero in 1906, the fourth at Buenos Aires in 1910, the fifth at Santiago in 1923, the sixth at Havana in 1928, the seventh at Montevideo in 1933, and the eighth at Lima in 1938.

In addition, some or all of the American nations have consulted together in scores of other international conferences dealing with such various subjects as the codification of the inter-

[4] From article by Donald Marquand Dozer, Department of History, University of Maryland. *World Affairs Interpreter.* 11:378-85. Winter, 1941.

national law of the Americas, the status of women, the promotion of the sciences, the construction of a Pan-American highway, commercial aviation, health and sanitation, and the welfare of their children. For the past several decades they have thus formed, though somewhat slowly it must be admitted, the habit of talking over their common problems together.

But the present procedure of consultation is different. It represents something new in inter-American relations and has been forced upon the Western nations by the grinding necessities of the international situation. Forming as they do the largest bloc of neutral nations in the world, they are employing the procedure now in an effort to maintain their collective solidarity.

They first took steps in this direction at the extraordinary Inter-American Conference for the Maintenance of Peace, which assembled at Buenos Aires in December 1936, at the suggestion of President Roosevelt. While the threats of the European dictators were daily becoming more inflamatory, all the twenty-one American republics agreed in this conference that if their peace was menaced either by a war between the American states or by an international war outside America they would consult together to preserve the peace of the American continent. This "Convention for the Maintenance, Preservation, and Re-establishment of Peace" has been called "the strongest assurance of peace which this continent has ever had." In an "Additional Protocol Relative to Non-Intervention" the representatives at Buenos Aires agreed that if any American state intervened in the internal or external affairs of another they would hold mutual consultation in order to find methods of peaceful adjustment. And in a third important act, the "Declaration of Principles of Inter-American Solidarity and Cooperation," they broadly declared "that every act susceptible of disturbing the peace of America affects each and every one of them and justifies the initiation of the procedure of consultation." Thus, the conference at Buenos Aires introduced the new principle into the inter-American peace machinery. But the delegates made no specific provisions as to the times or methods of employing it.

When the American republics again assembled two years later in the eighth Pan-American conference at Lima, they were confronted with the dire and imminent prospect of war in Europe. Accordingly, they re-affirmed their continental solidarity in the "Declaration of Lima" and agreed that "in case the peace, security or territorial integrity of any American Republic" should be threatened they would make their solidarity effective by means of the procedure of consultation. In order to define this procedure the Argentine delegation, significantly enough, proposed that the foreign ministers of the American republics or representatives designated by them meet to discuss problems of common interest whenever they deemed it advisable. The conference approved this proposal and thus provided that the consultations should take the form of meetings of the foreign ministers of the American nations convening "when deemed desirable and at the initiative of any one of them." They also broadened the scope of the consultations to include "any economic, cultural or other questions" in "which American States may have a common interest." Several months before the beginning of the present European war the American nations thus determined to preserve their collective neutrality and to strengthen their common interests through a defined procedure of consultation.

Scarcely had Germany marched across Poland's frontiers last September when the American governments began to make plans for a consultative meeting of their foreign ministers in accordance with the arrangements made at Buenos Aires and Lima. The Pan-American Union drew up a short program for the meeting under three heads: (1) neutrality, involving a consideration of the rights and duties of neutrals and belligerents, (2) protection of the peace of the Western Hemisphere "whether on land, in the air, within territorial waters, or within the area of the primary defense of the Western Hemisphere," and (3) economic cooperation to safeguard "the economic and financial stability of the American Republics." All the American governments sent delegations, many of which were headed by their ministers of foreign affairs, to the historic first consultative meeting which convened in the National Institute in Panama City on September 23, 1939. During its ten-day sessions experienced observers felt that no inter-American conference had ever revealed such complete unanimity of purpose as this Panama meeting. As a result of their consultations the delegates approved a Final Act containing sixteen resolutions and declarations.

On the subject of neutrality the Panama meeting expressed the unanimous intention of the American republics not to become involved in the European conflict and set forth the general principles of neutrality which they intended to follow. They agreed, for example, to prevent their territories from being used as bases of belligerent operations, to prevent the recruiting of troops within their jurisdictions for the aid of the belligerents, to control the passage of belligerent aircraft over their territories, and in general to enforce a uniform neutrality as far as possible. To this end they established for the duration of the war an Inter-American Neutrality Committee composed of seven experts in international law to study and submit to the American governments recommendations on the changing problems of neutrality. This Committee began its sessions in Rio de Janiero last January 15 and has since presented recommendations on neutral mails, internment, the treatment of auxiliary craft, and other problems arising out of the war.

For the protection of the peace of the Western Hemisphere the foreign ministers and their representatives at Panama urged cooperative action by the American nations to repress the unlawful activities of their inhabitants in favor of a foreign belligerent state and to eradicate doctrines that jeopardize "the common Inter-American democratic ideal." As a further measure of protection they forbade European belligerents to commit hostile acts within a "zone of security" extending from 300 to 600 miles to sea around the American continents excepting only "the territorial waters of Canada and of the undisputed colonies and possessions of European countries within these limits." They agreed to ask the belligerents to respect the zone defined in this "Declaration of Panama" and declared that they would consult together whenever they considered it necessary to take further action to secure its observance. They arranged also to hold another consultative meeting whenever the transfer of a European colony in this hemisphere to another state should occur and so threaten the security of the American continent.

And, finally, in order to promote the economic cooperation of the American republics the conference set up an Inter-American Financial and Economic Advisory Committee in Washington consisting of an economic expert from each of the American countries. They instructed this committee to provide for the interchange of economic information among the American nations and to propose measures for inter-American cooperation to offset the commercial and financial dislocations caused by the war. In this first consultative meeting the American republics thus established two committees, which have since been regularly functioning, and they agreed upon other measures which set a new high standard of inter-American cooperation. Before adjourning they recommended that another consultative meeting be held at Havana on October 1, 1940, "without prejudice to an earlier meeting if this should be found necessary."

An earlier meeting was found to be necessary as a result of the exigencies of the European situation. After the adjournment of the conference the European belligerents committed hostile acts not only in the "zone of security" but even in the territorial waters of American nations, and in January and February three of the principal belligerents officially informed the American governments that they would not respect the zone. Moreover, the position of all members seemed to become more precarious after the successive collapse of Norway, Denmark, Holland, and Luxembourg; and the fate of the Dutch and later the French islands in the Western Hemisphere became a problem of immediate concern to all the American nations. Accordingly, the second meeting of the American foreign ministers, which convened in Havana last July 21 at President Roosevelt's suggestion, approved some of the most far-reaching measures ever enacted in a Pan-American gathering.

In order to preserve their common neutrality the Havana conference asked the Inter-American Neutrality Committee to draft a convention completely embodying the principles of neutrality applicable to the American nations in the present conflict, and they urged that the governments not only ratify this convention but also incorporate the Committee's recommendations in their domestic legislation. More significant, however, was the conference's action against "fifth-column" activities in the Americas, for they instructed the Pan American Union to convoke an inter-American conference of jurists and police authorities to draft measures for "the most complete and effective defense against acts of an unlawful character, as well as against any other unlawful activities which may affect the institutions of the American States." They also agreed that the American governments should suppress activities of foreign governments and individuals tending to subvert their domestic institutions or to alter "their existing democratic systems," and they arranged to consult together if such activities menaced the peace of any of the American republics. The delegates further provided for the national interchange among their foreign ministers of confidential information on such activities and reaffirmed the Panama resolution calling for the eradication from the Americas of doctrines which jeopardize the "common inter-American democratic ideal." In pursuance of these agreements the United States has compiled considerable data on the activities of suspected agents of foreign governments in Latin-American countries.

In order to protect the Western Hemisphere against more direct action by the belligerents the delegates at Havana urged the Inter-American Neutrality Committee to draft a convention setting forth the present status of the security zone, and they collectively reprobated hostilities within this zone and within their territorial waters. They agreed to consider any attempt by a non-American state against the integrity or inviolability of an American nation as an act of aggression against all of them and to resort to the procedure of consultation and to prepare for mutual defense against such aggression. They also expanded the powers of the Inter-American Financial and Economic Advisory Committee to provide for closer financial and economic cooperation among the American governments.

But probably the "Act of Havana concerning the provisional administration of European colonies and possessions in the Americas" was the most momentous enactment of the conference. It continentalized the traditional "no-transfer principle" of the United States, which runs back for at least a century and a quarter and has been deemed to be throughout that long period an exclusively unilateral commitment of the Washington government. In the "Act of Havana" the American nations collectively agreed to set up a provisional administration over European colonies in this hemisphere threatened with transfer to other European governments. If the danger of such transfer is immediate, this administration will be exercised by an emergency committee composed of one representative of each of the American republics, and when the danger ceases to exist these administered areas will either be organized as autonomous states or restored to their previous colonial status.

In a separate draft convention, which is open to ratification by the American nations, the delegates at Havana sought to provide a treaty basis for the administration of these regions. Declaring that the transfer of European colonies in this hemisphere to other European countries is "against American sentiments and principles" and will not "be recognized or accepted by the American Republics," the convention creates an Inter-American Commission on Territorial Administration," composed of one representative from each of the ratifying states. This Commission will ask one or more states to undertake the task of administering these colonial regions and will supervise the administration "in the interest of the security of the Americas and for the benefit of the region under administration." Though not called by the same name, this provisional administrative region bears interesting resemblances to the mandatory system established in the Covenant of the League of Nations. Secretary Hull referred to it as "a collective trusteeship" in his opening address to the conference, and probably the term mandate was avoided because Japan's treatment of her mandated areas in the South Pacific has brought it into disrepute. Then, too, the purposes of the two systems are different. The League's mandatory system was intended as a tutelage for "peoples not yet able to stand by themselves under the strenuous conditions of the modern world," whereas the "Act of Havana" seeks to checkmate "attempts at conquest, which have been repudiated in the international relations of the American Republics" and which might threaten their security.

MAIN DRIVE BEHIND JAPANESE NATIONAL POLICIES [5]

The third impelling idea behind Japanese imperial policy is that East Asia and the adjacent island world should be organized as an autonomous and self-sufficient regional unit under the hegemony of Japan. This may be called the practical application of the Master-state concept. The idea of regionalism did not originate in Japan: it is simply an Oriental version of the Pan-American doctrine of the United States, and of the regional organization of Europe which Aristide Briand envisioned years ago, and about which Nazi leaders lately have been talking. Regionalism harmonizes with ambitions long cherished by Japan, and serves to justify her present ruthless

[5] From article by Galen M. Fisher, Christian worker in Japan. *Pacific Affairs*. 13:388-91. December, 1940.

measures in China. Publicists in Japan have been discussing and popularizing the idea for several years, but it was not until Foreign Minister Arita's radio address of June 29 that it received the official imprimatur. He said:

It seems to be a most natural step that peoples who are closely related with one another geographically, racially, culturally and economically should first form a sphere of their own for co-existence and co-prosperity and establish peace and order within that sphere, and at the same time secure a relationship of common existence and prosperity with other spheres. The causes of strife mankind has hitherto experienced lie generally in the failure to give due consideration to the necessity of some such natural and constructive world order and to remedy the irrationalities and injustices of the old. The countries of East Asia and the regions of the South Seas are geographically, historically, racially and economically very closely related to one another. They are destined to cooperate and minister to one another's needs for their common well-being and prosperity, and to promote peace and progress in their regions. The uniting of all these regions under a single sphere on the basis of common existence and insuring thereby the stability of that sphere is, I think, a natural conclusion. I desire to declare that the destiny of these regions (East Asia and the South Seas)—any development therein, and any disposal thereof—is a matter of grave concern to Japan in view of her mission and responsibility as the stabilizing force in East Asia.

A more elaborate argument for regionalism in general, and for East Asian regionalism in particular is presented in an article by one of Japan's most eminent moderates, Iwao F. Ayusawa, in the July issue of *Contemporary Japan.* Dr. Ayusawa writes out of a wide experience in Europe and America, first as a graduate student in Columbia University, and later as an official of the International Labor Office. He says:

Nationalism is being discredited and will have to be superseded by something else as a result of this catastrophic war. This may be one of the few things Europe will gain from the conflict. The substitute for nationalism—for the time being—is *regionalism,* a system of ensuring security, order and peace, not for the whole world at once, as the League attempted to do and failed, but within three or four separate regions of the earth such as America, Asia, Western and Eastern Europe, etc. Whether we "recognize" it or not, various systems of regional cooperation are developing rapidly as a natural course of events under our own eyes. Suppose Germany and Italy gain a decisive victory in the present conflict and that a wide area of Europe now occupied by them falls under the hegemony of those two powers! It is presumable then that a regional order in that part of the world will come much sooner than one would have reasonably expected—though, of course, its duration may be questioned. It is our belief, in any case, that when a regional order of one kind or another is established in Europe, something similar to it will develop, or *must* develop, in other regions of the world as well. In order to ensure that such a development shall take place spontaneously without cooercion—though persuasion will be necessary—we must not fix too many details arbitrarily in advance.

In these words Dr. Ayusawa has set forth the Japanese conception of regionalism at its best. I say "at its best," for the average occidental reader can hardly restrain a smile when he compares the ideal of a regional order set up "spontaneously without coercion" with what appears to the outsider to be the harshest coercion now being applied to China as the first step in the process. Be that as it may, it must be admitted that the idea is worthy of the most serious consideration, both on its intrinsic merits, and also on the score of its controlling influence in Japanese policy.

The slogan "A Monroe Doctrine for Asia" has been eagerly seized upon by Japanese protagonists of the eviction of occidental domination from Eastern and Southern Asia. Some of the more liberal minds in Japan have sought to equate an "Asiatic Monroe Doctrine" with the regional idea as it is expounded by men like Dr. Ayusawa, but most of its advocates have used the magic name Monroe to camouflage a policy of Japanese hegemony of the Orient, to be achieved by consent, where practicable, but to be imposed by force, if necessary. Even so intelligent a writer as the well-known journalist Mr. Katsuji Inahara persists in assuming that the American Monroe Doctrine, even today, means that the United States is forcing its will upon the other American republics. President Roosevelt may have spoken inadvisedly when he said, on July 6: "This government would ask no voice in the disposition of French Indo-China because of its place in the sphere of Asiatic influence. For instance, in the case of French Indo-China, we think the disposition should be decided among the Asiatic countries." But he does, in this statement, emphasize the crucial principle of consent, which animates the Monroe Doctrine, and which many Japanese spokesmen overlook. If Japan in Manchukuo had given more convincing evidence of abiding by the spirit of Premier Konoye's pledge to take neither indemnities nor territory from a defeated China, then occidentals might be more inclined to take at face value the proposed Monroe Doctrine for Asia, and to welcome an East Asian regional federation founded upon the free consent of the members.

EXCERPTS

Peace in the Americas must be attained through regionalism. The greater regionalism implies cooperation between the states of this hemisphere in the maintenance of peace and security. Lesser regionalism implies cooperation between a small number of states for the adjustment and solution of problems common to them, but not of concern to the entire hemisphere.

The greater regionalism, properly organized, must seek to maintain the neutrality of the nations of this hemisphere, through a deliberate policy of keeping out of European wars, and by maintaining neutral rights through collective arrangements, and, if need be, by collective action.—*Charles E. Martin, University of Washington. American Society of International Law. Proceedings,* 1940. *p.*18.

To begin with the philosophical origin of the United States of Europe. Many sociologists consider that the creation of the League of Nations has resulted in a complete stage in the evolution of the world being skipped. They consider that between the groups of governments and the Universe there should have been an intermediate category: the continent. This purely theoretic idea has no corresponding reality, but it has figured in the writings of numerous advocates and by its simplicity has caught the imaginations of eminent thinkers. On the other hand, as a practical proposition, the example of the Pan American Union has suggested the idea that it would be a good thing to develop an analogous union in Europe and thus to establish the League of Nations on a more solid basis.—*William Martin, Foreign Editor of the Journal de Genève. Contemporary Review. Mr. '30. p.291.*

The movement for a Federated Europe to build a permanent peace after the end of the present war has aroused great enthusiasm. It is daily gaining momentum not only in the United States but among the warring nations themselves. British opinion, particularly among labor and liberal circles, has been leading this tendency, and the first governmental endorsement of the idea came in cautious statements by Halifax and Chamberlain. The Pope in his Christmas address to the College of Cardinals pointed in the same direction. Premier Daladier granted recognition to the idea, when in praising the British-French economic cooperation, adopted for war purposes, he said that it would be open to other nations, and hinted at the effort to establish a continental unity after the conflict.—*Editorial. New Republic. Ja. 8, '40. p.38.*

Let the United States make vital contact with the countries of the Western Hemisphere in the interest of a democratic international order. These are not empire-building nations. They could really become the basis for a new internationalism. Let us work first of all for a league of nations in this hemisphere. If there can be a European league of nations and an Asiatic league of nations, well and good. But if there is to be one league, let it rest not upon the impossible base of Western Europe, but on the base of the nations of the Western Hemisphere where democracy will be unimpaired by the war, and whose vitality, reinforced by association with one another, offers the best chance of being able to carry on in the future.

This proposal is in harmony with the historic policy which starts with freedom from European involvements. It projects world government without using empire capitalism as its foundation.—*Arthur E. Holt, Professor of Social Ethics, Chicago Theological Seminary and in the Divinity School, University of Chicago. Christian Century. Je. 26, '40. p.819.*

Next time, let man try to advance from the lesser to the greater organization. Regional combinations, in Western Europe, the Americas and the Far East, will be hard enough to bring into effective organization. Russia, I agree, "is itself a federation of peoples."

So far, so good. But a stumbling block already appears—the European imperial systems. I do not see how the British Commonwealth (if that is defined as the great self-governing Dominions) can exist as an interregional federation, including areas in North America, Australasia and South Africa. Nor do I see how the British Crown Colonies and the French and Dutch possessions can fairly be integrated with the federation of Western Europe. It would be better for all types of government in a region to belong to that regional federation. Thus it would be necessary to set up federations for Africa and for Australasia (including the southwestern Pacific).

I should hope that such federations would be organized under the simplest kind of machinery, with due balance between authority and responsibility. A central clearing house, which might take over the present functions of the League of Nations, could coordinate information and supply experts.

And as a first step toward solving some of the economic problems which have been provocative in the past I would suggest that every unit which is not self-governing should be open to the commerce of the world, on a most-favored-nation basis. This would stop the exploitation of subject peoples for the benefit of the commerce and industry of their imperial masters.—*Payson J. Treat, Professor of History, Stanford University. Asia. Jl. '40. p.392.*

Of the two concepts of the future, the two projects for a new order in Europe, one has been tried out; as yet the other has not. Temporarily and in limited measure the ultra-powerful empire of mastery and servitude, the empire of the self-enslaved superior race which sets its heel upon the subjugated helot races, has been tried out: the whole world knows approximately what it will be like. The picture of this peace stands before our eyes in the shape of a "Greater Germany" and its protectorates, set up by villainous madmen. In the unspeakable atrocities which are taking place in Poland and the Bohemian Protectorate those "subjects of the German people" who are still at liberty—the Danes, the Dutch, the Swiss, and whoever else may be regarded as occupying the German "living space"—can envisage their own fate.

The other "new world" has not been tried out; it is only a promise, and a precarious promise, of a peace to which each country would have to make equal sacrifices of national sovereignty and national self-determination, of a world of international cooperation, political and economic, where liberty is subject to social bonds and limitations, the Commonwealth, the Confederation of Europe. It is an optimistically humanitarian prospect of welfare, freedom, regard for law, individual happiness, the blossoming of culture; and consequently—for one must realize with what harshness and self-contempt man is apt to look upon himself—it is at a certain moral and intellectual disadvantage as against the tragically pessimistic and realistic idea of a black, bloody, and violent future.—*Thomas Mann, German Author. Nation. F.* 10, '40. *p.*176.

For the immediate future, both biological analogy and historical experience demand a step-by-step advance. Some functions are sufficiently advanced to be put on a world footing without dislocation, while for others the step can only be on to a regional basis. The chief functions which could be stepped up to a world platform are those concerned with primary products and raw material, with certain aspects of research and of communications, and with sea-power. The chief functions for which we must be content with the intermediate regional step-up are the political, in the broad sense of the world.

Let me amplify the second point first. National culture and tradition, usually combined with language, is the strongest political force in the world today. So-called race problems, when analyzed, always turn out to owe their acuteness to differences in culture and economic level which happen to be associated with quite minor genetic differences.

It is wholly premature to envisage any immediate world government which could stand up to the tensions introduced by existing differences in national culture. Regionally, however, there is hope.

The U.S.S.R. has already established a federal system over one-sixth of the world's land area. Pan America is beginning to emerge. The present struggle between Japan and China could without too great difficulty be forgotten in a Far Eastern federation. Malaya and tropical Africa are destined by nature to take their place as world regions as their inhabitants progress toward economic efficiency and political self-government. And finally there remains Europe. I use the word Europe in a cultural sense, as that region where western civilization arose and where it still flourishes, however impeded by barriers of nationalism and the counter-currents of totalitarian philosophy; regionally, the geographic Europe minus European Russia but plus the Asiatic and African fringes of the Mediterranean Sea.

The most urgent political post-war task is the settlement of this European region. It is here that the greatest number of powerful nationalisms occur, here that they are most crowded, here that the ownership of tropical territories is chiefly concentrated. Geography and history alike indicate a regional solution for this area, now torn by war. And the war is a civil one, between different representatives of the European tradition—the tradition based on Greece, on the Roman empire, on western

Christianity, on representative government, on the spirit of modern science, on technology.

Yet the differences between the various nations or groups of nations within Europe are so great, their separate traditions within the enfeebled European tradition so strong, that it would be hopeless to attempt at one bound a full-fledged federal system like that of Switzerland or the U.S.A.

Let us not attempt any ideal or complete plan, and grandiose scheme for which the world is not ripe. That was one of the causes of the League's failure; it was an attempt to impose an ambitious ready-made plan of world citizenship, for which public opinion was insufficiently prepared. Rousseau and the Encyclopedists had been preparing opinion for a radical change in society for half of the eighteenth century; without that preparation, the French Revolution would have been a fiasco. In 1918, the idea of supernational organization had not penetrated beyond a limited circle of intellectuals, and even they had not had time to work out the idea in detail, before Wilson sought to impose it in reality. Today we have at least had twenty years of discussion, together with some bitter if salutary experiences. If the leaders of thought in the various nations can now work out a less pretentious but more workable plan, and at the same time can prepare public opinion for the idea of a dual citizenship, national and world, this war may be the occasion for taking a small but decisive step away from war and towards a world organization of humanity.—*Dr. Julian Sorrell Huxley, English Biologist. Science. F.* 16, '40. *p.*154-5, 158.

Some commentators on the idea of a federated Europe have argued that the diversity of interests, the heritage of bitterness, and the unevenness in the stage of social development among the countries of that continent present problems too difficult to be overcome within a reasonable period of time. It is suggested that groups of small countries adjacent to one another are better fitted by community interests to embark upon a federal experiment first, and that a general continental union might emerge from an association of these regional units with the Great Powers. Dr. Eduard Benes, former President of Czechoslovakia, urges "*a kind of federative reorganization, first perhaps in certain regions* (the Danubian region, the Baltic region, the Balkans, or northern Europe) which [he hopes] will be extended later to the whole of Europe.

Illustrations of this possibility are found in the cooperation of the Scandinavian states in what is known (since 1932) as the Oslo group, and in the formation of an agreement between Turkey, Greece, Rumania, and Yugoslavia in 1934, which has gradually developed into a sort of Balkan entente. It is true that until Bulgaria becomes a member the group remains, to some extent, a defensive alliance against the revisionist claims of the one Balkan state conspicuously absent.

Although frequently discussed as if they were identical, the two ideas of a Danubian federation and of a Balkan union tend to be mutually exclusive. The former would reincorporate the territories of what was formerly the Austro-Hungarian Empire along with other areas forming part of the Danubian basin into a single association, allowing national, cultural, and such other autonomy as they deem fit to the separate parts. This might include Austria, Bohemia-Moravia, Slovakia, Hungary, Rumania, and Yugoslavia. In order to overcome the bitter Hungarian-Rumanian conflict, the district of Transylvania (which is the bone of contention) might be set up as an autonomous unit. In defense of such a political experiment, it may be said that these communities (1) have, for a considerable part, once known a common government (although a monarchy), (2) form a natural economic unit within the Danubian basis, and (3) would create together an effective counterbalance against German or Russian power in south central Europe. Should Austria remain under German control, the remaining states would still explore the conditions of cooperation. Long ago, in the 1860's,

Louis Kossuth dreamed of such a non-German confederation along the Danube when he said:

> Any state of the lower Danube, should it ever be successful in rallying around itself all its racial brethren now belonging to other states, could be in the best case only a state of second rank, the independence of which would be continuously menaced and inevitably subjected to foreign influences. However if the Magyars, the southern Slavs, and the Rumanians would adopt this plan [of confederation], they would become a wealthy, powerful state of first rank with thirty million inhabitants which would have a heavy weight on the scales of Europe. . . . Unity, concord, fraternity between Magyars, Slavs and Rumanians! This is my most ardent wish, my most sincere advice.

A Balkan federation, while proposing the inclusion of Rumania and Yugoslavia, would reach southward to Turkey and the former territories of the Ottoman Empire (Greece, Bulgaria, and possibly Albania). Stretching across an area of vital strategic importance, and of some economic value, such a union might reduce the vulnerability of the Balkans to Great Power domination.

With regard to both the Danubian and the Balkan proposals it may be said that, no matter how chimerical the ideas might seem, the problem of achieving stability in those regions is of vital importance to the whole of Europe and to the world. Shattered into fragments by political and economic nationalism, and by the confusion of racial minorities, southeastern Europe presents an open invitation to the intrigues of stronger powers seeking economic or political advantage. United, one or the other, or even a partial blending of the two, might achieve internal peace in that quarter of the world and participate on more equal terms in the endeavors of the powers to develop a European, or larger, federation.—*"European Plans for World Order," by William P. Maddox, Associate Professor of Political Science, University of Pennsylvania. American Academy of Political and Social Science. Mr. '40. p. 43-4.*

SUMMARY OF THE ARGUMENTS

RESOLVED: *That an international federation of the democracies should be instituted.*

INTRODUCTION

A. Among the many projects for a better world order to which men's minds have turned, in part as an outcome of recent world events, attention has been given to an increased extent to some form of international cooperation.
   1. Various suggestions have been made as to the form such cooperation among nations might take when peace has been won, among which have been:
      a. A reformed League of Nations that will more effectively serve law and order.
      b. Some form of international federation or union among nations.
         (1) Such projected possibilities have ranged through regional, continental, oceanic or world unions.
         (2) Our Pan American accord has been pointed out as an outstanding example of the possibilities of regional ties.
         (3) A European federation has been visualized from time to time and of late particularly stressed as a need of post-war Europe.
         (4) Japan has visualized the attainment of an Asiatic Union.
         (5) Some support has been given to proposed federation of other regional units.
   2. One of the most prevalent suggestions, both to implement the peace when it comes and also proposed as an immediate step in helping win the war, is for a union of the democracies.
      a. Various forms of closer British-American ties have been proposed in late years.
      b. The plan of Union Now by Clarence Streit, revised since the fall of several democracies abroad and now proposed more explicitly as Union Now With Britain, has received wide publicity and discussion.

B. The plan for a union of the democracies as projected under Union Now, would provide more fundamentally:

1. An international organization analogous, in the international field, to the Federal Government in our Union of States.
2. A supreme body that would govern international affairs and resolve conflicts and dissensions between nations.
   a. It would be called upon to regulate, in the main, delegated matters, among which have been proposed international trade, citizenship, money, communications and world defense.
   b. Outside of matters voluntarily given to it nations would retain full sovereignty and autonomy.
3. The supreme law would act directly on individuals and not, as in the League of Nations, on nations as a unit.
4. The initial nucleus of nations, however constituted, would take in other nations as fast as they might be fitted for such inclusion.
5. The ultimate ideal is one of world unity.

C. Definitions:
1. By "democracies" is meant more particularly nations which can conform to certain democratic principles and ways of life, rather than a strictly political form of government.
   a. Fundamentally and practically conditions would necessitate its application to Britain, her self-governing Dominions, and the United States.
   b. Nations adopting democratic ideology and a minimum of fundamental rights for their citizens would be considered "democratic" for the purposes of union.
2. By "instituted" is implied the taking of steps for its realization.

AFFIRMATIVE

I. It is highly desirable that a federation of the democracies be established.
A. Some more effective form of international cooperation among nations which retain the ideals fundamental to democratic nations is vitally necessary.
1. No effective world organization now exists that can protect the interests of these nations.
   a. The League of Nations has proved totally inadequate to deal with such crucial world affairs as afflict us today.
      (1) It has lacked adequate powers.
      (2) Its inadequacy is intrinsically bound up with its form, which makes it fundamentally a collection of nationalities.

(a) The political control rests in the national governments constituting it.

(b) It is not, and cannot be in its present form, a true community of peoples devoted to common welfare.

b. No other organization exists for the effective protection of the common interests of the democratic nations.

2. The lack of such an effective international cooperation among the liberal-minded nations has been one of the strongest factors leading to the present straits of other continents and constituting a threat to our own.

a. The disunity of nations has been the chief encouragement of totalitarian advance.

(1) It offered no obstacle to lawless powers.

(2) Nations, relying on false promises and neutrality, were picked off with impunity one by one.

(3) The Axis advance, augmented by extensive conquests and vast new resources, now presents a formidable threat to the British Empire.

(4) Our own country would be gravely threatened in case Britain should be vitally weakened or overcome.

b. The strength and power of dictatorship can be adequately met only by an international front equivalent to or surpassing the dictatorship strength.

3. Isolation is no longer practicable.

a. The world is now interdependent as never before.

(1) Under technological change distances have been annihilated and the world has shrunk.

(2) Even a nation trying to uphold isolationist and neutrality policies cannot avoid the economic and social effects of conditions in other regions.

b. No nation can maintain isolation and be assured of ultimate freedom while other nations are violating all principles of international law.

B. A federation of the democracies would be ideologically desirable.

1. It would link constitutionally nations already linked to a great extent in a close community.

a. Britain and the United States have a like-minded community of spirit.

b. They have largely a common culture and common standards of life.

c. They have close economic relations.

2. It would unite a group having long experience of democracy.
   a. It would unite nations which have experience in representative self-government.
   b. A closer union would be instituted between nations which have the same basic ideas of freedom and its responsibilities.
3. It would unite nations having the closest trust and confidence.

C. Close cooperation with Britain and her Dominions is in accord with our present tendencies.
1. We have the closest of ties with Canada.
   a. Every consideration of western hemispheric welfare includes Canada.
   b. We have set up with Canada a Permanent Defense Board.
2. We are already tied up militarily with Britain.
   a. We have furnished her 50 destroyers.
   b. Vast quantities of arms and supplies are being furnished her in "all-out" aid.
   c. Britain has leased us various naval bases for ninety-nine years.
3. On the safety of the British fleet and nation depend in great measure our own.
   a. Should Britain be conquered we should have to face both Atlantic and Pacific powers alone.
   b. If the English fleet should be taken over the Axis powers would have a formidable oceanic power with which to menace not only us but the entire world.

D. A federated union of nations would be a logical and natural development in international relations.
1. It is a natural next step in the evolutionary principle of social organization.
   a. Social groups have evolved successively from small to increasingly large cooperative associations, through family, tribe, city, state and nation.
   b. The present age points predominantly to an international order.
      (1) It has taken form widely in the minds of men.
      (2) It is only logical to cement with stronger ties the international cooperation in which we must in any case engage.
2. The idea of international federation is not revolutionary or new.
   a. The federation of large independent political groups has been practically realized in a number of cases.

b. The League of Nations was an effort to realize a federation of the nations of the world.
c. The proposed federation is but one additional step.

E. A union of the democracies would for all time do away with international aggressions and thus definitely promote security and peace.

1. It would contribute vitally to peace in the present war if established now.
   a. It would be of substantial aid to Britain at this crucial time.
      (1) The joining of our forces industrially, economically, financially would present a formidable front to the advancing Axis.
      (2) It would unite the full potentialities of the democratic nations behind Britain.
   b. It would tend to check and gradually to undermine the totalitarian powers.
      (1) It is questionable if they would have the incentive and will for further advance if opposed by united strength surpassing their own.
      (2) The democracies would control a preponderance of practically every war essential.
      (3) The Axis powers would be deprived of many essential products and in time vitally undermined.
   c. It would contribute vitally to morale.
      (1) The democracies themselves would be strengthened in their morale.
      (2) Every country whose liberty is or might yet be manaced and every captive nation which retains a suppressed spirit of revolt would be given courage to hold on.
2. It would contribute to lasting peace when the war is over.
   a. Such a federation would contain the means of henceforth regulating threats to peace.
      (1) Such threats would be dealt with in their initial stages.
      (2) The federation would stand as a unit in backing action.
   b. It is unlikely cause for war would arise within such a federation.
      (1) If constituted on the lines proposed various world problems that give rise to conflict would be taken care of so as to give equitable opportunities and rights to all.
      (2) It would contain means of meeting common problems in a justiciable way.

c. It is unlikely serious threats would come to such a federation from nations outside.
   (1) It would present formidable strength at the outset that other nations would hesitate to challenge.
   (2) It would unite to itself other democratic nations and thus grow in strength and resources.
d. The democracies would be given to the principles that uphold law and order everywhere.

II. The proposed federation would be the most practicable and best means of establishing union among the nations for the purposes of a better world order.
   A. International cooperation by means of other forms of association have usually been found inadequate.
      1. Alliances, wherever tried, have always eventually failed.
      2. Balances of power carry the germs of their own defeat.
         a. They are in a continual state of moral warfare.
         b. They cannot maintain a stable equilibrium.
            (1) They always overbalance one way or the other.
            (2) If equilibrium is attained it takes little to put it out of balance once more.
         c. They may delay wars but seldom prevent them in the end.
      3. Confederations of nations lack the power to effectively promote international ends.
      4. The League of Nations has failed in various respects.
   B. Other forms of international federation would be less adequate for our needs than a federation based on the democracies.
      1. A Western Hemispheric union however valuable in itself, is inadequate to take the place of a wider union such as would be realized under a union of the democracies.
         a. Pan American interests relate more specifically to our regional interests.
         b. In many ways we have stronger ties with Canada and Great Britain than with our southern neighbors.
         c. Our real interests are inter-regional and in many respects co-extensive with world interest.
      2. A European union would be far less successful and desirable than one based on the democracies.
         a. It would have to unite diverse governments, many the reverse of democratic.
         b. England and Ireland would find it difficult to choose between such a continental type of union and their extra-European ties.

c. The chances of a European union succeeding would be small.
   (1) If the totalitarian nations were left out such a union would be virtually a new balance of power and lead to eventual war.
   (2) The inclusion of totalitarian peoples would probably lead to bitter controversies and civil war.
      (a) It would constitute a union of people who had little confidence or trust in each other.
      (b) A large proportion of its people would be people of little or no experience in self government and ill-equipped to run it.

d. If such a union worked effectively it would be greatly to our disadvantage.
   (1) It would be virtually a world union.
      (a) The European nations comprising it would have colonies in various parts of the world.
      (b) With the British commonwealth associated with it, it would be world wide.
   (2) We should find ourselves at its mercy.
      (a) It would give its members tremendous economic and other advantages.
      (b) We should have no influence in shaping its policies and actions.

3. A union of the democracies would be more practicable for establishment at this time than a union projected outright on a plan of world federation.
   a. A world federation is premature under world conditions today.
      (1) There is no possibility of immediately bringing in the extensive and strong Axis nations in any case.
      (2) It is out of question to include for the present captive, neutral or weak nations.
         (a) They lack the freedom to associate with it.
         (b) Until world conditions are more settled their positions would be further jeopardized.
      (3) The formation and groundwork of such a union should be supported only by such nations as can contribute definite strength and stability.

b. Nations not brought in at the outset would be eligible for later admission under probably more advantageous conditions.
(1) By qualifying themselves as to certain minimum but beneficial essentials they would be admissible.
(2) They could unite with a union already working harmoniously and effectively.
c. The ideal of a union of democracies is to promote a union of the world as fast as that would be practicable.

C. A federation of the democracies would be practicable and sound.
1. Wherever union has been tried along democratic lines it has succeeded.
a. The French and English of Canada have succeeded.
b. The French, Italians and Germans of Switzerland have succeeded.
c. The Dutch and English of South Africa have united successfully.
d. Federation underlies our own Constitution and gives in the United States the most important instance of its success.
2. The projected international federation would be largely along the same lines that have proved practicable and sound in the past.
a. It would be strong and elastic.
b. It would provide a unified government for the entire region or nations covered.
c. It would interfere only to a minor extent with the sovereignty of nations.
(1) The international government would be given certain delegated powers and rights.
(2) Except for such delegated power the nations would retain their full sovereign rights.
d. It would rest upon the peoples of the nations rather than on their governments.

III. A new order such as could be realized under a federation of the democracies would bring widespread benefits.
A. Such a union would greatly benefit our country.
1. It would bring us vast economic benefits.
a. It would open up extensive markets and resources for the enhancement of our national economy.
(1) We should have tariff-free access to the markets of the countries constituting it and their colonies.
(2) Their markets would be open to our goods.

b. It would make available a politically safeguarded field of investment.

2. The pooling of defensive equipment would save us billions in naval construction and the building of other military defense.
3. It would give us moral leadership.
4. Such a union would remove danger of a clash should a regional federation develop without us.

B. It would have important political results.

1. It would provide a united front of the world's liberal-minded nations to keep totalitarian doctrines to nations whose people really want them.
2. It would have as an objective the implementation of such intention by economic and military cooperation if called for.

C. Such a federation would contribute fundamentally to a new world order when the peace is won.

1. It would facilitate the problems of reconstruction that will undoubtedly exist at the end of the war.

a. A channel would be provided for effective aid in rehabilitating the nations ravaged by the war.

(1) Public works could be instituted and employment established on a wide international scale.

(2) Communications, highways, railroads, waterways and airways could be restored, coordinated and extended.

(3) In these and other ways the worst effects of post-war depression might be avoided and the best welfare of the nations conserved.

b. It would provide a superior and effective means for removing long-standing economic and other problems between the nations.

(1) Barriers to trade, travel, etc. could doubtless be removed under such an international union.

(2) Racial and other questions would be more readily and more beneficially resolved.

2. It would regulate the problem of colonies and dependencies along new and more acceptable lines.

a. The control of colonies would pass to the federation.

b. Their regulation would be under an enlightened policy that would take full account of their welfare.

(1) If kept under mandate because of backward development they would be subject to regular inspection.

(2) Exploitation and other abuses would be eliminated.
(3) They would be developed for their general welfare and their peoples prepared for eventual self-government.

c. Colonies would become eligible for membership in the federation when ready, just as western states were admitted into the United States.

d. The benefits of such a policy would accrue to the whole world instead of to particular nations.
(1) Economic privileges and tariff and other preferences would be done away with.
(2) Raw materials would be open to all nations on equal terms.

3. It would provide a political framework adequate to promote and protect the principles of freedom and progress.

a. It would be fundamentally constituted to preserve the democratic ways of life.

b. The common responsibility of nations would assure an effective world order.
(1) Under their common effort and protection law and order would be enhanced.
(2) Such responsibility would protect against incipient outbreaks, adjudicate injustices and in other ways preserve sound relations between the nations.

c. It would tend to bring about a world outlook with its enhanced benefits for all.
(1) A habit of world cooperation and of considering problems from an international collective standpoint would come to supplant the nationalistic view.
(2) International planning would be extended as a logical concommitant of such new orientation.
(3) The populations of the world would come to forge more and more strongly the bonds of a common world citizenship and of spiritual brotherhood.

NEGATIVE

I. A plan of international federation of the democracies at this time is not desirable.

A. The time is not propitious for the realization of an international union.

1. Our first need is to avoid international entanglements and preserve the peace in our part of the world.

2. The difficulties of establishing an international union would be many.
    a. Nations are jealous of their sovereignty and would find it difficult to sacrifice any part of it to the common cause.
    b. Conflicting practices, economic, financial and otherwise, would present many problems in bringing about unification.
    c. Entrenched interests in every country would oppose change as detrimental to their interests and prestige.
3. It is doubtful if the United States could be brought to join such a plan.
    a. This country was unwilling to enter a League of Nations with its limited powers or to cooperate with the World Court on an effective basis.
    b. It is doubtful if political opposition would not prevent the still more extensive steps the proposed union would call for.
4. No effective international organization can well be established before peace is won.
    a. The world is in too unstabilized a condition.
    b. We don't know what pattern will predominate in the world when the war ends.

B. It is open to question whether international federation will be essential to the world when peace is attained.
1. If the Axis wins we shall not need to concern ourselves with the peace.
2. Under an Allied peace it will be possible to acceptably adjust most world problems without the proposed organization.
    a. Cooperation on a voluntary basis for rehabilitation and a better world would in any case be widespread.
        (1) Self interest, if nothing else, would dictate that effects of conditions prevailing in other countries and which are felt in our own be removed.
        (2) Common humanity and an awakened world conscience would alike contribute to a more widespread international helpfulness.
    b. Economic planning might well be expected to be taken up on an international scale.
        (1) The war has given a widespread realization of the vital need of regulating economic opportunities and resources on a more equitable plan than nationalistic control provides.

(2) Such international planning can be worked out effectively and with regard to common welfare by means of international commissions or other temporary or more permanent bodies.

c. Under liberal ministries at the end of the war it will doubtless be possible to put over more far-reaching reforms than would be possible at another time.

3. The problems of armed nations without doubt will be more effectively taken care of than in the past.

a. The nations will be too exhausted for a long time to undertake further armament.

b. After the experience of this war governments will be more amenable to making pacts that are really effective and that prevent any return on the part of ambitious nations to militaristic control.

C. A British-United States link on a federation basis would not be advisable at this time.

1. It is not an opportune time to establish a political link of any kind along sound lines.

a. It would be more or less subject to present crucial exigencies instead of to sound, deliberative action.

b. It would to a great extent be experimental.

2. The intrinsic need of such a union for winning the war has been overstressed.

a. Such a federation, if instituted at this time, would almost certainly involve us in the war.

b. We can give as effective or better aid to Britain by staying out.

3. Such a union would react to our political detriment.

a. Any war involvement would expose us to the risk of sacrificing our own democracy.

b. Such a link-up would react more to the political interests of Britain than to ours.

D. A democratic ideology is not the best foundation on which to base an international union.

1. It ignores realistic considerations.

a. It cuts across considerations of geographic and economic unity.

(1) It includes the British dominions in a far-flung, scattered empire.

(2) It ignores Britain's close economic and other relations with Europe.

(3) It ignores our own vital Western Hemispheric ties.

b. It ignores the more realistic requirements of defense.

(1) Defense should more logically be based on a continuous stretch of territory, regional or continental.
(2) Under a democratic union it would be necessary to defend scattered territories and colonies in all parts of the world.

c. A democratic union would tend to sharpen the ideological conflicts of the world.

2. To base the admission of countries on their possession of democratic attributes would be objectionable.
a. Such designation of proposed member nations has been arbitrary and in some cases contrary to fact.
(1) It has been proposed to include nations whose governments have been the reverse of democratic.
(2) The line between democracies and other nations is not clear in all cases.
b. It would give the original member nations of such a union a potential power to change the form of government of other nations which might wish to unite.
c. Britain itself is not really democratic in our sense.
(1) Britain is first of all an empire.
(2) Britain holds the vast Indian empire and its peoples under a control the reverse of democratic.

3. The exclusion of other countries from such a federation raises problems.
a. It would create a new balance of power or alliance.
(1) It would leave outside some 50 nations, including great states like Germany, Russia, Italy, Japan, and the Latin American republics.
(2) It would establish great opposing combinations, democratic and totalitarian.
b. The combination proposed would very likely result in greater wars and conflicts than we have yet known.
(1) The excluded autocracies would eventually attempt to secure by war and conquest their share of the wealth and resources from which such union excludes them.
(2) The democratic union might find it essential to become a dictatorship itself in order to completely unify its strength to meet such a contest.

II. A federation of the democracies is not a practicable and sound form on which to base effective cooperation among the nations.
   A. The analogy between such a federation and the union formed by our thirteen American colonies is misleading.
      1. In the American Union all the original colonies united on equal terms to form it.
         a. There were no exclusions.
         b. There were no attempts to question the internal governments or ideologies of the uniting states.
         c. It was an example of real democracy.
      2. The plan for a democratic union would be defective as to a really democratic basis.
         a. Only a few nations would be taken in in the beginning.
         b. Nations would be expected to have their governments and ideologies scrutinized and possibly modified to conform to concepts acceptable to the others before admission.
         c. Admission would rest on arbitrary decisions and votes of the original nations.
   B. There is no assurance it would be practicable for the realization of far-reaching reforms.
      1. Great Britain and her dominions would probably have preponderant power.
         a. Britain's empire would probably entitle her to the control of more votes than we should have.
         b. If the controlling power for the adoption of any act is in the Senate, as has been proposed, Britain would have the deciding vote.
      2. By joining with imperialistic nations the non-imperialistic democracies would only unite to perpetuate imperialism with its subjection of unwilling peoples.
      3. There is no assurance such a federation would grow into a universal union with world influence for reform.
         a. That other nations would hasten to adopt democratic ways and unite with it is pure assumption.
         b. Its enthusiasms would probably soon wear off and frictions and reactionary forces gain ascendency.
   C. The plan projected would place an immense and illogical burden on the United States.
      1. We should be compelled to transfer a substantial part of our resources to the Union.
         a. Nations would be obligated to transfer to it all non-self governing colonies.
         b. It would call for the pooling of all gold.
      2. It would compel us to assume heavy responsibilities as to other territories and nations.

   a. We should be called upon to contribute to the protection and welfare of all territories held by it.
   b. We should be compelled to assume common defense of all its member nations, however far-flung their empire.

D. From the standpoint of initial limited scale federation it would be preferable to establish regional units for the time being rather than a proposed union of democracies.
   1. Continental and other regional units would be along more natural and more practicable lines.
      a. They would consist of natural and continuous geographic units.
      b. They would comprise areas already having close ties, historical, cultural, social, economic.
      c. Such groupings would be based on the theory that nations should solve the problems of their own regions.
   2. Our Pan American Union represents in the Western Hemisphere an outstanding example of such regional cooperation.
      a. The cooperation and solidarity established by it have been of high value to the Americas.
      b. It has constituted an effective body for mutual action in connection with other nations, particularly in recent critical events.
      c. It has not prevented both the Latin American countries and our own having many interests and contacts outside.
   3. A European federation has been widely proposed as having possibilities of great advantage.
      a. It would answer within its own region all the requirements of a larger grouping.
      b. Such a union would provide solutions to problems that have so long made Europe a field of conflict.
         (1) It would apply its intrinsic understanding and common effort to the permanent solution of such problems as *lebensraum,* race, excessive nationalism and the like.
         (2) Equitable economic cooperation could be attained, at least to the point of limiting customs barriers and providing natural distribution of industries within its area.
      c. Sources of fear and distrust would tend to eliminate themselves.
         (1) A common understanding and spirit would tend to become pervasive.

(2) Balance of power would be abolished.
(a) The inclusion of Germany when she returns to a better standard of morals would eliminate the chief threat to unbalance.
(b) The area would provide a continuous and strong territory for defense.
d. Britain could as readily and advantageously join a European federation as an oceanic one.
(1) She has had in the past many intimate relations with the European countries.
(2) Her leadership would contribute to European unity.
(3) She could, at the same time, be a bridge between regional units of different continents, by reason of her ties of empire.
4. Such regional groupings could cooperate interregionally as called for, and could eventually unite on a world scale.

III. It is wiser that we look to other immediate steps, rather than to a union of democracies, in projecting the attainment of a new world order.
A. Before we aim at taking a substantial part in international affairs we should look to our own more immediate internal social and other problems.
1. Federation must be preceded by a new bill of rights for men.
a. Such a bill to ensure individual freedom, social justice and the greater pervasiveness of economic opportunity is fundamental to any new order.
b. The Bill of Rights proposed by H. G. Wells would meet this need.
2. Until we attain such essential reforms within it is futile to expect to beneficially reform the rest of the world.
B. A framework of international federation, when instituted, would be most wisely established on a world basis.
1. It is logical that such an order should be open to all nations without discrimination.
a. Under technological progress the world has merged into a single region.
b. Problems between nations are analogous and interrelated in their effects on every continent.
2. A world order alone would be free from military and other menace.
a. There could be no excluded nations to unite in military opposition.
b. There could be no resentments keeping alive the divisions of peoples.
(1) Cooperation would be closely established.

(2) Common problems would be mutually resolved.

3. Such an organization would hasten the realization of a common World Brotherhood.

C. A practical world federation could be established on the foundation of machinery already existing.

1. A reconstituted League of Nations could probably take us far toward its realization.

a. The League could be reconstructed in the light of experience gained by twenty years of trial and error.

b. We could ourselves join with it and strengthen it.

(1) Our keeping out has been one important factor of its weakness.

(2) Our moral leadership would give it new life.

2. An international tribunal or the World Court could be made a fully effective part of our international machinery for adjudicating problems not otherwise resolved, if we use our influence to make it so.

D. A world police, with or without other constituted federation of nations, could be made a strong and practicable agency for ensuring lasting peace.

1. Such an international police could be organized on a fully effective basis.

a. It could be established on oceanic islands given over to it, apart from the territories of any nation.

b. All armaments and war equipment could be turned over to it and controlled solely by it.

c. Control of its functions could rest in two wholly independent bodies, each having sole jurisdiction over its particular sphere.

(1) Each would have as members an equal number of representatives from every nation.

(2) All members would be internationalized.

2. Its power to act could be constituted along fully effective lines.

a. It would not be a talking or debating organization.

b. Its one basic function would be to preserve the peace wherever it was threatened in the world.

(1) The freedom of the seas would be preserved.

(2) Aggressions by any nation would be prevented.

(3) Other causes of war would be dealt with.

3. Such an international police could be constituted beyond control or abuse.

a. It could be made financially independent of all nations through automatic assignment of permanent bonds.

b. It could not become a super-militaristic power.

BIBLIOGRAPHY

An asterisk (*) preceding a reference indicates that the article or a part of of it has been reprinted in this book.

BIBLIOGRAPHIES

Carnegie Endowment for International Peace. Library. Collective security. M. Alice Matthews, comp. 6p. mimeo. (Brief reference list no.15) The Endowment. 700 Jackson Pl. Wash. D.C. Ap. 20, '39.

Carnegie Endowment for International Peace. Library. Federalism; select list of references on federal government, regionalism, etc., and notable examples of federations and unions of states. M. Alice Matthews, comp. 11p. mimeo. (Select bibliographies no.8) The Endowment. 700 Jackson Pl. Wash. D.C. Mr. 15, '38.

Carnegie Endowment for International Peace. Library. League of American nations. M. Alice Matthews, comp. 4p. mimeo. (Brief reference list no.11, revised) The Endowment. 700 Jackson Pl. Wash. D.C. O. 31, '38.

Carnegie Endowment for International Peace. Library. New world order; select list of references on regional and world federation; together with some special plans for world order after the war. Helen L. Scanlon, comp. 17p. mimeo. (Select bibliographies no.10) 700 Jackson Pl. Wash. D.C. D. 12, '40.

Introductory bibliography on federalism as applied to international organization. 1p. Campaign for World Government. Room 811, 166 W. Jackson Blvd. Chic. n.d.

Lyons, Jacob G. Union now; [annotated] bibliography on the federal union of nations. 12p. mimeo. Washington Association for Union Now. 1819 G. St. N.W. Wash. D.C. '40.

Pan American Union. Columbus Memorial Library. American league of nations. *In its* Bibliographic series no.21. p. 1-4. mimeo. The Union. Wash. D.C. F. 1, '39.

What world organization do we need? 1p. mimeo. International Affairs Literature Service. League of Nations Society in Canada. 124 Wellington St. Ottawa. '40.

See also notes to other references.

GENERAL REFERENCES

Books and Pamphlets

***American Society of International Law. Proceedings. 1940:104-15. Post-war organization. J. Eugene Harley.**

Barnes, Rosswell P. and others. Alternative to international anarchy; the Christian contribution to political world order. 20p. Federal Council of the Churches of Christ in America. 297 4th Av. N.Y. '38.

Beard, Charles A. Foreign policy for America. 154p. Alfred A. Knopf. N.Y. '40.

Brailsford, Henry Noel. From England to America. 130p. Whittlesey House. N.Y. '40.

Brailsford, Henry Noel. Olives of endless age; being a study of this distracted world and its need of unity. 431p. Harper & Bros. N.Y. '28.

Brown, Francis James; Hodges, Charles; and Roucek, Joseph Slabey, eds. Contemporary world politics; an introduction to the problems of international relations. 718p. John Wiley & Sons. N.Y. '39.

Brunauer, Esther Caukin. Revival of internationalism; a brief study guide. 12p. mimeo. (International Problem of the Month, Vol. 4, no.8) American Association of University Women. 1684 I St. Wash. D.C.

Butler, Nicholas Murray. Family of nations. 400p. Charles Scribner's Sons. N.Y. '38.

*Butler, Nicholas Murray. Toward a federal world. 17p. Division of Intercourse and Education. Carnegie Endowment for International Peace. 405 W. 117th St. N.Y. '39.

Address before the Parrish Art Museum, September 9, 1939. *Same.* Monetary Times. 103:338-40, 370, 396. S. 16-30, '39; Vital Speeches of the Day. 5:714-18. S. 15, '39.

Butler, Nicholas Murray. Why war? essays and addresses on war and peace. 323p. Charles Scribner's Sons. N.Y. '40.

California. University. Committee on International Relations. Problems of war and peace in the society of nations; six lectures. 155p. University of California. Berkeley. '37.

Carr, Albert H. Z. America's last chance. 328p. Thomas Y. Crowell Co. N.Y. '40.

Carr, Edward Hallett. Twenty years' crisis 1919-1939. 313p. Macmillan & Co. Lond. '39.

Prospects of a new international order. p. 287-307.

Chaning-Pearce, M. ed. Federal union; a symposium. 336p. Jonathan Cape. Lond. '40.

Chase, Stuart. New western front. 196p. Harcourt, Brace & Co. N.Y. '39.

Cheng, Seymour Ching-Yuan. Schemes for the federation of the British empire. 313p (Studies in History, Economics and Public Law, no.335) Columbia Univ. Press. N.Y. '31.

*Commission to Study the Organization of Peace. Preliminary report. 14p. The Commission. 8 W. 40th St. N.Y. N. '40.

Commission to Study the Organization of Peace. Study of the organization of peace, based on the Preliminary report. 32p. The Commission. 8 W. 40th St. N.Y. N. '40.

Curtis, Lionel. World order (Civitas Dei). 985p. Oxford Univ. Press. N.Y. '39.
Davies, David Davies. Problem of the twentieth century; a study in international relationships. 819p. Ernest Benn. Lond. '34.
Dulles, John Foster. United States and the world of nations. 16p. Federal Council of the Churches of Christ in America. 297 4th Av. N.Y. F. 27, '40.
Federalist; a commentary on the constitution of the United States. 618p. Modern Library. N.Y. '41.
Frank, Jerome. Save America first; how to make democracy work. 432p. Harper & Bros. N.Y. '38.
Fry, Varian. Bricks without mortar, the story of international cooperation. 96p. (Headline books no.16) Foreign Policy Assn. 8 W. 40th St. N.Y. '38.
Garnett, Maxwell. Inter-state and federal union. *In his* Lasting peace. p. 188-200. George Allen & Unwin. Lond. '40.
Gelber, Lionel and Gooch, Robert K. War for power and power for freedom. 32p. Farrar & Rinehart. N.Y. '40.
Greaves, H. R. G. Federal union in practice. 135p. George Allen & Unwin. Lond. '34.
Hill, Helen and Agar, Herbert. Beyond German victory. 117p. Reynal & Hitchcock. N.Y. '40.
Howard, Graeme K. America and a new world order. 121p. Charles Scribner's Sons. N.Y. '40.
Howe, William Stuart. Prospects for world unity. 256p. Four Seas Co. Bost. '26.
Hughan, Jessie Wallace. Study of international government. 401p. Thomas Y. Crowell Co. N.Y. '23.
Institute of World Affairs. Proceedings. 15:183-7. '37. European riddle, competing alliances or collective security. Everett Dean Martin.
Kant, Immanuel. Perpetual peace. 67p. Columbia Univ. Press. N.Y. '39.
Karve, D. G. Federations; a study in comparative politics. 318p. Oxford Univ. Press. Lond. '32.
Knox, Frank; Laves, Walter and Spencer, William. After the next armistice—what? radio discussion. p. 1-24. (Round Table. No.87) Univ. of Chicago. Chic. N. 12, '39.
Laves, Walter H. C. ed. Foundations of a more stable world order. 193p. Univ. of Chic. Press. Chic. '41.
Madariaga, Salvador de. Theory and practice in international relations. 105p. University of Pennsylvania Press. Phila. '37.
Maddox, William P. European plans for world order. 44p. (James-Patten-Rowe pamphlet series no.8) American Academy of Political and Social Science. Phila. '40.
Markham, R. H. Future prospects of democracy: here and abroad. 10p. mimeo. Institute of Public Affairs. University of Virginia. Charlottesville. Je. 19, '40.

Marriott, John A. R. Commonwealth or anarchy? a survey of projects of peace from the sixteenth to the twentieth century. 227p. Columbia Univ. Press. N.Y. '39.

Meade, J. E. Basis of a durable peace. 192p. Oxford Univ. Press. N.Y. '40.

Middlebush, Frederick A. and Hill, Chesney. Elements of international relations. 498p. McGraw-Hill Book Co. N.Y. '40.

Mitrany, David. Progress of international government. 176p. Yale Univ. Press. New Haven. '33.

National Policy Committee. Special Committee. Memorandum of the Special Committee on steps toward a durable peace. 28p. The Committee. Wash. D.C. '40.

New Larned history for ready reference, reading and research. Vol. 4, p. 3064-9. Federal government, federations. C. A. Nichols. Springfield, Mass. '23.

Newfang, Oscar. United States of the world; a comparison between the League of Nations and the United States of America. 284p. G. P. Putnam's Sons. N.Y. '30.

Patterson, Ernest Minor. Economic bases of peace. 264p. Whittlesey House. N.Y. '39.

Phelps, Edith M. ed. Basis of a lasting peace. *In her* University debaters' annual, 1939-40. Vol. 26. p. 11-50. H. W. Wilson Co. N.Y. '40.
Bibliography. p. 42-50.

Rappard, William E. Quest for peace since the world war. 516p. Harvard Univ. Press. Cambridge. '40.

Rauschning, Hermann. Redemption of democracy; the coming Atlantic empire. 243p. Alliance Book Corp. N.Y. '41.

Remington, Woodburn Edwin. World states of the machine age. 279p. Gilbert Ptg. Co. Columbus, Ga. '32.

Schuman, Frederick L. Future of the western state system. *In his* International politics. p. 722-47. McGraw-Hill Book Co. N.Y. '37.

Schuman, Frederick L. Night over Europe; the diplomacy of nemesis, 1939-1940. 600,i-xix p. Alfred A. Knopf. N.Y. '41.

Scott, James Brown. James Madison's notes of debate in the federal convention of 1787 and their relation to a more perfect society of nations. 149p. Oxford Univ. Press. N.Y. '18.

Scott, James Brown. United States of America: a study in international organization. 605p. Oxford Univ. Press. N.Y. '20.

Sharp, Walter R. and Kirk, Grayson. Organization of peace. *In their* Contemporary international politics. p. 749-76. Farrar & Rinehart. N.Y. '40.

Shotwell, James T. On the rim of the abyss. 400p. Macmillan Co. N.Y. '36.

Steed, Wickham. Our war aims. 215p. Secker & Warburg. Lond. '39.

Steiner, H. Arthur. Principles and problems of international relations. 835p. Harper & Bros. N.Y. '40.

Strausz-Hupé, Robert. Axis America; Hitler plans our future. 274p. G. P. Putnam's Sons. N.Y. '41.
Tracy, M. E. New world challenge to imperialism. 395p. Coward-McCann. N.Y. '40.
Vinacke, Harold M. International organization. 483p. F. S. Crofts & Co. N.Y. '34.
Warburg, James P. Peace in our time? 76p. Harper & Bros. N.Y. '40.
Woolf, Leonard Sidney. International government. 388p. George Allen and Unwin. Lond. '29(?).

PERIODICALS

*American Journal of International Law. 24:738-42. O. '30. American background to Briand's vision of a united Europe. James Brown Scott.
American Journal of International Law. 35:114-17. Ja. '41. Organization of peace; report of the Commission to Study the Organization of Peace. Arthur K. Kuhn.
American Political Science Review. 12:215-40. My. '18. Background of American federalism. Andrew C. McLaughlin.
Annals of the American Academy. 174:15-21. Jl. '34. Is nationalism opposed to internationalism? George Paish.
Annals of the American Academy. 198:9-14. Jl. '38. Power economy versus welfare economy. Eugene Staley.
Annals of the American Academy. 210:1-144. Jl. '40. When war ends; a consideration of the conditions necessary to bring about a lasting peace. ed. by Thorsten Sellin.
*Page, Ralph W. Designs for a world order. p. 50-6.
Aryan Path. 11:180-4. Ap. '40. Future of the League; Asiatic liberations. Norman Angell.
Asia. 40:291-4. Je. '40. Formula of federation. Felix Morley.
Same. Congressional Record. 86:(current) 10290-2. My. 23, '40. *Discussion.* Asia. 40:294-5. Je.; 392. Jl. '40. Harry D. Gideonse; Stephen Duggan; Payson J. Treat; Quincy Wright.
Atlantic Monthly. 166:189-94. Ag. '40. We tried to enforce peace. A. Lawrence Lowell.
British Industries. 23:209-16. Ag. '39. New world order.
Christian Century. 58:214-18, 248-50, 278-81, 311-13, 351-4. F. 12-Mr. 12, '41. Search for a lasting peace.
Christian Science Monitor. p. 18. F. 10, '40. Federation for two worlds; editorial.
Commonweal. 31:236-9. Ja. 5, '40. Civilization and sovereignty; this war points to the need for a new international organization. E. I. Watkin.
Commonweal. 31:335-6. F. 9, '40. Federation or else.
Congressional Record. 87:(current) A57-8. Ja. 9, '41. International anarchy or an ordered world society. Elbert D. Thomas.
Contemporary Review. 156:160-7. Ag. '39. Rebuilding world order. Maxwell Garnett.

Contemporary Review. 157:385-92. Ap. '40. After the war. Meston.
Contemporary Review. 157:513-24. My. '40. Federalism: a hook for leviathan. George Young.
Contemporary Review. 158:537-43. N. '40. Nationalism and Europe. Reinhold Aris.
Contemporary Review. 159:1-10. Ja. '41. Principles of economic federation. George Young.
Contemporary Review. 159:128-37. F. '41. Procedures of economic federation. George Young.
Edinburgh Review. 226:1-27. Jl. '17. National federations and world federation. Walter Alison Phillips.
Fabian Quarterly. no.26:10-17. Summer '40. Socialism and federation. Barbara Wootton; D. N. Pritt.
Fortnightly. 153 (n.s.147):117-26, 256-65. F.-Mr. '40. Beyond the war. H. A. L. Fisher.
Fortnightly. 153 (n.s.147):453-61. My. '40. Principles of reconstruction. Archbishop of York.
Fortnightly. 154 (n.s.148):541-7. D. '40. National sovereignty and industry: a step towards the new order in Europe. Balbus, pseud.
Fortune. 20:42-3. D. '39. War and peace; U.S. must now choose among retreat, isolation, and international leadership.
Future: the Magazine for Young Men. 3:19-20. O. '40. Defense against war. Milton Lomask.
Harper's Magazine. 180:297-304. F. '40. Struggle for peace. C. Hartley Grattan.
Hibbert Journal. 15:199-203. Ja. '17. Is international government possible? J. A. Hobson.
Independent Woman. 20:3-4+. Ja. '41. How build lasting peace? Clyde Eagleton.
International Conciliation. 325:589-621. D. '36. Alexander Hamilton and the reform of the League. L. P. Jacks.
Life. 10:61-5. F. 17, '41. American century. Henry R. Luce.
New Commonweal Quarterly; a review devoted to research into problems of a new world order. New Commonwealth Institute of World Affairs. Lond.
New Commonwealth Quarterly. 5:131-49. S. '39. Economic conditions of inter-state federalism. F. A. von Hayek.
New Commonwealth Quarterly. 5:150-6. S. '39. Economic problems of federal union. Barbara Wootton.
*New Republic. 102:176-7. F. 5, '40. Paradox of sovereignty. W. B. Curry.
New Statesman and Nation. 20:154-5. Ag. 17, '40. Open letter to H. G. Wells. C. E. M. Joad.
Reply. H. G. Wells. New Statesman and Nation. 20:180. Ag. 24, '40.
New York Times. p. 42. Mr. 16, '41. Aid to the democracies; radio address. Franklin D. Roosevelt.
*New York Times. Sec. 4. p. 8, 9. F. 2, '41. Axis defeat first but not ultimate road to peace. James P. Warburg.

Newsweek. 15:22-3. F. 12, '40. Pax Britannica; union, dismembered groups talk terms if, as, and when.
Oriental Economist. 7:146-8. Mr. '40. Regional world new orders.
Political Science Quarterly. 34:79-103. Mr. '19. Difficulties of world organization. Frederick F. Blachly and Miriam E. Oatman.
Quarterly Review. 274:325-43. Ap. '40. Nationalism and federalism. J. A. R. Marriott.
Science. 91:151-8. F. 16, '40. Science, war and reconstruction. Julian Sorell Huxley.
Science News Letter. 38:54-5. Jl. 27, '40. Conflict can be eliminated in community of nations. George M. Stratton.
Social Studies. 25:434-41. D. '34. Development of imperial federation. Constance Field Stecher.
Spectator (London). 165:492-3. N. 15, '40. New orders.
Survey Graphic. 29:599-601. D. '40. World is being born. Ernest Jäckh.
Time. 34:27. N. 20, '39. No paper plan.
Town Meeting (Bulletin of America's Town Meeting of the Air). 6:3-25. D. 2, '40. What kind of world order do we want? H. G. Wells, Hu Shih, Ray Lyman Wilbur and John T. Flynn.
Unpopular Review. 6:1-15. Jl. '16. Spread of federalization.
Vital Speeches of the Day. 6:197-201. Ja. 15, '40. Matters of common interest; British government is not trying to drag you into the war. Marquess of Lothian.
Vital Speeches of the Day. 6:208-9. Ja. 15, '40. Towards a new world order. P. J. Noel Baker.
Vital Speeches of the Day. 6:702-4. S. 1, '40. Education for world unity. Hans Kohn.
World Affairs. 103:138-41. S.'40. World constitution.
World Affairs. 103:216-18. D. '40. Early suggestion of union between Britain and America. Charles F. Mullett.
World Affairs. 104:18-21. Mr. '41. Planning for peace. Philip Marshall Brown.
*World Affairs Interpreter. 11:287-95. O. '40. World organization. E. Guy Talbott.
World Order. 5:263-72. O. '39. Concept of federation. Sirdar D. K. Sen.
World Unity. 4:50-64. Ap. '29. World citizenship. Carl A. Ross.
World Unity. 5:231-44, 299-310, 387-98; 6:31-42, 90-103, 171-82, 257-68, 318-33, 390-404. Ja.-S. '30. World community. John Herman Randall.
World Unity. 8:369-84. S. '31. Institutions and processes for the advancement of international peace: an evaluation. Charles E. Martin.
World Unity. 11:163-5. D. '32. World federation. Oscar Newfang.
Discussion. World Unity. 11:345-50, 419-28; 12:41-8. F.-Ap. '33.
World Unity. 14:193-8, 259-78. Jl.-Ag. '34. World unity questionnaire on peace. Horace Holley.

FEDERATION OF DEMOCRACIES

References more particularly for or against a plan of Federal Union are marked (F) or (A).

Books and Pamphlets

*Basic facts on union of free peoples. 12p. Congress of American Professions. 829 Provident Bank Bldg. Cincinnati, O.; and American Council of Public Affairs. 1734 Eye St. Wash. D.C. '40.

Beveridge, William. Peace by federation? 35p. (Federal tracts no.1) Federal Union. 44 Gordon Sq. Lond. W.C. 1, Eng. '40. (F)

Beveridge, William. Peace by federation. *In* Deeper causes of the war and its issues. p. 156-206. George Allen & Unwin. Lond. '40. (F)

Boothe, Clare and Streit, Clarence K. Beginning or the end for world democracy? 4p. Federal Union, Inc. 10 E. 40th St. N.Y. '40. (F)

Brailsford, H. N. Federal idea. 16p. Federal Union. 44 Gordon Sq. Lond. W.C. 1, Eng. n.d. (F)

Breckinridge, Mary. Frontier nurse speaks out. 6p. Federal Union, Inc. 10 E. 40th St. N.Y. '40. (F)

Brunauer, Esther Caukin. Building the new world order. 44p. (International relations series) American Association of University Women. 1634 I St. N.W. Wash. D.C. D. '39.

Curry, W. B. Case for federal union. 213p. Penquin Books. N.Y. '39. (F)

Davies, A. Powell. New plan to end war. 7p. The Author. Community Church of Summit, N.J. Mr. 12, '39. (F)

Griessemer, Tom. System of Hitler, Stalin or Streit, which is America's choice? 14p. New York Committee of Federal Union, Inc. 10 E 40th St. N.Y. '40. (F)

Humphreys, John H. Problems of federal union: I. elections; II. government. (8p.) Proportional Representation Society. 82 Victoria St. Lond. S.W. 1, Eng. '40.
Reprint from Federal Union News.

Institute of World Affairs. Proceedings. 17:223-7. '39. Constructive forces in the present world situation. Chester H. Rowell.

Jennings, W. Ivor. Federation for western Europe. 208p. Macmillan Co. N.Y. '40. (F)

Kennedy, Sinclair. Pan-Angles; a consideration of the federation of the seven English-speaking nations. 244p. Longmans, Green & Co. N.Y. '15.

Law, Richard. Federal union and the League of Nations. 4p. Federal Union. 44 Gordon Sq. Lond. W.C. 1. n.d.

Let's not make the same mistake twice. 19p. Federal Union, Inc. 10 E. 40th St. N.Y. n.d. (F)

Lothian, Philip Henry Kerr. Ending of Armageddon. 18p. Federal Union. 44 Gordon Sq. Lond. W.C. 1, Eng. n.d. (F)

Maddox, William P. Federal union of the democracies. *In his* European plans for world order. p. 31-3. American Academy of Political and Social Science. Phila. '40.

Munroe, David Hoadley. Hang together; the Union now primer. 98p. Union Press. 10 E. 40th St. N.Y. '40. (F)

Nash, Vernon. It must be done again; thirteen American states point the way for the nations now. 45p. Federal Union, Inc. 10 E. 40th St. N.Y. '40. (F)

Nichols, Egbert Ray, ed. Alliance of the democracies of the world. *In his* Intercollegiate debates. Vol. 20. p. 125-62. Noble & Noble. N.Y. '39.
Bibliography. p. 158-62.

Nichols, Egbert Ray, ed. Alliance with Great Britain. *In his* Intercollegiate debates. Vol. 19. p. 1-48. Noble & Noble. N.Y. '38.
Bibliography. p. 45-8.

Nichols, Egbert Ray, ed. International federal union of the democracies. *In his* Intercollegiate debates. Vol. 21. p. 157-92. Noble & Noble. N.Y. '40.
Bibliography. p. 192.

O'Malley, Raymond. Peace and prosperity for the asking. 8p. Federal Union, Midland Branch. 89 Macdonald St. Birmingham, Eng. n.d. (F)

Phelps, Edith M. ed. Anglo-American mutual assistance pact. *In her* University debaters' annual, 1937-1938. Vol. 24. p. 105-48. H. W. Wilson Co. N.Y. '38.
Bibliography. p. 142-8.

Phelps, Edith M. ed. Anglo-American alliance. *In her* University debaters' annual, 1938-1939. Vol. 25. p. 65-109. H. W. Wilson Co. N.Y. '39.
Bibliography. p. 101-9.

Pritt, D. N. Federal illusion? 152p. Frederick Muller, Ltd. Lond. '40. (A)

Ross, Carl A. Union now and peace now. 16p. The Author. 1310 U.S. 12 East. Albion, Mich. (F)
Bibliography. p. 15-16.

Saerchinger, Cesar. Can Britain and France unite? radio address. 12p. mimeo. (Story Behind the Headlines no.26) Ap. 19, '40.

Schwimmer, Rosika. Union now for peace or war? the danger in the plan of Clarence Streit. 19p. The Author. 105 W. 73d St. N.Y. Ag. '39. (A)

Sternberg, Fritz. Fivefold aid to Britain, to save her and keep us out of war. 76p. John Day Co. N.Y. '41.

Stewart, Marguerite Ann. Pros and cons of a federation of nations. 10p. mimeo. Foreign Policy Association. 8 W. 40th St. N.Y. '39.

Streit, Clarence K. Constructive proposal: a federal union now of democracies. 21p. mimeo. Institute of Public Affairs. Univ. of Virginia. Charlottesville. Ja. 10, '39. (F)

Streit, Clarence K. Essence of union now. 86p. Union Press. 10 E. 40th St. N.Y. '40. (F)

Selections from chapters 1, 9 and 12, Annex 1, and the "Last Word" of the author's *Union Now.*

Streit, Clarence K. For union now. 34p. Inter-Democracy Federal Unionists. 445 W. 23d St. N.Y. '38. (F)

Reprint of Chapter I of *Union Now,* together with an added preface.

Streit, Clarence K. Need for union now. 90p. Union Press. 10 E. 40th St. N.Y. '40. (F)

Includes chapters 2, 3, 12, Annex 5, and parts of chapters 1 and 4 of the author's *Union Now.*

Streit, Clarence K. Of freedom and union now. 35p. Federal Union, Inc. Union House. 10 E. 40th St. N.Y. '41. (F)

Reprint of Chapter 13 of the author's *Union Now.*

Streit, Clarence K. Union now; a proposal for a federal union of the democracies of the north Atlantic. 315p. Harper & Bros. N.Y. '39. (F)

**Also shorter version.* 256p. Harper & Bros. N.Y. '40.

Streit, Clarence K. Union now with Britain. 234p. Harper & Bros. N.Y. '41. (F)

Streit, Clarence K. World government or anarchy? our urgent need for world order. 57p. World Citizens Assn. 86 E. Randolph St. Chic. '39. (F)

Reprint, with an added preface, of chapters 2 and 3 of the author's *Union Now.*

Streit, Clarence K. and Sherwood, Robert E. Half-way measures won't keep Hitler out. 4p. Federal Union, Inc. 10 E. 40th St. N.Y. '40. (F)

Summers, H. B. comp. Anglo-American agreement. 374p. (Reference Shelf. Vol. 12, no.1) H.W. Wilson Co. N.Y. S. '38.

10 facts about the proposal to unite 15 democracies in a federal union. 6p. Inter-Democracy Federal Unionists. 445 W. 23d St. N.Y. n.d. (F)

Walch, J. Weston. Complete handbook on an Anglo-American alliance. 154p. Platform News Pub. Co. Portland, Me. '38.

Bibliography. p. 24-30.

Wells, Herbert G. Fate of man. 263p. Alliance Book Corp. N.Y. '39. (A)

Wells, H. G. New world order. 145p. Alfred A. Knopf. N.Y. '40. (F)

PERIODICALS

American Forum of the Air. 2, no.61:1-14. D. 1, '40. Shall the United States form a union with Great Britain and her commonwealths. Clarence K. Streit, John B. Trevor, John F. O'Ryan, Quincy Howe.

Annals of the American Academy. 204:93-101. Jl. '39. Atlantic union plan and the Americas. Clarence K. Streit.

Asia. 40:63-6. F. '40. World must federate! Hans Kohn. (F)

Discussion. Asia. 40:126-8, 172. Mr.-Ap. '40.

Asia. 41:7-16. Ja. '41. Things that could happen; if America enters the war? if America stays out? Edgar Snow.
Association of American Colleges. Bulletin. 26:15-19. Mr. '40. Union now. Clarence K. Streit. (F)
Atlantic Monthly. 165:445-8. Ap. '40. Program for peace. Paul Reynaud.
Atlantic Monthly. 166:531-9. N. '40. For mutual advantage. Clarence K. Streit. (F)
Also separate. 11p. Federal Union, Inc. Union House. 10 E. 40th St. N.Y.
Catholic World. 151:452-8. Jl. '40. Commonwealth of mankind. Henry Somerville. (A)
Chinese Social and Political Science Review. 23:463-72. Ja.-Mr. '40. Can there be a war to end war? Leyton Edwards.
Christian Century. 56:574. My. 3, '39. Union now, by C. K. Streit; review. Ernest H. Wilkins. (F)
Christian Century. 56:1494-6. D. 6, '39. Federated Europe?
Christian Century. 57:506-8. Ap. 17, '40. Case for federal union. Vernon Nash. (F)
Christian Science Monitor. p.18. Mr. 15, '41. Pacific federation; Australia and New Zealand. Guy Natusch.
Christian Science Monitor Weekly Magazine Section. p. 1-2+. N. 10, '37. Anglo-American front? D. Graham Hutton; Raymond Leslie Buell.
Christian Science Monitor Weekly Magazine Section. p. 7. My. 6, '39. United States of the world; review of Union now, by C. K. Streit. Marquis of Lothian. (F)
Christian Science Monitor Weekly Magazine Section. p. 2. F. 17, '40. Federalism for peace. Oscar Jászi. (F)
*Christian Science Monitor Weekly Magazine Section. p. 7+. O. 12, '40. English-speaking union. Mallory Browne. (F)
Churchman. 155:12-13. F. 1, '41. Plan for federal union. Betty Gram Swing. (F)
Collier's. 105:74. My. 11, '40. What is this Union now? editorial.
Collier's. 106:82. D. 14, '40. Question for Americans: union now. (F)
Congressional Digest. 17:193-229. Ag. '38. Should the U.S. establish an alliance with Great Britain? with pro and con discussion.
Congressional Record. 87:A1601. Mr. 31, '41. Union with Britain? editorial from New York Daily News. (A)
Contemporary Review. 158:267-74. S. '40. America and the British cause. R. B. Mowat.
Contemporary Review. 158:459-63. O. '40. America and the western bases. George Glasgow.
Contemporary Review. 158:609-15. D. '40. Free trade versus federal union. George Peel.
Contemporary Review. 159:121-7. F. '41. America and the war. Josiah C. Wedgwood. (F)

Current History. 51:16-18. Mr. '40. Ten points for world peace; declaration of the rights of man should be the foundation of any post-war world. H. G. Wells. (A)

Current History and Forum. 52:14-17. O. 22, '40. Should the United States unite with the British empire now? Clarence K. Streit. (F)

Current History and Forum. 52:25-7+. Mr. '41. To save Latin America; Union now of English-speaking nations would keep the Latin countries out of the Nazi orbit. Michael Scully. (F)

Current History and Forum. 52:47-8. Mr. '41. Union now. (F)

Editorial Research Reports. p. 359-74. N. 16, '39. Federal union and world peace. Buel W. Patch.

English-Speaking World. 21:259-61. Je. '39. Federal union. Wickham Steed. (F)

Federal Union World; formerly Union Now Bulletin. Published monthly by Federal Union, Inc. Union House. 10 E. 40th St. N.Y. (F)

Federal Union World. 2:2+. N. '40. Union should be a main war aim. André Maurois. (F)

*Federal Union World. 3:1+. Ja. '41. This challenge to world democracy. Lewis Mumford. (F)

*Federal Union World. 3:1+. Mr. '41. Can any nation long endure alone? Dorothy Thompson. (F)

Food for Thought. no. 11:3-12. Ja. '41. Federal union—panacea or delusion? R. S. Lambert.

Foreign Affairs. 15:587-94. Jl. '37. Roughhew them how we will. Walter Lippmann.

Fortnightly. 151 (n.s.145):419-28. Ap. '39. British commonwealth and world order. Alfred Zimmern. (F)

Fortnightly. 152 (n.s.146):416-22. O. '39. Federal government. Patrick Ransome. (F)

Fortnightly. 152 (n.s.146):473-96, 585-614; 153 (n.s.147):34-54, 187-210. N. '39-F. '40. New world order. Herbert G. Wells.

Fortnightly. 152 (n.s.146):628-37. D. '39. In search of assured peace. Duchess of Atholl.
Same. Living Age. 357:524-30. F. '40.

Fortnightly. 153 (n.s.147):573-82. Je. '40. Illusion of the democracies. H. Noel Fieldhouse. (A)

Fortune. 19:66-7. Ap. '39. Business-and-government; Clarence Streit's vision; a gargantuan democracy of 280,000,000 people, a vast economic opportunity. (F)
Same abridged. Reader's Digest. 34:99-101. Je. '39. *Also separate.* 2p. Inter-Democracy Federal Unionists. 445 W. 23d St. N.Y.

Fortune. 22:50-4+. D. '40. U.S. foreign policy: short of war; asset and liability items in any alliance with Britain.

Forum and Century. 101:289-90. Je. '39. Union now. Henry Goddard Leach. (F)

Forum and Century. 102:28-30. Jl. '39. Shall we have union now? a debate. Clarence K. Streit. (F)
Forum and Century. 102:31-2. Jl. '39. Shall we have union now? a debate. Quincy Howe. (A)
Hibbert Journal. 38:13-23. O. '39. Federation of the free. M. Chaning-Pearce. (F)
Independent Woman. 18:378-80. D. '39. Amid war, we plan for peace on earth. Mildred Adams.
International Conciliation. 368:182-4. Mr. '41. Text of Prime Minister Winston Churchill's address to the Pilgrims, January 9, 1941.
Labour Monthly (London). 22:41-7. Ja. '40. Meaning of federal union. Richard Goodman.
*Life. 9:98-102. O. 7, '40. Plan for union; America's future lies in union of the English-speaking peoples. Robert E. Sherwood. (F)
Same abridged. Reader's Digest. 37:92-5. D. '40; *Discussion.* Life. 9:2+. O. 28, '40.
Living Age. 357:252-4. N. '39. Design for peace. Norman Angell. (F)
Living Age. 357:318-23. D. '39. Union now or never. Clarence K. Streit. (F)
Living Age. 359:102-4. O. '40. Is union possible? formal union of the United States and the British Empire.
Living Age. 359:501-2. F. '41. World over; possible effect on the war's outcome that might result from an immediate confederation. (F)
Nation. 149:711. D. 23, '39. Collective security must come. Oswald Garrison Villard.
Nation. 151:651-4. D. 28, '40. Between two worlds. Harold Nicolson. (F)
Nation. 152:229-30. Mr. 1, '41. Luce thinking; Luce-Thompson brand of imperialism. Freda Kirchwey.
Nation. 152:353-6. Mr. 22, '41. Economy for a new world. Keith Hutchison.
New Commonwealth Quarterly. 5:119-30. S. '39. League of nations and federal union. Clyde Eagleton. (A)
New Commonwealth Quarterly. 5:157-69. S. '39. Union now? summary of debate. Wickham Steed, Horsfall Carter and others.
*New Europe. 1:3-4. D. 1, '40. Meaning of democracy. Robert Morrison MacIver.
New Republic. 98:225. Mr. 29, '39. Union now, by C. K. Streit; review. John Chamberlain.
New Republic. 103:857-61. D. 23, '40. Alternative to fascism; proposal for American-British cooperation.
Reply. New Republic. 104:211-12. F. 17, '41. Union with Britain. Henry Smith Leiper.
New Statesman and Nation. 20:208. Ag. 31, '40. Mr. Wells and the future. C. E. M. Joad. (F)

New York Herald Tribune. p. 11. Jl. 18, '40. Defense now needs union now; a proposal that the U.S.A. and the six British democracies form a federal union before it is too late. (F)
New York Times. Sec.4. p. 9. F. 23, '41. Alliance for peace. Lloyd M. Crosgrave. (F)
New York Times Book Review. p. 14. Mr. 16, '41. Proposing union with Britain; review of Union now with Britain, by C. K. Streit. C. Hartley Grattan.
Rotarian. 55:14+. Ag. '39. Is the Union now plan practical? Yes! Clarence K. Streit. (F)
Rotarian. 55:15+. Ag. '39. Is the Union now plan practical? No! George H. Cless, Jr. (A)
Rotarian. 57:13-14. O. '40. Union now? Yes. Clarence K. Streit. (F)
*Rotarian. 57:14-15+. O. '40. Union now? No. Bennett Champ Clark. (A)
Round Table. 29:476-88. Je. '39. Union now.
*Round Table. 29:733-44. S. '39. Union: oceanic or continental.
Saturday Evening Post. 213:24. Mr. 8, '41. Bitter question.
Saturday Review of Literature. 21:12-14. F. 10, '40. Book and an idea; case history of Union now. George Catlin.
Scholastic. 33:29-30+. S. 17, '38. Hands across the sea; debate. Charles F. Hunter.
Scholastic. 35:29-30+. N. 6, '39. Federal union: for peace with freedom. David Hoadley Munroe. (F)
Science News Letter. 39:7. Ja. 4, '41. Counter-plan for small nations, urgent need of democracies.
Scribner's Commentator. 9:19-22. Mr. '41. Union now, for what? Howard M. Yates. (A)
Spectator (London). 162:412. Mr. 10, '39. Union now, by C. K. Streit; review. Wilson Harris. (A)
Time. 36:14. Jl. 22, '40. Union now; U.S. and the six British democracies.
Time. 37:15-16. Mr. 17, '41. Case for union.
Town Meeting (Bulletin of America's Town Meeting of the Air). 4:1-38. Mr. 13, '39. Would a union of democracies save world peace? Clarence K. Streit, Dorothy Detzer, Wickham Steed, George E. Sokolsky.
Town Meeting (Bulletin of America's Town Meeting of the Air). 5:3-34. D. 4, '39. What kind of peace can Europe make? Maurice Hindus, Friedrich Aughagen, Linda Littlejohn and John Gunther.
Town Meeting (Bulletin of America's Town Meeting of the Air). 6:3-31. F. 17, '41. Should the English-speaking democracies unite now? Dorothy Thompson; John A. Danaher.
Vital Speeches of the Day. 7:313-14. Mr. 1, '41. Rebirth of democracy; growing unification of the English speaking world. Thomas Mann. (F)

REGIONAL FEDERATION

EUROPE

BOOKS AND PAMPHLETS

Bingham, Alfred M. United States of Europe. 336p. Duell, Sloan and Pearce. N.Y. '40.
Selected bibliography. p. 325-6.

Borowik, Joseph A.; Hodges, Charles and Roucek, Joseph S. Baltic region. *In* Brown, F. J.; Hodges, C.; and Roucek, J. S., eds. Contemporary world politics. p. 298-325. John Wiley & Sons. N.Y. '39.

Coudenhove-Kalergi, Richard N. Europe must unite. 160p. Secker & Warburg. Lond. '40.

Coudenhove-Kalergi, Richard N. Pan-Europe. 215p. Alfred A. Knopf. N.Y. '26.

Czernin, Ferdinand. United States of Europe, a utopian dream? 15p. mimeo. Institute of Public Affairs. University of Virginia. Charlottesville. Je. 22, '40.

Davies, David Davies. Federated Europe. 141p. Victor Gollancz. Lond. '40.

Felix, Archduke of Hapsburg. First steps toward peace in Europe. 15p. University of Pennsylvania Press. Phila. '40.

Foerster, F. W. Europe and the German question. p. 428-34. Sheed & Ward. N.Y. '40.

Grotius Society. Transactions. Problems of War and peace. Vol. 25. p. 1-31. Commonwealth of European states. W. R. Bisschop. Sweet & Maxwell. Lond. '39.

Herriot, Edouard. United States of Europe. tr. by R. J. Dingle. 330p. Viking Press. N.Y. '30.

Hutchinson, Paul. United States of Europe. 225p. Willett, Clark & Colby. Chic. '29.

Institute of World Affairs. Proceedings. 16:250-6. '38. Idea of a United States of Europe. W. Ivor Jennings.

Institute of World Affairs. Proceedings. 17:135-42. '39. New Central Europe. Vlastimil Kybal.

Mackay, R. W. G. Federal Europe; being the case for European federation together with a draft constitution of the United States of Europe. 323p. Michael Joseph. Lond. '40.

Maddox, William P. Federal union of European states. *In his* European plans for world order; Regional federations within Europe. p. 34-44. American Academy of Political and Social Science. Phila. '40.

Middle States Association of History and Social Science Teachers. Proceedings, 1939. p. 8-18. Europe—which way to peace? John C. de Wilde.

Roucek, Joseph Slabey. Danubian and Balkan Europe. *In* Brown, F. J.; Hodges, C.; and Roucek, J. S., eds. Contemporary world politics. p. 326-55. John Wiley & Sons. N.Y. '39.
Salter, Arthur. United States of Europe and other papers. 302p. George Allen & Unwin. Lond. '33.
Stern-Rubarth, Edgar. Exit Prussia; a plan for Europe. 220p. Duckworth. Lond. '40.
Union University. Schenectady. Union College. Faculty papers of Union College. Vol. 2. p. 96-102. United States of Europe. W. Leon Godshall. My. '31.

PERIODICALS

*American Mercury. 50:276-84. Jl. '40. End of small nations; great empires or a federated Europe. H. N. Brailsford.
American Mercury. 50:391-400. Ag. '40. Hitler's blueprint for a slave world. Eugene Lyons.
Annals of the American Academy. 149:150-6. My. '30. Economic foundations of Pan-Europeanism. Harry D. Gideonse.
Asia. 40:269-71. My. '40. Toward world federation; need for a planned economic structure. Fritz Sternberg.
Canadian Forum. 19:274-5. D. '39. Union now? Frank H. Underhill.
Central European Observer. 17:176-7. N. 1, '40. Possibilities of Central European federation. Hubert Ripka.
Chinese Social and Political Science Review. 15:229-64. Jl. '31. United States of Europe. K. M. Tsu.
Christian Century. 57:103-5. Ja. 24, '40. America and a federal Europe.
Christian Century. 57:379-81. Mr. 20, '40. Hapsburg Trojan horse; Archduke Felix advocates democratic federation of the Danubian states, Austria, Czechoslovakia and Hungary. Matthew Spinka.
Christian Century. 58:248-50. F. 19, '41. Search for a lasting peace; Germany and Europe's chaos.
Christian Science Monitor. p. 3. F. 8, '41. Laborite asks federal union as first British peace aim. William H. Stringer.
Christian Science Monitor Weekly Magazine Section. p. 14+. D. 2, '39. Can Europe unite? Richard Nicholas Coudenhove-Kalergi.
Reply. Christian Science Monitor Weekly Magazine Section. p. 15. Ap. 13, '40. S. G. Rendel.
Common Sense. 9:12-15. Mr. '40. Toward a United States of Europe. Alfred M. Bingham.
Commonweal. 10:526-7. S. 25, '29. Can Europe be united? Carlo Sforza.
Commonweal. 31:544-7; 32:8-11. Ap. 19-26, '40. Europe and the federal idea. Jacques Maritain.
Reply. Commonweal. 32:62. My. 10, '40. John P. Schillo.
Communist International. no.8:505-16. Ag. '40. Federated Europe. J. Revai.
Contemporary Japan. 9:955-63. Ag. '40. Destiny of Europe. Sadaji Yabe.

Contemporary Review. 137:289-99. Mr. '30. United States of Europe. William Martin.
Contemporary Review. 138:14-21. Jl. '30. Disunited states of Europe. William Harbutt Dawson.
Contemporary Review. 143:94-101. Ja. '33. United States of Europe. Christopher Home.
Contemporary Review. 157:160-8. F. '40. What shall we make of Europe? W. Walter Crotch.
Contemporary Review. 157:284-90. Mr. '40. Danubian union. Frederick Hertz.
Current History. 31:317-21. N. '29. Disunited states of Europe. Albert Bushnell Hart.
Current History. 32:658-65. Jl. '30. Proposed federation of European states. Carlo Sforza; John B. Whitton.
Current History. 32:1176-86. S. '30. Briand plan for European union; with text. John B. Whitton.
Current History. 33:65-9. O. '30. Case against Pan-Europa. David Mitrany.
Dublin Review. 187:123-33. Ja.-Mr. '31. United States of Europe. Douglas Woodruff.
Foreign Affairs. 8:237-47. Ja. '30. Pan-Europe? Edouard Herriot.
Foreign Policy Reports. 16:178-92. O. 15, '40. Europe under Nazi rule. Vera Micheles Dean.
Fortnightly. 153 (n.s.147):68-79. Ja. '40. New Europe. Storm Jameson.
Same abridged with title Collapse of sovereignty. Living Age. 358:7-12. Mr. '40.
Forum. 83:19-23. Ja. '30. Our muddling world; the United States of Europe. Salvador de Madariaga.
Forum. 83:290-3. My. '30. U.S. of Europe; reply to S. de Madariaga. Frank Bohn.
Harper's Magazine. 181:597-604. N. '40. Germany's plans for Europe. Peter F. Drucker.
International Affairs. 18:623-40. S. '39. Europe to-morrow. R. N. Coudenhove-Kalergi.
International Conciliation. Special Bulletin. p. 325-53. Je. '30. Memorandum on organization of a regime of European federal union, addressed to twenty-six governments of Europe, by M. Briand, Foreign minister of France, May 17, 1930.
International Conciliation. 265:653-769. D. '30. European federal union; replies of twenty-six governments of Europe to M. Briand's memorandum of May 17, 1930.
International Conciliation. 365:411-19. D. '40. Economic reorganization of Europe in the event of a German victory. Joachim Stresemann.
International Digest. 1:44-6. Ja. '31. Pan-Americanism and Pan-Europeanism. Louis Guilaine.

*Labour (London). 1:9-13. F. '39. Pan-European movement. Count Coudenhove-Kalergi.
Life. 9:64-9. Jl. 22, '40. Economic consequences of a German victory. Walter Lippmann.
Literary Digest. 102:12. S. 21, '29. Briand's United States of Europe.
Literary Digest. 106:12-13. S. 27, '30. U.S.E. postponed for a year.
Literary Digest. 116:11. Ag. 5, '33. Possible harm in a United States of Europe.
Nation. 130:615. My. 28, '30. Briand plan.
Nation. 149:702-5. D. 23, '39. Menace of a united Germany. Robert Dell.
Reply, with rejoinder. Eliot Janeway. Nation. 150:83. Ja. 20, '40.
Nation. 149:705-7. D. 23, '39. United States of the Danube. Rustem Vambery.
Nation. 150:174-7. F. 10, '40. Two visions of peace; European confederation or supreme domination by a gigantic absolute state. Thomas Mann.
Nation. 152:334-7. Mr. 22, '41. Europe under the master race. Konrad Heiden.
New Europe. 1:5-8, 31-5, 60-1. D. 1, '40, Ja. 1, F. 1, '41. United States of Central Europe. Anatol Muhlstein.
New Europe. 1:11-12. D. 1, '40. Federal traditions in Central Eastern Europe. Oscar Halecki.
New Europe. 1:25-6. Ja. 1, '41. Hitler's new order—slavery. John W. Wheeler-Bennett.
New Europe. 1:35-7. Ja. 1, '41. Problems of federal organization. Erich Hula.
New Europe. 1:54. F. '41. Is federation in the Baltic-Aegean area possible? Hubert Ripka.
New Europe. 1:95-6. Mr. '41. Balkan regionalism. Ernest Jackh.
New Republic. 63:356-7. Ag. 13, '30. Britain says yes and no.
New Republic. 101:227. D. 13, '39. Federation for Europe; Labor party's slogan, federate or perish. H. N. Brailsford.
New Republic. 102:38-40. Ja. 8, '40. Toward European federation.
New Republic. 102:204-7. F. 12, '40. Utopia for Europe; four-state subdivision based on natural environment. Derwent Whittlesey.
New Republic. 102:366-7. Mr. 18, '40. Can Europe federate? H. N. Brailsford.
*New York Herald Tribune. p. 17. My. 31, '40. World Germanica. Dorothy Thompson.
Same. Reader's Digest. 37:115-18. Jl. '40.
New York Times Magazine. p. 10+. Ja. 28, '40. Blueprint for a post-war world; Julian Huxley tries the scientific approach to the problem of a federated Europe. R. L. Duffus.
New York Times Magazine. p. 12+. Ja. 26, '41. New order, but not Hitler's; cooperation of all free nations. A. Visson.
Nineteenth Century. 127:536-48. My. '40. German International. L. B. Namier.

Open Court. 37:396-401. Jl. '23. United States of Europe—why not? Victor S. Yarros.
Pan American Magazine. 42:142-3. O. '29. New continental system? K. A. Bratt.
Pan American Magazine. 42:144-8. O. '29. British commonwealth, America and Europe. Wickham Steed.
Political Science Quarterly. 46:424-33. S. '31. Can Europe unite? Francis Deak.
*Round Table. 29:733-44. S. '39. Union: oceanic or continental.
Saturday Evening Post. 202:25+. F. 15, '30. United States of Europe. Winston Churchill.
Saturday Review of Literature. 22:6-7+. My. 25, '40. What kind of peace for Europe. Clarence K. Streit; Freda Utley.
Socialist Review (London). 12:451-65. Ja.-Mr. '15. United States of Europe; some historic proposals. Francis Johnson.
Statist. 135:506-7. My. 11, '40. Future of Europe.
Today's Challenge. 1:26-31. N. '39. Design for peace; a United States of Central Europe. Friedrich E. Auhagen.
World Unity. 5:365-74. Mr. '30. United States of Europe; representative European views.
World Unity. 7:167-79. D. '30. Europe in the coming world order. F. S. Marvin.
World Unity. 7:293-9. Ja. '31. United States of Europe. John Herman Randall, Jr.
Yale Review. n.s.20:217-33. D. '30. Pan-European problem. Hjalmar Schacht.
Yale Review. n.s.29, no.2:248-72. (D) '39. European trouble zone. George Vernadsky.

Pan Americanism

Books and Pamphlets

American Society of International Law. Proceedings, 1940. p. 18-53. Regionalism and neutrality as the bases of peace in the Americas. Charles E. Martin.
Beals, Carleton. Pan America. 545p. Houghton Mifflin Co. Bost. '40.
Butler, Nicholas Murray. Pan America. *In his* Family of nations. p. 323-31. Charles Scribner's Sons. N.Y. '38.
Nichols, Egbert Ray, comp. Western hemisphere defense. 398p. (Reference Shelf. Vol. 14, no. 5) H. W. Wilson Co. N.Y. Ja. '41.
Bibliography. p. 379-98.
Pan American Union. Eighth International Conference of American States, Lima, Peru, December 9, 1938. Special handbook for the use of delegates. p. 20-8. Creation of a league or association of American nations. The Union. Wash. D.C. '38.

Phelps, Edith M. ed. American league of nations. *In her* University debaters' annual, 1937-1938. Vol. 24, p. 149-95. H. W. Wilson Co. N.Y. '38.
Bibliography. p. 184-95.

Showman, Richard K. and Judson, Lyman S. comp. Monroe doctrine and the growth of western hemisphere solidarity. 302p. (Reference Shelf. Vol. 14, no. 7) H. W. Wilson Co. N.Y. Mr. '41.

Whitaker, Arthur P. New Latin America. *In* Brown, F. J.; Hodges, C.; and Roucek, J. S., eds. Contemporary world politics. p. 278-97. John Wiley & Sons. N.Y. '39.

Williams, Mary Wilhelmine. Regional groupings and world relationships of Latin America. *In her* People and politics of Latin America. p. 816-36. new ed. Ginn & Co. Bost. '38.

PERIODICALS

Annals of the American Academy. 204:1-237. Jl. '39. Democracy and the Americas, ed. by Ernest Minor Patterson.

Annals of the American Academy. 210:127-32. Jl. '40. New orientation of the Western hemisphere. Stephen Duggan.

Bulletin of the Pan American Union. 75:117-24. F. '41. Pan Americanism or the New World's new order. William Sanders.

Christian Century. 57:818-19. Je. 26, '40. Democracy and world capitalism. Arthur E. Holt.

Congressional Digest. 20:37-64. F. '41. Should the American republics form a permanent union? with pro and con discussion.

Foreign Affairs. 19:12-21. O. '40. Hemisphere solidarity; some economic and strategic considerations. Alvin H. Hansen.

*Foreign Affairs. 19:481-94. Ap. '41. Myth of the continents. Eugene Staley.

Geographical Review. 30:525-8. Jl. '40. Geography of the Monroe Doctrine and the limits of the Western hemisphere. Lawrence Martin.

Inter-American Quarterly. 3:28-35. Ja. '41. Scientific basis of Pan Americanism. Arthur Ramos.

International Digest. 1:44-6. Ja. '31. Pan-Americanism and Pan-Europeanism. Louis Guilaine.

Living Age. 337:767. F. 15, '30. Pan-America and Pan-Europe.

Living Age. 359:511-13. F. '41. Canadian asks union with U.S.; a North American federation would prove invulnerable to all aggressors. Jean-Charles Harvey.

Nation. 151:24-5. Jl. 13, '40. Needed, an American league of nations. Freda Kirchwey.

Nation. 152:8-11, 67-71. Ja. 4, 18, '41. Choice for the Americas. Lewis Corey.

New Commonwealth Quarterly. 6:208-21. Ja. '41. Pan American system an illustration of regional organization for peace. Samuel Guy Inman.

North American Review. 248, no. 2:219-33. (D) '39. Should Canada join Pan America? Horace Donald Crawford.
Quarterly Journal of Inter-American Relations. 1:25-36. Ja. '39. Toward an American association of nations. Ricardo J. Alfaro.
Scholastic. 37:14+. O. 28, '40. On a new order in the world; difference between our democratic Monroe Doctrine and the totalitarian conquests. Walter Lippmann.
Survey Graphic. 30:102-8. Mr. '41. Peace without empire. A. A. Berle, Jr.
Survey Graphic. 30:120-3+. Mr. '41. Our common defense. Frank R. McCoy.
United States. Department of State Bulletin. 1:659-63. D. 9, '39. Cooperative peace in the western hemisphere. Adolf A. Berle.
United States. Department of State Bulletin. 2:57-63. Ja. 20, '40. Relation of the Union of American republics to world organization. Warren Kelchner.
United States. Department of State Bulletin. 3:374-81. N. 2, '40. Political and economic solidarity of the Americas. Lawrence Duggan.
World Affairs. 101:158-70. S. '38. American league of nations. Ricardo J. Alfaro.
World Affairs. 102:26-41. Mr. '39. Lima and American solidarity. George Howland Cox.
World Affairs. 104:39-41. Mr. '41. Interparliamentary conference for the western hemisphere. Arthur Deerin Call.
World Affairs. 104:47-9. Mr. '41. Monroism and the new world order. Raul d'Eça.
*World Affairs Interpreter. 11:386-96. Ja. '41. Pan America consults. Donald Marquand Dozer.
World Unity. 7:265-77. Ja. '31. Pan-America in the coming world order. Graham H. Stuart.
Yale Review. n.s. 30, no. 2:291-30. (D) '40. Latin America and the new hemisphere front. John I. B. McCulloch.

Asia

Institute of World Affairs. Proceedings. 16:22-6. '38. Problem of Pan-Asianism. André Lobanov-Rostovsky.
Kohn, Hans. Near East. *In* Brown, F. J.; Hodges, C.; and Roucek, J. S., eds. Contemporary world politics. p. 356-69. John Wiley & Sons. N.Y. '39.
Smith, Robert Aura. Our future in Asia. 306p. Viking Press. N.Y. '40.
Amerasia. 4:518-24. Ja. '41. Shiratori speaks. Robert W. Barnett
China Weekly Review. 94:149-52. O. 5, '40. Dr. Sun Yat-sen's doctrine of pan-Asianism and its perversion by the Wang Ching-wei clique; with text of Dr. Sun's pan-Asianism speech of Nov. 23, 1924.

Fortnightly. 154(n.s. 148):390-7. O. '40. New order in East Asia. Gerald Samson.

Living Age. 357:176-8. O. '39. Mikado doctrine; Japanese Monroe Doctrine. Hikamatsu Kamikawa.

Living Age. 358:438-43. Jl. '40. Arab-Jewish federated state; union now proposed for Palestine, Transjordania and Lebanon. Joseph Wechler Eaton.

*Pacific Affairs. 13:381-92. D. '40. Main drive behind Japanese national policies. Galen M. Fisher.

WORLD ORGANIZATION

Books and Pamphlets

Brewer, William C. Permanent peace. 264p. Dorrance & Co. Phila. '40.

Bridgman, Raymond L. World organization. 172p. Ginn & Co. Bost. '05.

Common questions about the future United States of the world. 12p. Committee on World Government. Women's International League for Peace and Freedom (United States Section). 1734 F. St. N.W. Wash. D.C. '40.

*Landone, Brown. Which road to permanent peace. 48p. Landone Foundation. Orlando, Fla. '40.

Lemieux, Pierre. Universalism, the ideal state. 215p. The Author. Montreal, Can. '34.

Lloyd, Lola Maverick and Schwimmer, Rosika. Chaos, war, or a new world order? 7p. Campaign for World Government. 166 W. Jackson Blvd. Chic. My. '38.

Madariaga, Salvador de. World's design. 291p. George Allen & Unwin. Lond. '38.

Newfang, Oscar. Road to world peace; a federation of nations. 372p. G. P. Putnam's Sons. N.Y. '34.

Newfang, Oscar. World federation. 117p. Barnes & Noble. N.Y. '39.

Randall, John Herman. World community; the supreme task of the twentieth century. 294p. Frederick A. Stokes Co. N.Y. '30.
Bibliography. p.293-4.

Reddick, Olive I. World organization; an outline of some problems and recent proposals for federation for use of study groups or general reading. 36p. Women's International League for Peace and Freedom. 1924 Chestnut St. Phila. '41.

Wright, Quincy. World Citizens Association; statement of its purpose. 10p. The Association. 86 E. Randolph St. Chic. '39.

Periodicals

Century. 120:203-10. Ap. '30. World government. Salvador de Madariaga.
Chinese Social and Political Science Review. 22:28-41. Ap. '38. World conference, world domination or world government? H. C. E. Zacharias.
Christian Science Monitor Weekly Magazine Section. p. 1-2. My. 12, '37. For world government. Salvador de Madariaga.
Christian Science Monitor Weekly Magazine Section. p. 2. F. 24, '40. Hurdles before world federation. Hugh Dalton.
Common Sense. 8:12-15. Jl. '39. Union now or never. Robert Heckert.
Congressional Record. 85:(current) 2227-30. N. 3, '39. After the war, peace! John G. Alexander.
Congressional Record. 86:(current) 21467-8. D. 12, '40. New world order. John G. Alexander.
*Conscience. (India). 2:special sup. O. 31, '40. World union.
Forum. 84:246-9. O. '30. Disunited states of Europe. Salvador de Madariaga.
Forum and Century. 98:123-5. S. '37. Citizens of the world. Salvador de Madariaga.
National Education Association. Journal. 27:267-70. D. '38. Toward world cooperation. Eugene Staley.
School and Society. 50:823. D. 23, '39. Manifesto by English educators urges a federal union of all nations.
Spectator (London). 150:175-6. F. 10, '33. World patriotism. Evelyn Wrench.
*Talks. 5:41-5. O. '40. Post-war world. Arthur Sweetser.
World Order. 4:386-90. Ja. '39. World federal state. Lothar Von Wurmb.
World Unity. 5:375-86. Mr. '30. Phases of world citizenship. Carl A. Ross.
World Unity. 8:177-86. Je. '31. World citizenship and governments. Carl A. Ross.
World Unity. 8:238-46. Jl. '31. World citizenship and exterritoriality. Carl A. Ross.
World Unity. 8:310-19. Ag. '31. Transforming war debts into world credits. Carl A. Ross.
World Unity. 8:408-18. S. '31. Is world citizenship visionary? Carl A. Ross.
World Unity. 9:41-52. O. '31. World organization—parliament or federal? Carl A. Ross.
World Unity. 12:138-47. Je. '33. Advocating a federated world. C. W. Young.
World Unity. 12:195-204, 282-91, 347-56; 13:12-18, 98-107, 149-60, 235-41, 292-9, 342-7; 14:47-56. Jl.-D. '33; Ja.-Ap. '34. World citizenship. Carl A. Ross.

World Unity. 14:113-21. My. '34. Parliament of a federated world. C. W. Young.

World Unity. 14:207-16. Jl. '34. World conscience, an international society for the creation of world peace; scheme for an international city. Hendrik Christian Andersen.

The League of Nations

Garnett, Maxwell. World unity. 32p. Oxford Univ. Press. Lond. '39.

Haile, Pennington. League of Nations. *In* Brown, F. J.; Hodges, C.; and Roucek, J. S., eds. Contemporary world politics. p. 431-51. John Wiley & Sons. N.Y. '39.

Keeton, George W. National sovereignty and international order. 191p. Peace Book Co. Lond. '39.

Landone, Brown. League of Nations. *In his* Which road to permanent peace. p. 20-7. Landone Foundation. Orlando, Fla. '40.

League of Nations. Development of international co-operation in economic and social affairs; report of the special committee. 22p. The League. Geneva. Ag. '39.

Maddox, William P. Reorganizing the League of Nations. *In his* European plans for world order. p. 20-7. American Academy of Political and Social Science. Phila. '40.

Newfang, Oscar. Fulfilment of the conditions of world peace. *In his* World federation. Pt. 3. Barnes & Noble. N.Y. '39.

Newfang, Oscar. United States of the world; a comparison between the League of Nations and the United States of America. 284p. G. P. Putnam's Sons. N.Y. '30.

Shotwell, James T. Changing League. *In his* On the rim of the abyss. p. 287-355. Macmillan Co. N.Y. '36.

Steiner, H. Arthur. League system. *In his* Principles and problems of international relations. p. 459-580. Harper & Bros. N.Y. '40.

International Conciliation. 363:333-69. O. '40. Causes of the peace failure 1919-1939; survey by the International Consultative Group of Geneva.

An International Police

Baker, Philip Noel. International air police force. *In* Jameson, Storm, ed. Challenge to death. p. 206-39. Constable & Co. Lond. '35.

*Landone, Brown. League of Nations. *In his* Which road to permanent peace? p. 20-7. Landone Foundation. Orlando, Fla. '40.

Maddox, William P. Proposals for an international police force. *In his* European plans for world order. p. 28-30. American Academy of Political and Social Science. Phila. '40.

Van der Leeuw, J. J. Why a world peace is inevitable. 18p. (Pamphlets Ser.B. no.4B.) New Commonwealth. Thorney House, Smith Sq. Westminster, Lond. S.W.1. Mr. '37.

Catholic World. 152:44-52. O. '40. Give peace a sword. A. R. Bandini.

Christian Science Monitor Weekly Magazine Section. p. 1-2. Ag. 12, '36. International police? a debate. Lord Davies; Lord Londonderry.

Discussion. Christian Science Monitor Weekly Magazine Section. p. 18. S. 16; 12-13. S. 23; 14. S. 30; 18. O. 7; 15. N. 4; 18. N. 18, '36; 15. Ja. 20, '37.

Fortnightly. 146 (n.s. 140):397-402. O. '36. International force. L. P. Jacks.

Forum. 96:177-82. O. '36. International air force. Vyvyan Adams.

Forum and Century. 102:74-7. Ag. '39. Roads to peace; a debate on the international-police proposal. Sarah Wambaugh; Nathaniel Peffer.

International Conciliation. 323:479-86. O. '36. World police for world peace. Viscount Allenby.

Scholastic. 33:14S+ D. 17, '38. Why not an international police force? Clyde Eagleton.

World Affairs. 102:19-26. Mr. '39. As to an international military force. Arthur Deerin Call.

World Tomorrow. 17:32-3. Ja. 18, '34. International police? H. N. Brailsford.